A Word From the Authors

We welcome you with the sixth edition of the *Walker Washington Guide*.

For over 30 years the authors have participated actively in the day-to-day life of the capital, seeing it progress from a relaxed, uncomplicated town to what is now referred to as "the most important city in the most important country in the world."

The purpose of this *Guide* is to share with the reader the increasing wealth of sights, activities and cultural attractions to be enjoyed in Washington. The list continues to grow at a dizzying pace. The $8–$10 dinner at a fancy restaurant and the $20 a night room at a luxury hotel described in our 1963 edition are dim memories. In their place, however, stand choices of varied cuisines from around the world and hosteleries to rival those of any capital city.

John Walker spent his professional career as a Washington lawyer, dealing on a daily basis with the powers and frustrations of the institutions of government. Katharine Walker has supplemented her hours at the typewriter with hours on the town as a guide-lecturer with groups from here and abroad.

Stephen Kraft, the illustrator and book designer, is an Adjunct Professor of Art at the American University.

May this *Guide* help you enjoy this remarkable city and appreciate your capital.

A Word From the Authors

We welcome you with the second edition of the Bittersweet Harvest from China.

In over 20 years, the authors have attempted to portray the day-to-day life of the people as they find it ... from a relatively complete tour. It is while it may not be so ... the most important of the most important country in the world.

The purpose of our guide is to share with the reader the ... interesting wealth of ... cultural and cultural attraction, to be enjoyed by the reader ... the locations to partake of ...

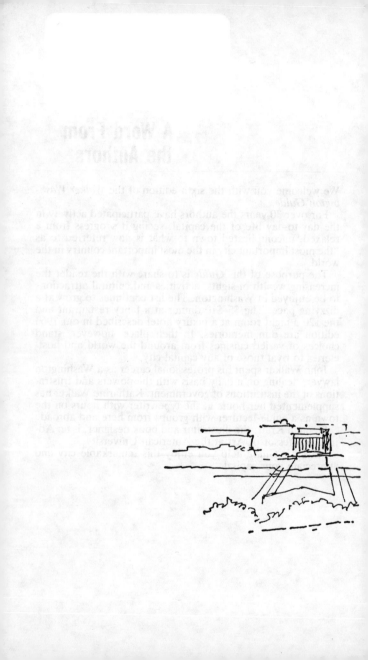

The Walker
WASHINGTON
GUIDE

John and Katharine Walker

Designed and illustrated by Stephen Kraft

EPM PUBLICATIONS, McLean, Va.

Acknowledgments

Outstandingly well-qualified people have contributed to virtually every section of the editions of our *Guide*, and the authors acknowledge a pleasant debt of gratitude to them. We have been the beneficiaries of so much enthusiastic help in revising the earlier editions that we can only thank the many private and public agencies and their distinguished officers by this expression of appreciation and by entering the substantial improvements in the text their revisions have made possible.

Library of Congress Cataloging-in-Publication Data

Walker, John Stanley, 1920–
  The Walker Washington guide.

  Includes index.
  1. Washington (D.C.)—Description—1981–   —Guidebooks.   I. Walker, Katharine Davidson, 1921–
II. Title.
F192.3.W3   1987   917.53′044   87-9175
ISBN 0-914440-96-9

EPM Publications, Inc., 1003 Turkey Run Road,
  McLean, Virginia 22101

Printed in the United States of America

Foreword

Since the first edition of this *Guide* in 1963 the federal government and its capital city have undergone dramatic changes:

The 1963 federal budget of just over $100 billion doubled by 1969 to $200 billion and now has risen to the $1 trillion range.

The U.S. federal budget deficit has risen from $4.8 billion in 1963 to $220.5 billion in 1986.

The population of the greater Washington area (including the suburbs of Maryland and Virginia) has risen by 5.5 percent since the Guide's *last edition. It stands at 3,348,000.*

For the first time in over 100 years, Washington now has an elected mayor, an elected city council with legislative powers and a non-voting delegate in Congress.

Extensive construction in the downtown area, the southwest redevelopment and the professional district has changed the appearance of the city. Metro, the subway, is the most expensive single city public works venture ever undertaken in this country. It has already had a big impact on the city's development.

To the city's museums in the 1970s there were added the Hirshhorn Museum and Sculpture Garden; the Renwick Gallery; the National Museum of American Art; the National Portrait Gallery; the National Air and Space Museum; the new East Building of the National Gallery of Art; and the Museum of African Art. The performing arts have been enriched by the Kennedy Center and Wolf Trap Farm Park.

In recent years a qualitative and quantitative change seems to have come to Washington. There has been a great enhancement of living values, and more physical development downtown than in the entire previous history of the city. The federal government becomes ever more powerful. These are heady changes that contain enormous challenges and pressures with respect to the evolution of the capital.

John Walker

Contents

Part III   Special Features

Part I

Introduction to Washington

Welcome to Washington

WELCOME TO WASHINGTON! Many of us who live here consider our city unique in the world—as a focus of world issues, a repository of our heritages and as a planned city of physical beauty.

You will not have time to see more than a few sights. Even lifelong residents will not have seen all of the items discussed in this *Guide*. It is designed, therefore, to help you make the most of your visit(or life here) by enabling you to choose what to do and how best to do it.

Remember that Washington is on the move. As a result, hours, exhibits and telephone numbers are subject to change and you are wise to check the matters of greatest interest to you so as not to be disappointed by a last minute or temporary change.

You will find it surprisingly easy to find your way around Washington. The Federal District was laid out as a square, ten miles on each side, with the corners oriented exactly north-south and east-west. Andrew Ellicott surveyed the boundaries and pinpointed the location for the dome of the U.S. Capitol exactly at the center.

Pierre Charles L'Enfant, the French-born "artist of the Revolution," planned central Washington in imaginative detail. A comparison of his 1791 plan done by Ellicott with a map of today shows how much of his concept has been carried out. Note that:

north-south streets are numbered from the Capitol
east-west streets are lettered from the Capitol
the broad avenues, named for the states, run diagonally

Washington owes a literal debt to its designer, L'Enfant. He was never paid for his work. Shortly after making his plan, L'Enfant became embroiled in a running controversy with property owners in the federal area. He was blamed for the slow sale of lots, upon which depended the successful financing of the Federal District, and resigned under fire in 1792. Except for one interlude as architect for Fort Washington, L'Enfant lived out the rest of his life in obscurity. By the time of his death in 1825, he was no longer recognized as the designer of the city. His plan was also in danger of being

11

passed over. Development of the Federal City lagged badly. For almost the entire first half of its history, the capital remained a backward town, one of the slowest to grow in the entire country. Only after the Civil War did the city really begin to develop, and only then was the initiative regained to carry out the original plan. Belated recognition of L'Enfant came in 1909, when his obscure grave was moved to its present site at Arlington House, overlooking the city he shaped.

A statement attributed to John F. Kennedy characterizes Washington as having all the charm of a northern city and the efficiency of a southern town. To the extent true, this description relates to the past.

As observers of and participants in Washington's recent history, we noted a qualitative and quantitative change occurring in the late 60s. With the opening of the Kennedy Center and Wolf Trap Farm Park a host of stage and cultural groups came here to perform, often for the first time. Six major museums were started. Good restaurants began to proliferate, many of them small, with real ethnic qualities.

At about the same time Washingtonians began to think of themselves in a new way: as residents privileged to partake of the capital's special resources; as people living in the center of the national activity and world power; and as fortunate citizens with a wide range of cultural activities and life styles available to them.

It is evident that others perceived these changes, and large numbers of businesses have followed their inclinations by moving here. In the 70s more than 900 trade associations established their national headquarters in Washington. Office space has increased 50 percent in the last decade, and the rate of increase continues to spiral upwards. The development in the capital's downtown area during the past decade probably exceeds that of the entire previous history of the city.

The solid lines of new office buildings in the professional district are visible evidence (perhaps too visible) of this recent growth (the professional district is centered on K Street and parallel streets from 14th Street west to Rock Creek Park). The Pennsylvania Avenue Development Corporation has made dramatic improvements along Pennsylvania Avenue between the Treasury Building and the Capitol. Stunning additions to the area are the two new parks in the grand squares from 13th Street to 15th Street.

Washington's "newest tradition" is the Pavilion at the Old Post Office, 1100 Pennsylvania Ave., where shops, restaurants and daily (including lunchtime) entertainment attract office workers and tourists to this beautifully renovated Romanesque style building, completed in 1899.

The Washington Convention Center, opened in January 1983 at 900 9th St.,N.W. on a 9.7 acre site, is having a great impact on the downtown area. The space in the four exhibit halls and 40 meeting rooms is so vast that 26,000 people can be accommodated simultaneously. This happened in the spring of 1986 during the Billy Graham crusade.

The Metro subway, now two-thirds completed, is among the greatest forces shaping the entire metropolitan area. Already, the face of the suburbs has been affected, with once quiet neighborhoods near Metro stops overwhelmed by high-rises looming over small classic American homes.

Looking ahead to the summer of 1988 we will see the re-opening of the resurrected Union Station, the imposing Roman style classical building completed in 1908, and once the gateway to the city. Inside the giant complex will be movie theaters, restaurants, 100 shops, and a fast-food arcade, with Amtrak service in a separate building.

With growth and change come special challenges. From its earliest days Washington was conceived as a horizontal city, dominated by the Capitol. Today the pressures of population and need for office space have all but exhausted available accommodations in the prime business area. Within 15-20 years the renewal of land east of 14th Street and north of Pennsylvania Avenue may use up another important area. Changes adjacent to the monumental core already threaten the city's wide vistas and thus the horizontal character of Washington.

Tips to the Wise Visitor

TELEPHONE TIPS

Area codes: DC 202; MD 301; VA 703
Telephone Information 411
Local Weather 936-1212
Time of Day 844-2525
Dial-a-Park 426-6975
   (information about activities in National Capital Parks)
Dial-a-Museum 357-2020 (current exhibitions and
   programs at the Smithsonian)
Dial-a-Phenomenon 357-2000
   (space and earth phenomena)
Dial-an-Event 737-8866
Tourist Information Center 789-7000
Washington Convention and Visitors Assoc.
   789-7000
District Medical Bureau 466-1880
Dental Referral Service 686-0803
National Archives 523-3000
Tourmobile 554-7950 (routes and information)
City-wide EMERGENCY number 911
IVIS (International Visitors Information Service)
   783-6540
Capitol 224-3121
Metro-Metrobus Information 637-7000

Note: Much useful information is available in the front pages
of the D.C. telephone book (White Pages) and the Maryland
Suburban book (Yellow Pages).

FIRST STOPS

The *Tourist Information Center*, in the Department of Commerce Building at 14th St. and Pennsylvania Ave., N.W.,
offers maps, directions and other information 9:00 A.M. to
5:00 P.M., Monday through Saturday. Volunteers from the
International Visitors Information Service and Travelers Aid
Society are on hand to answer questions.

HOW TO GET AROUND

Under "Transportation" you will find taxi tips, comments on driving your own car in the city, information about buses, boats, sightseeing tours and the Metro subway.

Arm yourself with a good map of the city.

Walk as much as you can; the "area maps" in this *Guide* will show you where you will see and savor more on foot.

Use taxicabs in the downtown area. You can hail a cab without waiting (except perhaps during rainstorms) and the price in the downtown zone (where most popular sights are) is reasonable. The *Metro* subway (look for this symbol **M**) provides a fast and pleasant way to move about the city. With limited (and expensive) parking downtown, cars may prove to be a nuisance. The *Tourmobile* is a transportation alternative.

WHAT TO WEAR

In any season, bring rain gear and comfortable shoes. Ladies should leave at home (or in the suitcase) shorts, halters and all lounging or beach wear. Such dress is inappropriate for sightseeing and is a mark of disrespect for our national monuments. Need we say that hair rollers in public are inappropriate at any season or for any occasion? Do have a sweater handy even on the hottest summer days; air-conditioning is often overdone. Men should reserve loud sport shirts and shorts for home barbecues or mowing the lawn.

SOME GENERAL TIPS

Sightseeing is tiring; everyone is tempted to do too much. You will have more fun and remember more by doing less than your energies allow.

The *Washington Post* (particularly the Friday *Weekend* section), the *Washington Times* and the monthly *Washingtonian* magazine will keep you informed of special events each day and of sports and amusements. These publications provide a good supplement to this *Guide* in making sure you don't miss anything while you are here.

See the city at night. The lighted monuments provide an unforgettable sight.

This Week and *Where*, weekly publications available free at hotels and motels, will inform you of current entertainment highlights.

INFORMATION KIOSKS

Look for the distinctive Information Kiosks operated by the National Park Service in the Mall and Monument area. They are manned by Park Guides who provide general information about Washington and vicinity. You will find them open 8:30 A.M.–5:00 P.M., June 1–Sept. 1.

A FINAL TIP

Scan this entire book before starting on your sightseeing. The material at the end will give you ideas on everything from "Areas of Interest" to "Where to Stay, Eat and Shop."

Special Events:
A Calendar

January

The first week marks the opening of Congress. Every fourth year, on January 20, a new President takes the oath of office on the west front of the Capitol. The inaugural parade, sometimes lasting four hours, follows. Route is from Capitol down Pennsylvania Avenue past White House.

The third Monday in January is a federal holiday celebrating Martin Luther King Jr.'s birthday. The event is marked with speeches, dance and choral performances.

February

Abraham Lincoln's birthday on February 12 is celebrated by special services at the Lincoln Memorial. On February 22, George Washington's birthday, services are held at Mount Vernon, and Old Town Alexandria celebrates with the nation's largest George Washington Birthday Parade, featuring military bands, fife and drum corps, bagpipe bands and floats. This day is also celebrated by city-wide bargain sales in shops and department stores all over town.

Late February–early March

The Chinese New Year is celebrated in Chinatown with firework displays, dragon dancers and Chinese dancers making their way through the streets. The area's restaurants offer special holiday menus.

March (late, or early April)

Cherry Blossoms: white single blossoms around Tidal Basin (and Kenwood, Maryland) appear first; pink double blossoms, mainly around Hains Point, appear about two weeks later. The Flower Show comes to the Washington Convention Center. Forsythia appears on hillsides, banks and terraces at Dumbarton Oaks Gardens.

The Cherry Blossom Festival is held; the festivities include band concerts, parades, lighting of the Japanese lantern at the Tidal Basin, the crowning of a princess and a ball.

The Men's Professional Tennis Tournament is held at the Smith center, George Washington University.

Smithsonian sponsors annual Kite Festival on the Mall.

April (or late March)

Easter sunrise services in Arlington National Cemetery, Carter Barron Amphitheater and on the grounds of Walter Reed Army Hospital. Easter Monday egg rolling on White House lawn attracts scads of children, with adults admitted only when accompanied by a child.

A spectacular display of azaleas is on view at the National Arboretum—whole hillsides are covered with thousands of azaleas of every color and variety.

The Washington Craft Show, a sales exhibition of work by 100 juried exhibitors, is sponsored by the Smithsonian Associates in late-April at the Departmental Auditorium, 1301 Constitution Ave., N.W.

House, Garden and Embassy Tours held throughout the month offer a rare opportunity to see the interior of some of Washington's most elegant embassies and private homes. The Georgetown House Tour (usually the last weekend in April) features seven homes each weekend day; tickets at St. John's Church, 3240 O St., N.W. 338-1796).

The Georgetown Garden Tour (usually a Saturday in mid-April) offers 10–11 gardens. Tickets at 3224 N St., N.W. (338-4229).

Vassar Book Sale (usually last week of April) takes place at central downtown location. Thousands of used books sold at bargain prices. (Information: 797-3638)

A once-a-year chance to visit the open hangar of the Smithsonian's Air and Space Museum's collection of aircraft housed in the Paul E. Garber Facility in Suitland, MD. Open house the last week in April; tours; call 357-2700 for information.

May

The annual Azalea Festival is held on the grounds of the Landon School for Boys, Bethesda, MD (late April or early May). (320-3200)

Outdoor fair on grounds of Washington Cathedral, rain or shine; colorful booths with international flavor. (first Friday)

(Third Sunday) Armed Forces Day, when military installations in area have open house.

Memorial Day—special services at Arlington National Cemetery; President lays wreath at Tomb of the Unknown Soldier.

June

Washington moves outdoors, with outstanding (free) events sponsored by the Summer in the Parks program; outdoor concerts are presented at noon and during the evenings.

Outdoor performances begin at *Wolf Trap Farm Park*, Vienna, VA (and continue through August).

At *Glen Echo Park*, MacArthur Blvd. and Goldsboro Rd., Glen Echo, MD, music and dance performances are offered.

The Service Bands start their summer-long series of free concerts almost every night on the West Lawn of the U.S. Capitol, the Sylvan Theater on the Washington Monument grounds and the West Terrace of the Air and Space Museum.

For three weekends in June an annual Potomac Riverfest is held on the Southwest Waterfront, featuring a parade, music, crafts, ethnic food, water events and tall ship visits. Information: 673-7660.

Annual Festival of American Folklife, a celebration of American heritage, is held on the Mall between 12th and 14th Sts. Information: 357-2700 (Smithsonian Institution). Usually late June, early July.

July

July 4: The National Symphony Orchestra plays on the West Lawn of the U.S. Capitol at 8:00 P.M. preceding the spectacular firework display on the Washington Monument Grounds.

The Sovran Bank/D.C. National Tennis Classic is held at 16th and Kennedy Sts., N.W.

Musical offerings at Wolf Trap Farm Park, Kennedy Center, Glen Echo Park, Fort Hunt Park (Alexandria, VA) and Merriweather Post Pavilion.

July 14: Dominique's Bastille Day Race on Pennsylvania Ave., N.W.

August

Music and dance performances continue both outdoors and indoors; service band concerts and Summer in the Park presentations offered.

September

A free Labor Day concert is presented by the National Symphony Orchestra on the West Lawn of the U.S. Capitol at 8:00 P.M.

Adams Morgan Day (the second Sunday in September) is known as the biggest block party on the eastern seaboard, featuring ethnic food, crafts, bands and dancing.

International Children's Festival at Wolf Trap Farm Park for four days, mid-September (chance for children to join professionals in opera, dance, theater and crafts).

Free Sunday evening (7:00 P.M.) concerts resume in East Garden Court of National Gallery of Art (usually continue until June).

October

In mid-October the Annual White House Garden Tour affords visitors an opportunity to view the Rose Garden and East Lawn with background music of military bands. Call 472-3669.

With the opening ceremony of the Supreme Court, Washington traditionally starts off its full schedule of social and cultural events. Many free concerts, films and lectures offered at museums, galleries and Library of Congress.

November

The annual Marine Corps Marathon, with world-class runners, begins at the Iwo Jima Memorial the first Sunday in November. (640-2741)

Veteran's Day services held at Arlington National Cemetery Amphitheatre, and at the Vietnam Veterans Memorial.

A month-long Decorators' Showhouse offers a unique opportunity to visit a Washington mansion decorated by top local talent. Information: 333-1122.

Mid-Nov. District of Columbia Antiques Show.

Washington, DC International (with many entries from abroad) takes place at Laurel Racetrack, Laurel, MD.

December

Pearl Harbor Day ceremonies at Iwo Jima Memorial on December 7.

Christmas week, Pageant of Peace Christmas ceremonies held at the Ellipse (south of the White House); opens with President lighting Christmas tree; special events every day—carols, madrigal singers.

Kennedy Center offers "Twelve Days of Christmas" (starting about December 20) with galaxy of concerts, sing-ins, and special holiday treats (many of them free).

Annual Christmas Program at Wolf Trap Farm Park features free Christmas carols acocmpanied by a U.S. service band (a few days before Christmas).

WASHINGTON SEASONS AND WEATHER

Each of the seasons has some special advantage for the visitor. The cherry blossoms, azaleas and flowering fruit trees make spring the most popular season. The fall provides perhaps the city's finest weather and large crowds are not a problem. In winter there are the fewest tourists and sights can be contemplated at your leisure. Because of air-conditioning, summers are tolerable and this is the second most popular season.

Normal monthly highs and lows and the average mean temperatures run as follows:

	Jan.	Feb.	Mar.	Apr.	May	June	July	Aug.	Sept.	Oct.	Nov.	Dec.
Normal High	42.6	44.4	53.0	64.2	74.9	82.8	86.8	84.4	78.4	67.5	55.1	44.8
Normal Low	27.4	28.0	35.0	44.2	54.5	63.4	68.0	66.1	59.6	48.0	37.9	29.8
Mean Temp.	35.0	36.2	44.0	54.2	64.7	73.1	77.4	75.3	69.0	57.8	46.5	37.3

Rainfall is evenly distributed throughout the year.

Part II
What to See and How to See It

Alexandria, Virginia

WHERE   25-min. car ride south of
        Washington, DC.

HOW   By car (Washington Memorial
        Parkway or Route 1) or by Metro,
        King Street stop.

Alexandria, founded by Scottish merchants in 1749, flourished as a major port of the eastern seaboard well before the
Federal City was ever proposed. While successive generations
have imposed their modern and commercial structures on the
colonial landscape of Alexandria, it still has more original
houses than Williamsburg and more old homes than Georgetown. By leaving the main traffic arteries for a visit to the old
section of the city (which lies to the east, on the banks of the
Potomac), you will greatly increase the number of structures
of exceptional historic and architectural merit you can see.
We suggest a walking tour as the best way to enjoy the pleasant
ambiance. (See Map 1.)

Especially noteworthy are:

Christ Church, Cameron and Columbus Sts. (open weekdays
9:00 A.M.–4:00 P.M., Sunday services, 8:00 A.M. and 10:30 A.M.),
a beautiful example of Georgian church architecture, dates
from 1773. Silver plaques mark the pews of Washington, who
served as a vestryman, and of Robert E. Lee. The ancient
tombstones in the churchyard with their interesting inscriptions mark graves of early Alexandria residents. (See
"Churches.")

The *Old Presbyterian Meeting House*, 321 South Fairfax St.
(open 9:00 A.M. to 4:00 P.M., weekdays; closed Saturday; Sunday service at 11:00 A.M.) finished in 1774, is the oldest Presbyterian church in Virginia. You may gain admittance from
the church office in the rear. Many of Alexandria's founders
were Scot-Presbyterians; their tombs are in the graveyard, as
is the *Tomb of the Unknown Soldier of the Revolutionary War*.

The *Stabler-Leadbeater Apothecary Shop*, 107 South Fairfax
St. (open weekdays 10:00 A.M.–4:30 P.M., Mon.–Sat.), was

founded in 1792 and remained in business under the Stabler family until 1933. Today this unique museum looks much as it did when Washington and Robert E. Lee were customers. The collection of pharmaceutical glass is noteworthy. Here Lee received his orders to go to Harpers Ferry to quell the rebellion led by John Brown.

Gadsby's Tavern Museum, 134 North Royal St. (open 10:00 A.M.–5:00 P.M., Tues.–Sat.; 1:00 P.M.–5:00 P.M., Sun.) erected in 1752, provides one of the best remaining examples of Georgian architecture. The handcarved woodwork is especially fine. Gadsby's was noted as one of the finest taverns in the colonies and served Alexandria as an important meeting place and hostelry for many years during the 18th century. Washington used it as his military headquarters at least three times during the French and Indian War. Here on February 22, 1799, he attended the last public celebration of his birthday. The Tavern has been restored. On the 30-minute tour you will see the ballroom (Assembly Room), typical bedrooms, the Tap Room and the Game Room. At Gadsby's Tavern you may enjoy homemade fare in an authentic colonial atmosphere.

The *George Washington Masonic National Memorial Association*, between King and Duke Sts., off Russell Rd. (open 9:00 A.M.–5:00 P.M., daily) offers one of the finest views of Washington plus an extraordinary collection of Colonial-era treasures. This was the site originally proposed for the national capitol building. More than three million Masons contributed funds to build this national home of Freemasonery. Don't miss the trowel used by President Washington in laying the cornerstone of the Capitol in 1793. Fourteen of our Presidents have been Masons.

The Robert E. Lee Boyhood Home, 607 Oronoco St. (open 10:00 A.M.–4:00 P.M., Mon.–Sat.; NOON–4:00 P.M., Sun. Closed Dec. 15–Jan. 31. Admission fee.) "Light-Horse Harry" Lee, father of Robert E. Lee, brought his wife and five children here before the War of 1812; he died in 1818. His widow, Ann Hill Carter, lived here until 1825. General Lafayette visited her in 1824 while in the city. The early Federal architecture is noteworthy as are the charming interiors and furnishings.

Captain's Row, on Prince St., between Union and Lee Sts., provides Alexandria's greatest concentration of picturesque, unpretentious 18th-century houses. Hessian prisoners laid the cobblestone streets in 1785 after the Revolutionary War.

Other fine houses, recently open to the public, are well worth a visit because of their architectural and historical interest.

The *Carlyle House*, 121 N. Fairfax St. (open 10:00 A.M.–5:00 P.M., Tues.–Sat.; NOON–5:00 P.M., Sun.; admission fee) is one of the most historic buildings in America. John Carlyle, a Scottish merchant and town founder built the house. General Braddock used it as his headquarters in 1755 during the French and Indian War. (549-2997)

The *Lee-Fendall House*, 429 N. Washington St. (open 10:00 A.M.–4:00 P.M., Tues.–Sat.; NOON–4:00 P.M., Sun.; admission fee) was built in 1785 by Philip Fendall. A long line of Lees lived in this house. (548-1789)

The *Lloyd House*, 220 N. Washington St. (open 9:00 A.M.–5:00 P.M., Mon–Sat.) is known for its fine Georgian architecture. An extensive collection of rare books, records and displays on Alexandria and Virginia history is available for historic research. (838-4577)

The *Visitors Center* of the Alexandria Tourist Council is housed in the Ramsay House, 221 King St., 549-0205. Known as "Alexandria's Oldest House," it served as the home of the town's first Mayor, William Ramsay, and dates back to 1751.

Open 9:00 A.M. to 5:00 P.M., daily (except holidays) the Tourist Council provides brochures on a walking tour of Alexandria, information and maps of other tourist attractions, a calendar of events, and guides to restaurants, antique stores, shops, lodging and art galleries. This should be your first stop. Walking tours lasting an hour or more are highly recommended. A block ticket for admission to four historic houses costs $5.

Visit, too, *The Lyceum* at the corner of Washington and Prince Sts. This renovated structure serves as an interpretive center for Alexandria's history from Colonial days to the present. You will see here paintings, antiques and artifacts, and may obtain maps, brochures, and help in obtaining accommodations. Open daily, 9:00 A.M. to 5:00 P.M. (838-4994)

The *Athenaeum, The Northern Virginia Fine Arts Association* at 201 Prince St., presents a series of exhibitions representative of fine arts, past and present, lectures, children's and adult programs including concerts and cinema. The building itself is one of Alexandria's two surviving examples of Greek neo-classical architecture. Open 10:00 A.M. to 4:00 P.M., Tues.–Sat.; 1:00 to 4:00 P.M. on exhibit Sundays. Closed Mondays and during the summer months.

For information on lodging, restaurants, shops and attractions write: Alexandria Tourist Council, 221 King S., Alexandria, VA 28314.

A favorite place to browse is the *Torpedo Factory*, 105 North Union St. (838-4565), where sculptors, potters, printmakers, jewelers, textile artists, and painters create and sell their works.

The *Annual Scottish Christmas Walk* takes place the first Saturday in December and features kilted bagpipers, Highland dancers, caroling, horses and dogs parading through the streets and many other holiday events.

A SOUTHERN EXCURSION

Having visited Alexandria for a taste of the "old South" you will probably plan Mount Vernon as your next stop. Press on! We urge you to continue down State Highway 235, just east of Route 1 near Fort Belvoir to see *Washington's Grist Mill* (open 10:00 A.M.–6:00 P.M., daily, June through August; closed in winter.) This handsome reconstruction of the grist mill built in 1770 by George Washington, will show you how an historic 18th-century mill looked and operated. In his day the nearby water permitted shipment of the wheat and corn to England and the West Indies. Interpretive exhibits explain how the machinery worked, and picnic tables nearby are for public use.

Continue on a short distance to *Woodlawn*, the hilltop plantation of Nellie Custis Lewis, Martha Washington's granddaughter, and her husband, Lawrence Lewis, George Washington's nephew. (See "Historic Homes.")

Follow Route 1 to *Pohick Church* (open 9:00 A.M.–5:00 P.M., daily) which served as Washington's and George Mason's home church. Washington surveyed for the site, drew the plans and served on the construction committee. Mason completed the interior of the building. During the Civil War the interior was used as a stable. The interior was fully restored before World War II, and today the church serves an active Episcopal congregation.

Your final stop will be at *Gunston Hall Plantation*, home of George Mason. A full description of this delightful estate appears in "Historic Homes."

A map of this area appears in the Map Section.

Arlington House

(THE ROBERT E. LEE MEMORIAL)

M Arlington Cemetery	WHERE	Arlington Cemetery, top of bluff due west of Memorial Bridge.
	WHEN	9:30 A.M.–4:30 P.M. daily, Oct.–Mar. (open until 6:00 P.M., Apr.–Sept.).
	HOW	Self-guided tours (except for groups by appointment.) Free.

Arlington House (also called "Custis-Lee Mansion") brings together the serenity of a southern plantation, the Washington and Lee families, and the drama of the Civil War. This was the home of George Washington Parke Custis, grandson of Martha Washington, and later the home of Robert E. Lee, his son-in-law. Arlington Cemetery is carved from the surrounding plantation lands. The view from the Mansion's portico on a high bluff overlooking the city, in itself merits a trip. You can see the impressive columns of the portico from many parts of downtown Washington.

The house and grounds have a particular charm that comes from age and distinction. The Mansion represents an outstanding example of classic Greek Revival architecture. George Hadfield, a talented young Englishman who came to America in 1795 to supervise work on the Capitol, worked on the plans of the house. The two-story central portion is flanked by two balanced wings, one story in height, with graceful, recessed windows. Foundations, walls and even the columns are of brick fired on the plantation, covered with stucco plaster on surfaces exposed to the weather. You can better appreciate the tour of the interior if you first walk around the building to see the fine old planting, the dominating portico of eight columns, Doric in style, on the river side and the extraordinary view.

The large central hall characterizes Virginia homes of the period. In the summer months the hallways of both the first and second floors were furnished with sofas and chairs for use as parlors. The winter kitchen under the north wing includes a large fireplace, a laundry and a wine cellar.

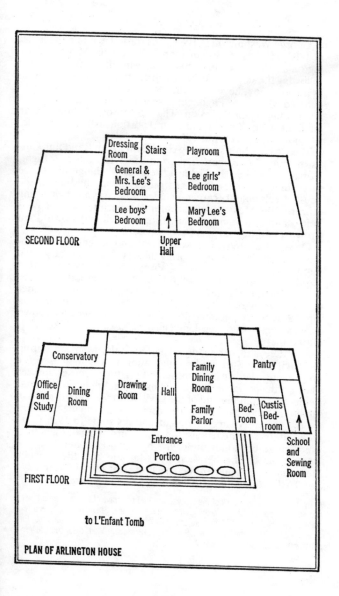

SECOND FLOOR

Dressing Room | Stairs | Playroom

General & Mrs. Lee's Bedroom | Lee girls' Bedroom

Lee boys' Bedroom | Mary Lee's Bedroom

Upper Hall

FIRST FLOOR

Conservatory | Pantry

Office and Study | Dining Room | Drawing Room | Hall | Family Dining Room | Bed-room | Custis Bed-room

Family Parlor

Entrance

Portico

School and Sewing Room

to L'Enfant Tomb

PLAN OF ARLINGTON HOUSE

George Washington Parke Custis started work on the house in 1802. He was the son of John Parke Custis, Martha Washington's son by her first marriage, who died of camp fever following the siege of Yorktown. Adopted by the Washingtons as a young boy, he grew up at Mount Vernon. In 1804 Custis married Mary Lee Fitzhugh; a year later they moved to the north wing of the Mansion. The custom of the time was to build the wings first and the central portion last. The structure was not completed until 1817.

The Custis's only surviving child, Mary Ann Randolph Custis, married Lt. Robert E. Lee in 1831. His father, "Light-Horse Harry" Lee, had been a friend of Washington's. In the succeeding 30 years the Lees raised seven children in the house. Lee's military career included service as an engineering officer in the Mexican War, a stint as superintendent of West Point, and command of the troops which put down John Brown's raid on Harpers Ferry.

On April 18, 1861, Lee was offered and declined field command of the Union army. During the next four years he gained fame as the brilliant leader of Virginia's military forces. On April 20 he resigned from the U.S. Army and left his home for Richmond. He never returned. Following the surrender of the Confederate forces at Appomattox Courthouse on April 9, 1865, Lee became president of the college now known as Washington and Lee University at Lexington, VA. He is buried there.

Mrs. Lee and her family abandoned the Mansion during the Civil War. Surrounding plantation lands, first used for army camps, later were confiscated for tax purposes and set aside for the burial of soldiers. Thus began Arlington National Cemetery. From the end of the Civil War until 1925 the house served as headquarters for the cemetery and living quarters for the cemetery superintendent and his staff. In 1925 Congress authorized the restoration and refurnishing of the house which continues today under the National Park Service.

On a direct line between the Mansion and the Lincoln Memorial is the grave of the late President John F. Kennedy. See "Arlington National Cemetery (Kennedy Graves)."

At the point of the best view of the city you will find the grave of Pierre L'Enfant, who laid out the Federal City at Washington's request. General Sheridan's grave is a few steps to the south, near a Monument to the Unknown Dead of the Civil War; also, the grave of John Clem, the "Drummer Boy of Chickamauga." Visit, also, the Old Amphitheatre, once used for Memorial Day services.

Arlington National Cemetery

(KENNEDY GRAVES)

M Arlington
Cemetery

WHERE   Directly west of Memorial Bridge in
        Arlington, VA.

WHEN   8:00 A.M.–7:00 P.M. every day
        (closes 5:00 P.M., Oct.–March).

HOW   By car, by cab, by Metro bus
        Tourmobile, or Metro subway.

*"Here rests in honored glory an American
soldier known but to God."*

Arlington National Cemetery covers the quiet and beautifully
landscaped hillsides overlooking the Potomac, directly west
of the Lincoln Memorial. Arlington House, visible from much
of downtown Washington, marks the heart of the cemetery.

A visit to the Tomb of the Unknown Soldier, the Memorial
Amphitheatre, and the Kennedy graves combines easily with
a trip to Arlington House.

The *Tomb of the Unknown Soldier* overlooks a green lawn
bordered by beech hedges. The monument of white marble
which marks the Tomb is of the most effective simplicity. The
sculptor was Thomas Hudson Jones and the architect Lorimer
Rich. Flat stones marking the Unknowns of World War II,
the Korean War and the Vietnam War flank the Tomb.

A solitary soldier paces out his guard of honor before the
Tomb. With the utmost precision the guard takes 21 steps,
stops, turns toward Washington, stands motionless for 21 seconds, turns and shifts his rifle to the shoulder away from the
Tomb, and again stands motionless for 21 seconds, before
retracing his steps. Every hour on the hour October through
March, and every half hour April through September, the
guard is ceremoniously changed. All sentries are selected from
the Army's 1st Battalion, 3rd United States Infantry (The Old
Guard) stationed at Fort Myer.

The *Memorial Amphitheatre* adjoining the Tomb follows
the design of Greek and Roman theaters. It provides the

official site for the Memorial and Veteran's Day Services attended by government leaders, members of the diplomatic corps, veterans groups and citizens. Carrère and Hastings designed the Amphitheatre. Completed in 1920 at a cost of $825,000, it has a capacity of 4,000.

The *Trophy Room* at the east end of the Amphitheatre houses decorations conferred on the Unknown Soldier by allied nations.

The mast towering to the west was salvaged from the *U.S.S. Maine*. The sinking of the battleship in Havana harbor provided the battle cry ("Remember the Maine") for the Spanish-American War.

Tomb of the Unknown Soldier

Arlington House has memorials of special interest close by. A granite slab engraved with his plan of Washington marks the grave of Pierre L'Enfant. A massive sarcophagus identifies the Tomb of the 2,111 Unknown Dead of the Civil War, near the grave of General Philip Sheridan. The wisteria-covered old amphitheatre formerly used for memorial services, is exceptionally lovely in spring.

On the sloping hillside below Arlington House is the *grave of the late President John Fitzgerald Kennedy*. The visitor approaches it by a granite walkway from the road below, and senses immediately the appropriateness of the monument by John Carl Warnecke. An imposing overlook, in essence a small, formal park defined by a low, curved wall inscribed with quotations from Kennedy's inaugural address, affords a

J.F. Kennedy Gravesite

magnificent view of the distant capital. Note the excellence of the incised lettering by calligrapher John Benson.

The rectangular grave area is conceived as a more personal part of the site. Five marble steps lead from the platform to the grave itself, marked by the eternal flame. Rough field-stones from Cape Cod cover the plot, contrasting strongly with the marble platform. Simple slate headstones mark the President's grave and those of his infant son and daughter. Mrs. Paul Mellon is responsible for the landscaping which combines a glorious variety of flowering trees—spring bloom-ing magnolias, cherry and hawthorne, and evergreens and plants. The monument is moving in its great beauty and sim-plicity.

The *grave of the late Senator Robert F. Kennedy* lies nearby. Arlington cemetery traces its origins to the Civil War. Until the war's outbreak, Robert E. Lee occupied the Mansion and farmed the surrounding plantation. In 1861, shortly after Lee declined command of the Northern forces and left to join the Confederacy, Union troops occupied his home and converted the surrounding fields into a Union army camp. In 1864 the Union acquired the 210 acres first set aside for the burial of soldiers under controversial circumstances: the government bought the land at public auction after refusing payment of taxes from an agent of Mrs. Lee's. By law it had been required that Mrs. Lee should appear in person to pay the taxes. After the deaths of both General and Mrs. Lee, their son sued for the return of the Custis Estate, claiming it by right of inheritance. The case was eventually settled by the Supreme Court, and he relinquished all rights to the property for $150,000. Additions have brought the cemetery acreage to its present size of 1,100 acres.

Memorial Bridge connects the capital city and the Lincoln Memorial with Arlington House and the National Cemetery, providing both a physical and symbolic reunification of the North and South. Interment is reserved for members of the armed services who die on active duty, recipients of the Medal of Honor, and retired members of the military, together with their wives and minor children.

One other President of the United States, William H. Taft, is buried in Arlington. Among the distinguished persons interred in the cemetery are General Omar Bradley, William Jennings Bryan, Rear Admiral Richard E. Byrd, Roger B. Chaffee and Virgil I. Grissom (astronauts), John Foster Dulles, Medgar Evers, James V. Forrestal, Oliver Wendell Holmes, Jr., Rear Admiral Robert E. Peary, General John J. Pershing and General Philip H. Sheridan.

Cars are not admitted to Arlington Cemetery. Ample parking is provided in a large lot near the entrance (free; two hours). Touring the cemetery on foot is possible, but distances are great. Tourmobiles are the only vehicles allowed to drive through the grounds. They leave from the Visitor's Center at regular intervals. The narrated tour takes about one hour, stops at the Kennedy Graves, the Tomb of the Unknown Soldier and Arlington House. Cost: adults $2.25; children (2–11), $1. The Tourmobile operates from 8:00 A.M. to 6:30 P.M. Apr. to Sept., and until 4:30 P.M. the rest of the year.

Bureau of Engraving and Printing

M Smithsonian

WHERE West side of 14th St. at C. St., S.W.

WHEN Visitor's Center: 8:30 A.M.–2:30 P.M., Mon.–Fri.; closed Sat., Sun., and holidays.

HOW Self-guided, admission-free tour; allow 25 min.

The Bureau of Engraving and Printing designs, engraves and prints all major items of a financial character issued by the United States Government. It produces paper currency, Treasury bonds, bills, notes and certificates; and postage, revenue, customs, documentary stamps and food coupons. In addition, the Bureau prints commissions, certificates of awards, permits and a wide variety of other miscellaneous items. Currency and postage stamps comprise the greatest volume of work produced. Engraved printings range in face value from the one-cent postage stamp to the $500,000,000 Treasury Note. Annually, the Bureau delivers approximately 40 billion security items having a face value of approximately $300,000,000,000.

Visitors to the Bureau enter by way of 14th Street and proceed up the bridge to the escalator entrance which leads to the glass-enclosed gallery. The tour is about one-fifth of a mile in length and terminates at the exit escalator on the 15th Street side of the building.

Along the tour visitors will observe the entire operation of producing currency, beginning with the printing of blank sheets of distinctive paper, continuing through the processes of sheet examining, trimming, overprinting (seals and serial numbers), cutting the sheets into individual notes, and making "star" note replacements, ending with the packaging of the notes for delivery from the Bureau. In addition, you may view the intaglio printing of multi-color commemorative postage stamps. An audio system explains the various operations.

The paper currency you have in your pocket was printed here by the engraved intaglio process. It takes approximately

15 days to produce a single note at an estimated cost of 2.4 cents per note. Under normal usage the average life expectancy of a one dollar bill is 18 months. Special security features which help to protect you against currency counterfeiting include, in part, special formula paper and printing inks and the engraved intaglio printing method employed in the manufacture of paper currency.

The Bureau of Engraving and Printing does not mint metal coins. These are produced by the Bureau of the Mint in Philadelphia, Denver and San Francisco.

While on tour, the taking of photographs is prohibited, and no smoking is allowed. Parking facilities are not available. Take public transportation, walk, or take one of the many bus tours which include the Bureau as one of the major attractions. During the peak tourist season (April–August) you are urged to arrive no later than 2:00 P.M. Inquiries regarding the prints (presidential portraits, seals, vignettes, etc.) available for sale to the general public should be referred to:

Bureau of Engraving and Printing
Public Affairs
14th and C Sts., N.W.
Washington, DC 20228
447-0193

The
Capitol

M Capitol
South

WHERE Capitol Hill.

WHEN 9:00 A.M.–4:30 P.M., daily. Closed
Thanksgiving, Christmas and New
Year's.

HOW Allow several hours; start with
excellent free conducted tours from
Rotunda every 15 min. until 3:45
P.M. Information: 225-6827.

See the Capitol, the most symbolic and representative building of our government, if it is the only thing you do in Washington. Here each year the U.S. Congress studies 18,000 bills,
enacts about 1,250 of them into permanent law, and in 1986
appropriated $979.9 billion to run the government.

Use the excellent conducted tour as your introduction to
the Capitol. The tours, discussed in detail below, leave every
15 minutes from the Rotunda and take about 45 minutes.

Try to make your visit during Congressional working hours.
You can then attend the House of Representatives and the
Senate in session and see "Congress in action" by attending
a hearing of a Congressional committee. Allow enough time
to take the tour, to attend a hearing and to follow up on your
own those aspects of the Capitol which interest you most.
Visitors not in tours must have a pass to the Senate or House
chambers. You may obtain one from your Senator or Congressman. Visitors from abroad may obtain a pass to the
Senate gallery from the office of the Sergeant at Arms of the
Senate by showing identification. Passes to the House of Representatives gallery may be obtained from the Doorkeeper of
the House on the gallery floor.

Congress convenes the first Monday in January and usually
adjourns late in the year. The normal hours for the House
and Senate on weekdays are from noon until late afternoon.
Session hours, however, frequently change. Committee hearings are usually scheduled during the morning or for other
hours when the Congress is not in actual session. (A committee must obtain special authority to sit while its chamber
is in session.)

To check on committee meeting times and places—and whether the hearings are open to the public or closed ("executive")—look for "In Congress," in the *Washington Post*, usually in the first section. You can check directly by telephone with any committee in which you are interested (224-3121), and ask for the committee.

One further word of introduction before you go on your tour. As you pass through the corridors on the Senate side, on the first-floor level, stop and admire the beautifully decorated panels on the walls by Constantino Brumidi, the "Michelangelo of the Capitol." The overall effect is extraordinary. Brumidi was an Italian who came to this country in 1852. He expressed his gratitude to his adopted country by devoting more than 25 years to decorating the interior of the Capitol. You will see his greatest work in the eye of the Dome and in the design of the frieze in the Rotunda.

TOUR OF THE CAPITOL

THE ROTUNDA

Groups now assemble in the *Rotunda*. The great central room has unusual proportions (180 feet high and 97 feet across). The softly colored fresco by Constantino Brumidi in the eye of the dome is the *Apotheosis of Washington*. It covers 4,664 feet of surface and shows the first President attended by Liberty, Victory and Fame. Female figures around him represent the 13 original states. Six allegorical groups stand for Commerce, Mechanics, Agriculture, War, Marine, and Arts and Sciences. Some of the figures are 15 feet tall; from the floor they appear life-size. If your neck troubles you, remember that the artist had to lie flat on his back on a scaffold 180 feet above the floor to execute this masterpiece.

Brumidi also started the 300-foot frieze which encircles the Rotunda 58 feet above the floor. Note the sculpture-like appearance of the figures of the fresco. For three years the aged artist worked on these scenes depicting important events in American history and completed the first seven. One day his chair slipped from the scaffolding; he clung desperately to the rung of a ladder until he was rescued some 15 minutes later. The shock of the accident resulted in his death soon afterward. Filippo Costaggini finished the next eight panels from Brumidi's sketches, but crowded them to make room for a design of his own. The last 30 feet remained empty until Allyn Cox

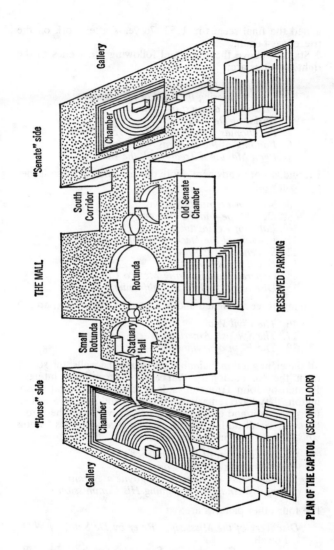

PLAN OF THE CAPITOL (SECOND FLOOR)

"Senate" side

Gallery

Chamber

South Corridor

Old Senate Chamber

THE MALL

Rotunda

RESERVED PARKING

Small Rotunda

Statuary Hall

"House" side

Gallery

Chamber

added the final scenes in 1953, 76 years after work on the frieze was begun.

Starting above the clock and following the scenes to the right the titles are:

1. *Landing of Columbus*
2. *Cortez Entering the Hall of Montezuma*
3. *Pizarro's Conquest of Peru*
4. *Burial of De Soto*
5. *Pocahontas Saving the Life of John Smith*
6. *Landing of the Pilgrims*
7. *Penn Making a Treaty with the Indians*

Brumidi's work ends here. Note the crowding in these scenes by Costaggini:

8. *Scene in Plymouth Colony*
9. *Oglethorpe and the Indians*
10. *Battle of Lexington*
11. *Reading of the Declaration of Independence*
12. *Surrender of Cornwallis*
13. *Death of Tecumseh*
14. *General Scott Entering Mexico City*
15. *Discovery of Gold in California*

The last three, designed and executed by Allyn Cox, are:

16. *The Civil War*
17. *The Spanish-American War*
18. *The Birth of Aviation*

Of the eight giant *oil paintings* encircling the walls, the scenes from the Revolutionary War are of exceptional interest. Painted by John Trumbull, aide-de-camp to General Washington, they have remarkable accuracy and detail. Washington, Jefferson and other leading figures were sketched from life. The small outline below each picture identifies "who's who." These four important pictures are:

The Declaration of Independence
The Surrender of Lord Cornwallis
The Surrender of General Burgoyne at Saratoga
General Washington Resigning His Commission

The four other pictures are:

Discovery of the Mississippi River by De Soto, by W.H. Powell
Landing of Columbus on San Salvador, by John Vanderlyn

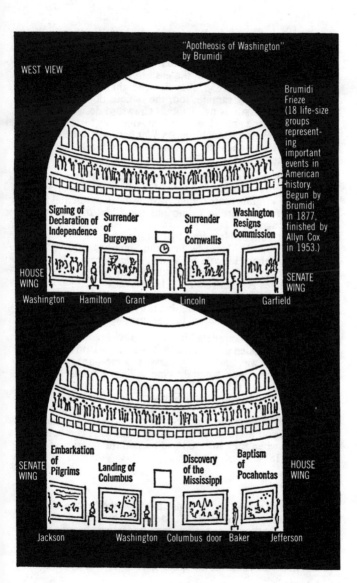

"Apotheosis of Washington"
by Brumidi

WEST VIEW

Brumidi Frieze (18 life-size groups representing important events in American history. Begun by Brumidi in 1877, finished by Allyn Cox in 1953.)

HOUSE WING

SENATE WING

Signing of Declaration of Independence

Surrender of Burgoyne

Surrender of Cornwallis

Washington Resigns Commission

Washington Hamilton Grant Lincoln Garfield

SENATE WING

HOUSE WING

Embarkation of Pilgrims

Landing of Columbus

Discovery of the Mississippi

Baptism of Pocahontas

Jackson Washington Columbus door Baker Jefferson

Embarkation of the Pilgrims, by Robert W. Weir
Baptism of Pocahontas, by John G. Chapman

Note the handsome *bronze doors* which form the main entrance to the Rotunda from the eastern portico. Modeled by Randolph Rogers in 1858, they depict eight scenes from the life of Columbus. Examine, too, the famous door at the entrance to the Senate wing. Thomas Crawford designed eight panels illustrating important events in American history, most of them scenes from Revolutionary War battles. Of the *statues* around the Rotunda, some are considered better than others. Those starred merit special notice:

★   1. Thomas Jefferson (at 33) by David d'Angers
★   2. George Washington (after Houdon's famous original in Virginia State Capitol). Shown in Continental uniform he wore as Commander-in-Chief of the Army at age 54
      3. Alexander Hamilton by Horatio Stone
      4. Ulysses S. Grant by Franklin Simmons
      5. Abraham Lincoln by Vinnie Ream Hoxie
      6. Roger Williams by Franklin Simmons
      7. James A. Garfield by C.H. Niehaus
      8. Andrew Jackson by L.F. and Belle Kinney Scholz
      9. Marquis de Lafayette, bust, by David d'Angers
   10. George Washington, bronze bust, by David d'Angers

The Rotunda was completed in 1827 and covered with a copper covered wooden dome until 1855, when work on the great cast-iron dome was started. The massive dome—a shell within a shell—weighs approximately nine million pounds; it was completed during the Civil War, in 1865.

Between the Rotunda and Statuary Hall you will pass a *Small Rotunda*, a circular room with domed ceiling and cupola, which reflects the simplicity of the Federal neo-classic school. As you leave, note the circular stairway, climbed by the British when they stormed and burned the interior of the Capitol in 1814.

HOUSE SIDE

Statuary Hall served as the legislative chamber of the House of Representatives until 1857. Designed by Benjamin Latrobe, this handsome, semicircular room features breccia marble Corinthian columns and a domed ceiling reminiscent of the Pantheon in Rome—but its acoustics are notoriously poor. A disc in the floor marks the spot where John Quincy Adams,

How the Capitol Grew ... 170 Years of Evolution

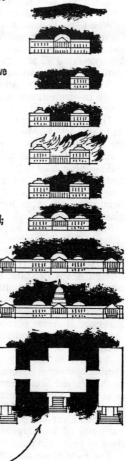

1790   First proclamation by Washington to acquire "Jenkin's Hill," former campsite of Powhatan Indians.

1793   Architectural plan of Dr. William Thornton accepted April 5 ... $500 award; cornerstone laid Sept. 18, 1793.

1800   North wing finished; House and Senate move from Philadelphia and crowd into it.

1801   Judiciary moves to Washington.

1811   South wing completed; joined to North by wooden passageway.

1814   British burn Capitol, August 24.

1819   Capitol again ready for occupancy.

1829   Restoration of North and South buildings completed and new central portion erected; cost $2,433,844 through 1827.

1857   Present House wing completed and House Chamber occupied.

1859   Present Senate Chamber completed and occupied.

1865   Present dome of cast iron completed, replacing old dome of wood, covered with copper.

1897   Library of Congress moved to its own building.

1935   Supreme Court Justices move from Old Senate Chamber.

1951   Restoration and modernization of House and Senate Chambers, roof and ceiling of wings ... first major changes in Chambers in 90 years.

1962   East Front extension of Capitol completed, adding 32½ feet; cost, including dome repairs, subway terminal and other work, $24,000,000.

1987   Replacement of deteriorated stonework on West Central Front.

the sixth President, was fatally stricken on February 21, 1848, at the age of 81. After serving as President he had returned to Congress as a member of the House, and served eight terms—from 1831 until his death.

When the House in 1864 voted to utilize the old House Chamber as a National Statuary Hall, each state was invited to contribute two statues of eminent citizens. To date 50 states have donated 92 statues. Because of their great weight, the statues have been spread over to the Hall of Columns, House and Senate corridors and elsewhere in the Capitol. The great range of size, stance, costume and artistic merit creates an extraordinary sight.

The *House of Representatives Chamber*, occupied in 1857 and remodeled 1949–51, is the largest legislative chamber in the world (139 feet long, 92 feet wide, 42 feet high to the oculus). In the center of the new stainless steel portion of the ceiling there is an oculus, the field of which is of curved glass and bronze outlining the figure of an eagle, illuminated from above. Painted plaster reproductions of the state seals have been installed, reproducing those seals formerly painted on glass in the old laylight ceiling removed from the Chamber.

Seats for the 435 Representatives are arranged in a semi-circle with Democrats on the Speaker's right, Republicans on his left, separated by the *aisle*. Joint meetings of the Senate and House are held here for such events as addresses by foreign heads of state, ministers, kings, diplomats and important public personalities. Only the President of the United States may address Congress in joint session.

When the House is called to order each day an assistant Sergeant at Arms places the Mace of the House of Representatives on a cylindrical pedestal of polished green marble at the right of the Speaker's desk.

Aside from the flag, the Mace provides the only visible symbol of federal government authority. It has no counterpart in the United States Senate, none in the Supreme Court. It is as old as the government itself, having been provided for in a resolution adopted by the House during the First Congress in 1789. Ever since it has served as the active symbol of authority of the Sergeant at Arms, who is charged with the duty of preserving order on the floor of the House.

The *First Floor* contains restaurants, transportation offices and a post office. The room directly below the giant Rotunda is known as the *Crypt*. Had not George Washington's relatives refused to have his body removed from Mount Vernon, he would have been re-interred below the crypt. The empty tomb

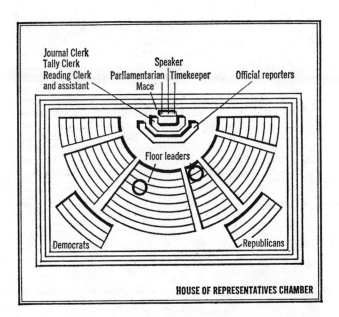

Journal Clerk
Tally Clerk
Reading Clerk
and assistant

Speaker
Parliamentarian | Timekeeper
Mace

Official reporters

Floor leaders

Democrats

Republicans

HOUSE OF REPRESENTATIVES CHAMBER

remains there today. The busts of the suffragettes Lucretia Mott, Susan B. Anthony and Elizabeth Cady Stanton, familiarly referred to as "Three Women in a Tub," are a Capitol landmark. The 24 million dollar extension project, initiated in 1956 and completed in 1962, extended 32½ feet to the Capitol's East Front. On the first-floor level, a new reception room has been created. Over 100 rooms were added.

SENATE SIDE

The *Old Senate Chamber*, on the Senate side of the Rotunda, was the meeting place of the Senate until 1859. Here Calhoun, Clay and Webster delivered their great speeches. The Supreme Court occupied the room from 1860 until it moved to the new Supreme Court Building in 1935. See also the original *Supreme Court Chamber*, which has been restored to its 1859 appearance.

The *Senate* has been located in its present chamber since 1859. The cream and dark red marble, mahogany desks and gold silk damask walls contribute an air of dignity and elegance to the chamber as remodeled in 1949–51. The chandelier in the hall outside the south entrance tells whether the Senate is in session. Two bulbs are attached to the lower part of the chandelier; the red one signals an executive session, the white, a regular session. Seating is assigned by seniority. Note the small crystal bottles on each desk. Used in former days as containers for sand to blot ink, they are continued today as a tradition and may have some usefulness as paperweights. The absence of portraits, paintings and frescoes is attributable to a resolution passed in 1884 that no such ornamentation should decorate the Chamber. You will, however, see busts of the Vice-Presidents in niches on the gallery level.

HOW THE CONGRESS WORKS

You can come closer to seeing government in action in the Capitol than any place else. You may well pass Senators and

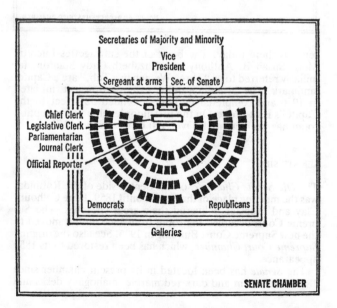

Congressmen in the corridors. Most of their legislative work takes place in the capitol and in the adjoining office buildings. (See "How to Pass a Bill," page 300).

Two simple rules will help you understand the practical side of how Congress functions. First: the several dozen committees of Congress do virtually all the legislative groundwork, including consideration of all bills introduced. Second: these committees are organized along party lines. For example, when the Democrats have a majority in the Senate, more Democrats than Republicans are appointed to each of the Senate committees and the senior Democrat becomes the chairman of the committee.

Very practical consequences flow from this committee-party system of operation. If a committee will not act on a bill ("bottles it up in committee") that almost always means the end of it. On the other hand, when a committee votes favorably on a bill, detailed legislative work on it has been largely completed.

As a result, routine bills need not be debated on the floor of Congress; on controversial bills the political parties have recognized and taken their positions on the issues well in advance.

Do not be disillusioned, therefore, when you find no great Webster-Clay debates occurring when you visit the House or Senate chambers. Your Congressman or Senator may not seem to be paying much attention to the proceedings. He may very well not be there. However, he knows what is happening; he has the committee reports on the bills under debate and knows his party's position on each one. He is represented on the floor by his party's floor leader, who follows the debate closely and summons him when his presence is necessary.

He also follows developments by a system of bells that you will hear throughout the Capitol and the office buildings during sessions.

Originally the Senate and the House embodied more divergent theories of government than they do now. The Senate at first stood for the idea of government through elected representatives and for state sovereignty. Until 1913, state legislatures elected the Senators from their state. Now, of course, Senators are elected by popular vote.

From the beginning, the House of Representatives stood for the democratic theory of direct representation of the citizenry. Since there was to be no taxation without representation, and only the House provided direct representation, the Constitution limits the origination of money bills to the House.

The Senate has the special power to "confirm" major Presidential appointments, which under the Constitution are to be made "by and with the advice of the Senate." The Senate rarely votes not to confirm, but from time to time enough resistance against an appointee has developed in the Senate to make the withdrawl of his or her name expedient.

The *closing days of Congress* provide one of the great shows of the Capitol. Congress acts on hundreds of bills before adjourning, cutting through issues accumulated throughout the rest of the session. Try to attend this free spectacle if you are in Washington during this time, particularly a night session. Remember that you must obtain a card from your Senator or Congressman to be admitted to the galleries.

There are more romantic ways to determine when Congress is meeting than to telephone the Capitol. A flag flies over the Senate wing and over the House wing whenever—day or night—that chamber is in session. Everyone within eyeshot of the Capitol can follow night sessions by looking at the upper dome of the Capitol, where a light burns whenever either House is meeting.

The colossal statue of *Freedom*, designed by Thomas Crawford, was erected atop the newly completed iron dome of the Capitol on December 2, 1863, with the hope that the ceremony "would provide inspiration for the dispirited Union troops." The 19½-foot figure of a woman in flowing draperies carries a sheathed sword, a wreath and a shield. Her helmet is topped by an eagle's head; flowing plumage suggests an American Indian headdress.

During your visit to the Capitol be sure to stroll to the West Front to admire the stunning vista of the Mall, the Washington Monument and, in the far distance, the Lincoln Memorial. It was here that Ronald Reagan took his oath of office in 1981 and 1985. The scaffolding and construction spanning the West Front of the building is part of a $49 million restoration project begun in 1983 to strengthen the foundation and underpinnings of the vaulted structure.

Before you leave home, and well in advance, write to your Congressman or Senator for tickets to the morning congressional tour. Request a Visitor's Pass, which will allow you to sit in the balcony of the House or Senate to view a session.

OFFICE BUILDINGS

Senate and House Office Buildings contain the office suites provided for each legislator, as well as most of the committee suites and hearing rooms. Unless you visit the office of one of your representatives, or attend a committee hearing, you will find the office buildings of no particular interest.

The *Old Senate ("Russell") Office Building* has been in use since 1909, the *New Senate ("Dirksen") Office Building* since 1958. The famous Senate *subway*, now completely modernized, connects the basements of the Senate office buildings with the Capitol. The public is welcome to a ride—"No charge!"

The *Cannon Office Building* was occupied in 1908, the *Longworth Office Building* in 1933, and the huge *Rayburn Office Building* in 1965, all named for former speakers of the House. Representatives and the public may ride the subway from the Rayburn terminal to the Capitol.

Cherry Blossoms

WHERE   Tidal Basin; Hains Point.

WHEN   About two weeks bet. Mar. 20 and
Apr. 20 for Tidal Basin; East
Potomac Park two weeks later.

HOW   On foot or by (bumper to bumper)
car.

You may be one of the 700,000 visitors who has made special plans to see the dramatic display of white (and some pink) cherry blossoms. You will need a bit of luck in timing your visit. The blossoms cannot be predicted accurately until about ten days before they are out. They usually appear between March 20 and April 15: over the years April 5 has been the average date. The trees remain in bloom for the better part of two weeks, barring high winds and frost.

Most blossoms around the Tidal Basin are of the single, white variety. These are the famous Yoshino trees, which form 90 percent of the Tidal Basin cherries. The other 10 percent are the Akebonos, which produce a single blossom of pale pink. They are the earliest of the cherries to flower.

Some six other varieties are planted in East Potomac Park (Hains Point). Double blossom cherries predominate. These are deep pink in color and appear about two weeks after the Yoshinos and Akebonos. The average date is April 22.

The city of Tokyo contributed this distinctive addition to the beauty of Washington in spring. In 1912, Tokyo sent 3,000 flowering cherries of a dozen varieties, all specially grafted for the transplanting. Our gratitude is also due to Mrs. William Howard Taft. She had expressed an interest in planting Japanese cherries soon after her husband became President and the gift was in response to her interest. Bronze markers commemorate the planting by Mrs. Taft and by Viscountess Chinda, wife of the Japanese Ambassador, of the first two trees on March 27, 1912. You will find the markers due west of the John Paul Jones statue, at the south end of 17th Street.

Tokyo's courtesy has been returned. The parent trees in suburban Tokyo deteriorated from lack of care during World War II. In 1952 the National Capital Parks was able to send cuttings from the gift trees to replenish the parent stock.

Each year a Cherry Blossom Festival is held. It opens with the lighting of a 300-year-old ceremonial lantern and includes a pageant, a parade and the crowning of a Cherry Blossom queen, chosen from princesses representing the 50 states. The planners of the festival must guess, even as you and I, when the blossoms will be out. If you mistime your visit, you may have official company.

Don't tour the blossom area by car unless you enjoy seeing as many cars as blossoms. Drive instead to Kenwood, MD, six miles northwest of the Tidal Basin, which has a superb stand of single white blossom trees. The Kenwood cherries line both sides of its several miles of streets and are more tightly massed than at the Tidal Basin.

Chesapeake and Ohio Canal

WHERE   The C&O Canal starts in
        Georgetown (½ block south of 30th
        and M Sts., N.W.) and parallels the
        Potomac River to Cumberland, MD,
        184.5 miles west.

HOW   Walks, talks and tours available
        year-round at various places around
        the city. Call Dial-a-Park for
        information: 426-6975.

Despite devastating damage to the Chesapeake and Ohio Canal committed by successive hurricanes, it is still possible to enjoy hiking, biking, fishing, canoeing and conducted nature hikes by volunteers and Park Service Rangers. *Kiosk*, a monthly calendar of events, details the rich program of events offered by the National Park Service from canoe lessons to wildflower walks, concerts and outdoor sketching. (To receive free copies write *Kiosk* Editor, Office of Public Affairs, National Capital Region, 1100 Ohio Drive, S.W., Washington, DC 20242.)

Hiking and biking along the towpath of the canal still provide a year-round pleasure. Start at the barge landing in Georgetown or at Great Falls (Maryland side). The restored Great Falls Tavern offers a museum illustrating canal history (open daily from 9:30 A.M. to 5:00 P.M.).

One and a half hour *mule-drawn boat trips* are available on the *Canal Clipper* (located in Potomac, MD) and *The Georgetown* (located between 30th and Thomas Jefferson Sts., N.W.). For schedule and reservations call 472-6685 (*Georgetown*) and 299-3614 (*Canal Clipper*).

Canoes, rowboats and *bicycles* are for rent at Fletcher's Boat House, 4940 Canal Rd., N.W., about three miles north of Georgetown on the left side of the road. Canoes may also be rented at Swain's Lock off River Rd., just north of the town of Potomac, MD.

Ice skating on the canal is a rare treat. The frozen canal provides a scene as beautiful as a Dutch painting.

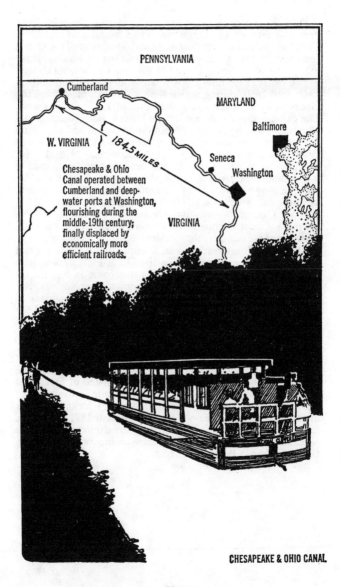

PENNSYLVANIA

MARYLAND

Cumberland

Baltimore

W. VIRGINIA

184.5 MILES

Seneca

Washington

Chesapeake & Ohio Canal operated between Cumberland and deep-water ports at Washington, flourishing during the middle-19th century; finally displaced by economically more efficient railroads.

VIRGINIA

CHESAPEAKE & OHIO CANAL

During most of the 19th century, waterways provided the principal arteries of commerce. The Chesapeake and Ohio Canal was one of the earliest and most significant of the canals constructed during the great canal-building era; today, it remains one of the least altered of the older American canals.

The canal as we now know it was under construction from 1828 until 1850, during which time it was extended from the Georgetown Division to Cumberland, MD, 184.5 miles west. The canal company succeeded the historic Potowmack Canal Company, which operated on both the Virginia and Maryland sides of the Potomac River between 1785 and 1828. George Washington invested $10,000 in this company. He also supervised much of the work: he was deeply interested in uniting the Atlantic seaboard colonies with the land west of the Alleghenies by means of the Potomac River. On his death, Washington's stock was left to found the university which has become George Washington University. Although the Potowmack Canal Company went bankrupt in 1828, the University survives as a leading eastern center of learning.

The older Potowmack Canal Company also made a great contribution to engineering. In the Great Falls area a drop of 76 feet in water level had to be overcome in less than a mile, without adequate construction tools or explosives. Before construction of the Great Falls locks, no engineer in America had even seen a canal lock and few understood the mechanical principles involved. Two of the original five locks that met this challenge remain in fair condition and are accessible to the public at Great Falls Park, VA.

Cargo in early years consisted of coal, stone, grain, whiskey, lumber and flour, but later was confined largely to coal. The mule-drawn barges moved at an average speed of four miles an hour. When not working, the mules rode in the bows of the boats. Between the terminal points 74 locks raised or lowered the barges over 600 feet. In the year 1871, 530 boats carried some 850,000 tons of coal. Thereafter the commerce of canals declined, under increasing competition from the faster and more flexible railroads.

Corcoran
Gallery of Art

M Farragut North
or West

WHERE   17th St. at New York Ave., N.W.

WHEN   10:00 A.M.–4:30 P.M.,
Tues.–Sun.; until 9:00 P.M.
Thurs.; closed Mon. and holidays.

HOW   Private Gallery; tours 12:30 P.M.,
Tues.–Sun. Free admission except
for special exhibitions.

The Corcoran Gallery of Art houses as a nucleus the great collections of William Wilson Corcoran and Senator William Andrews Clark. Although dedicated primarily "to the encouragement of the American genius," the Gallery goes well beyond native confines and has an excellent and representative group of European works.

The Corcoran paintings provide an illustrative "Who's Who" of American art. Early American portraitists include Smibert, Copley, Sully, Rembrandt Peale and other members of the gifted Peale family. You will see two famous portraits of George Washington by Gilbert Stuart, known as the Athenaeum portraits. They will be familiar to you because of their reproduction on the one-dollar bill and the one-cent stamp. Less familiar to most people will be the portrait of Abraham Lincoln by George Healy, painted in Springfield, Illinois, before he became President and before he grew his beard. The Hudson River School and the mid-19th-century genre painters are well represented, and in addition such late 19th-century American impressionists as Childe Hassam and Mary Cassatt. Note Samuel F.B. Morse's remarkable example of documentary realism, the large, detailed, richly colored *Congress Hall* (the Old House of Representatives) painted in 1822 before he turned to scientific invention. Study the 86 portraits in this imposing picture, for which each person sat. Of later American painters, you may enjoy works of Winslow Homer, James A. McN. Whistler, John Singer Sargent, Thomas Eakins, Albert Pinkham Ryder, John Sloan and George Bellows, as well as the better known contemporary artists.

The first floor west wing houses the varied collection of Senator Clark. Here you can see what may be the largest collection of Corot's paintings outside the Louvre, and an outstanding group of Dutch and Flemish paintings of the 17th century. The wing also includes English master portraits, stained-glass windows from France, faïence ware, and the magnificent Tournai tapestries in Gallery 31. The scenes of court life depicted in the tapestries give us a glimpse of activities engaged in by nobles during the reign of Louis XII in the late 15th century. Don't fail to see the Grand Salon from the Hôtel d'Orsay in Paris, built by Boucher d'Orsay in the reign of Louis XVI. It has been moved and reconstructed in its entirety.

Since 1907 the Corcoran has sponsored the Biennial Exhibition of contemporary American painting, a noteworthy national show held for six weeks.

William Wilson Corcoran, Washington banker and philanthropist, gave his collection to the city of Washington in 1869. Its original home was in the striking building at the corner of 17th St. and Pennsylvania Ave., designed by James Renwick (the architect of the Smithsonian Institution and St. Patrick's Cathedral in New York). The present neo-classic building dates from 1897; Ernest Flagg served as architect. Two bronze lions guard the entrance; they were cast from those modeled by Canova for the tomb of Pope Clement XIII in St. Peter's, Rome. The Clark wing was added in 1928 to carry out Senator Clark's desire to have his collection exhibited as a unit. The north part of the building houses the Corcoran School of Art.

The Corcoran regularly features exhibitions of fine art photography and works by artists of the Washington region.

Federal Bureau of Investigation

(J. EDGAR HOOVER
FBI BUILDING)

M Metro
Center

WHERE Between 9th and 10th Sts. and
Pennsylvania Ave., N.W., E St.
Entrance.

WHEN 9:00 A.M.–4:15 P.M., Mon.–Fri.,
exc. holidays.

HOW Free tours (allow 1¼ hours).
Reservations are suggested for
groups of 15 or more. (324-3447).

The FBI tour in the new J. Edgar Hoover FBI Building continues a long tradition in emphasizing the past achievements of the Bureau, the current challenges facing law enforcement and the need for teamwork among all citizens in preserving the public order. This tour has always been a favorite for tourists of all ages; prepare for a wait when Washington's season is in full swing.

A brief introductory motion picture featuring remarks by the FBI director will orient you to the work of the FBI. You will have a glimpse of historic FBI cases, such as those dating from the gangster era of the 1930s; national security and civil rights investigations of later decades; and other major cases depicting the wide range of FBI responsibilities.

One of the highlights of your tour will be a visit to the renowned FBI laboratory, where you will view scientific examinations involving evidence in cases currently being investigated by the FBI.

The tour ends with a bang. A special agent gives a firearms demonstration, firing a .38 caliber revolver and Thompson submachine gun. More than 5,000 visitors a day can be provided with a fascinating view of this important governmental agency at work.

Folger (Shakespeare) Library

M Union Station
or Capitol South

WHERE   201 E. Capitol St., S.E.

WHEN   10:00 A.M.–4:00 P.M. daily Apr. 15 to Labor Day. Closed Sun. rest of year.

HOW   Tours available. Exhibits self-explanatory.

The Folger is a library unlike any you have ever seen. The collection contains precious manuscripts, art works and 90,000 books on every aspect of Shakespeare's life, age and influence. The material dealing with British civilization for the period 1445–1715 is the finest outside Great Britain. Here, too, is a rich assemblage of theatrical material from the 16th through the early 19th century.

The Library building is remarkable, outside and inside. The exterior represents no bland imitation of Greek architecture, but a fresh blending of the classic with the modern. (Consider the problem of the architect, Paul Cret, in designing a building to go between the Delphic grandeur of the Supreme Court and the uncompromising Renaissance of the Library of Congress.)

The bas-relief panels along the East Capitol Street side complement the simplicity of the white marble exterior. These scenes from Shakespeare's plays are perhaps the finest work of the sculptor John Gregory. Do not overlook Brenda Putnam's Puck statue at the Capitol end of the building ("Lord, what fooles these mortals be!")

The interior style changes to Elizabethan, in accordance with the wishes of the donor, H.C. Folger. The exhibition rooms will give you the best flavor of Elizabethan times available on this continent.

The *Exhibition Hall* reproduces the great hall of an Elizabethan palace. Note particularly the oak paneling, the exceptional barrel-vaulted plaster ceiling with its design, and the floor characteristic of the period. The paintings, the decorations and the showcases in the Hall bring to life the manners, articles, apparel and activities typical of Elizabethan times. Each item is labeled and explained. Don't miss the Globe Playhouse model, built over a ten-year span by Dr. Adams to the scale of 1:24. The inner yard of the model has been paved with some 6,500 bricks cut to scale and the secondary roofs contain some 9,550 separate tiles!

The *Shakespearean Theatre* follows faithfully the public playhouses of Shakespeare's day, but does not copy any particular building. The Theatre allows you to see firsthand the amazing flexibility of the Elizabethan stage. The Shakespeare Theatre at the Folger performs here regularly. (See "Theater" section.)

This unique library and educational institution, run by Amherst College, is private. At the entrance you can purchase good quality, inexpensive paperbacks of Shakespeare's plays and a remarkable series of booklets on Elizabethan times (a popular example is *English Sports and Recreations*).

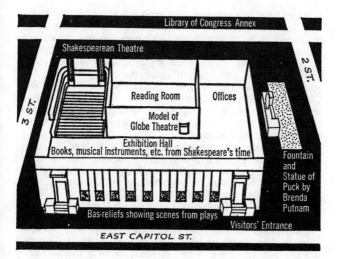

59

Ford's Theatre

M Metro Center
(11th St. Exit)

WHERE 511 10th Street, N.W.

WHEN 9:00 A.M.–5:00 P.M., daily.

HOW Admission free.

"I think I have done well." JOHN WILKES BOOTH

Ford's Theatre, the only theater in the country that is also a national monument, deserves your visit. Located in the heart of the downtown shopping area and within walking distance of the Mall attractions, the theater provides an opportunity to admire an historically accurate restoration of the building where Lincoln spent his last evening as President. You may also attend a live performance of a play most evenings throughout the year.

After Lincoln's assassination on April 14, 1865, the theater was not used as such until February 13, 1968, when it was reopened in its present form. Although the federal government purchased the building within a few months after the President's death, it was used for processing the records of Union soldiers, and later to house the Army Medical Museum—never as a place of entertainment. In 1964 the 88th Congress voted $2.7 million for full restoration of the building, using contemporary photographs, drawings, newspaper articles, official reports and samples of wallpaper and curtain material to ensure accuracy.

In the theater's basement you will find a museum of Lincoln memorabilia, grouped according to various aspects of his life—as husband and father, as politician, as President and statesman. The clothes he wore the night of the assassination, the 36-star flag that draped his coffin, Booth's confidential diary and the derringer pistol from which the fatal bullet was fired are on display.

Lincoln's assasination was part of a larger plot by the actor John Wilkes Booth and his Southern sympathizers directed toward General Grant, Vice President Johnson and Secretary of State Seward. The others escaped death, both Johnson and Grant later serving as Presidents of the United States. Johnson's assassin at the last moment found he could not go through with his assignment; Grant had a fortuitous change of plans and left the city the morning of April 14. Miss Clara Harris and her fiancé, Major Henry Rathbone, took General and Mrs. Grant's places in the Presidential party.

The occasion at Ford's Theatre was the presentation of Tom Taylor's *Our American Cousin,* a celebrated comedy of the day. As the Presidential party entered the flag-draped box, the audience cheered and the orchestra struck up "Hail to the Chief." At 10:15 Booth's shot rang through the theater. The assassin had entered Lincoln's box from the rear and fired at the back of the President's head with his single-shot derringer. Major Rathbone was stabbed while attempting to grapple with Booth, who then leaped to the stage, 11½ feet below. His spur caught in the Treasury Guard's Flag draped over the front of the box, causing him to fall and fracture a bone in his left foot. Eyewitnesses to the event quote Booth as shouting, "Sic Semper Tyrannis" (Ever Thus to Tyrants), as he dashed across the stage and out the rear door.

Pandemonium broke loose in the theater. Dr. Leale, a 23-year-old surgeon and specialist in gunshot wounds, rushed to the President's box. Fearful that the cobblestone ride to the White House would prove fatal to the President, he and two attending doctors ordered Lincoln carried across the street to the home of William Petersen, a Swedish tailor. Dr. Leale is credited with prolonging the President's life until 7:22 the next morning. To do so he used mouth-to-mouth artificial respiration.

Twelve days later, on April 26 at Port Royal, VA, Booth died of a gunshot wound inflicted by Bosten Corbett, a Federal cavalryman. All of Booth's accomplices were tried by a military commission. Four were hanged; three were sentenced to life imprisonment.

PETERSEN HOUSE

"Now he belongs to the ages."

After seeing Ford's Theatre and the Lincoln Museum, cross the street for a visit to the *Petersen House* at 516 10th St. (open the same hours). It was here that Abraham Lincoln died on the morning of April 15, 1865.

You will walk up the curved front steps over which the wounded President was carried, down the narrow hallway on the first floor. The sofa in the small, simple front parlor occupies the place it did when Mrs. Lincoln maintained her night-long vigil. The bedroom to which Lincoln was taken is strikingly small and starkly furnished. Because of his height

61

Lincoln on his deathbed, Petersen House, April 15, 1865

(6'4"), the President was forced to lie diagonally across the bed.

In the back parlor Secretary of War Edwin M. Stanton interviewed witnesses to the shooting. Lincoln lived through the night, but died at 7:22 the next morning. The quotation above is attributed to Stanton.

The house remains substantially as it was in 1865. William Petersen, a Swedish tailor, built the three-story red brick home in 1849. He kept his shop in the basement and rented the extra rooms. The government purchased the house in 1896. Five women's patriotic organizations assisted in refurnishing the house in 1932, using a diagram drawn shortly after Lincoln's death.

Freer Gallery of Art

M Smithsonian,
Mall Exit

WHERE   12th St. and Jefferson Drive, S.W.

WHEN   10:00 A.M.–5:30 P.M. daily
        (except Christmas Day).

HOW   Tours at 10:30 and 11:30 A.M.,
        1:00 and 2:00 P.M., Mon.–Sat.;
        1:00 and 2:00 P.M., Sun.

"A place to go and wash your eyes."

The Freer Gallery of Art houses one of the foremost collections of Far and Near Eastern art in the United States, and the world's largest collection of Whistler. The late art critic Aline Saarinen describes the gallery as "a pilgrimage spot for scholars in Oriental art and philosophy; a sight for. . .conscientious sighseers. . .; and for lovers of art. . .as John La Farge described it 'a place to go and wash your eyes.'"

The *Oriental* collections feature Chinese bronze, jade, painting, pottery, porcelain and sculpture; Greek, Aramaic and Armenian Biblical manuscripts; early Christian painting; Japanese ceramics, painting and sculpture; Korean pottery and bronze; Near Eastern painting, pottery, metalwork and sculpture; illuminated manuscripts, painting and sculpture from India; and sculpture, glass and metal-work from Egypt and Syria. The *Library* on the ground floor contains over 30,000 books and pamphlets on the arts and cultures of the East.

Western arts are represented by American artists of the generation of the donor, Charles Lang Freer (1856–1919), including paintings by John Singer Sargent, Gari Melchers, Abbot Handerson Thayer and Winslow Homer. The collection of works of Whistler, the expatriate American artist who was a close friend of Freer, includes over 1,000 of his pastels, lithographs, drawings, etchings, oils and watercolors. A representative selection of these is always on exhibition.

The *Peacock Room* (Gallery XII) shows Whistler's most ambitious and only surviving attempt at interior decoration. The story of it is both amusing and tragic. One of Whistler's

63

patrons, Frederick R. Leyland, remodeled his London town house in order to live in the style of a retired Venetian merchant prince. Henry Jeckyll, a decorator largely responsible for introducing Japanese methods of decoration into England, was chosen to do the dining room. The room as you see it was largely Jeckyll's creation. Whistler's oil painting, *Rose and Silver: The Princess from the Land of Porcelain,* was to have the place of honor over the fireplace. A crisis developed when Whistler saw the room; he objected strongly that the gilt leather covering the walls detracted from the delicate colors of his *Princess*. This was no ordinary leather, but richly gilded cordovan thought to have been brought to England 300 years before by Catherine of Aragon.

As Leyland was leaving for an extended trip, Whistler obtained permission to "touch up" the room. For six months during the fall and winter of 1876 and 1877, he worked furiously to paint the leather, completing all but the wall opposite the *Princess*. Blue peacocks and peacock feathers provided the sole motifs he used. Leyland returned to find his precious leather covered by paint. After a bitter argument, Whistler finished the incompleted panel, using the design of the "the rich peacock and the poor peacock" to show the relationship between artist and patron. One peacock (Leyland) clutches a mass of silver shillings, while the other (Whistler) prances and looks disdainfully at his adversary. Jeckyll was shocked and disappointed; he was committed to an insane asylum and died soon afterward. Leyland eventually grew to admire the decoration. Freer acquired the room at auction in 1904; it has been in the Freer Gallery since 1921.

The Gallery's donor, Charles Lang Freer, made a remarkable series of contributions to art: he is credited with initiating the present-day interest in Near and Far Eastern art; he assembled an exceptional collection of the works of American artists of his time; and by the gift of his collection and a building to house it, he paved the way for future gifts, such as Andrew Mellon's, which formed the nucleus of the National Gallery of Art.

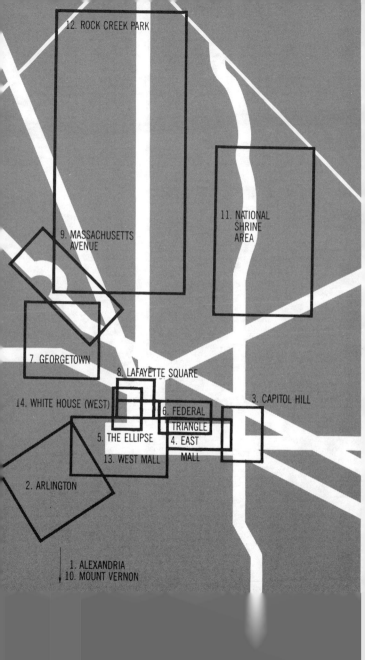

12. ROCK CREEK PARK

11. NATIONAL SHRINE AREA

9. MASSACHUSETTS AVENUE

7. GEORGETOWN

8. LAFAYETTE SQUARE

14. WHITE HOUSE (WEST)

3. CAPITOL HILL

6. FEDERAL TRIANGLE

5. THE ELLIPSE

4. EAST MALL

13. WEST MALL

2. ARLINGTON

1. ALEXANDRIA
10. MOUNT VERNON

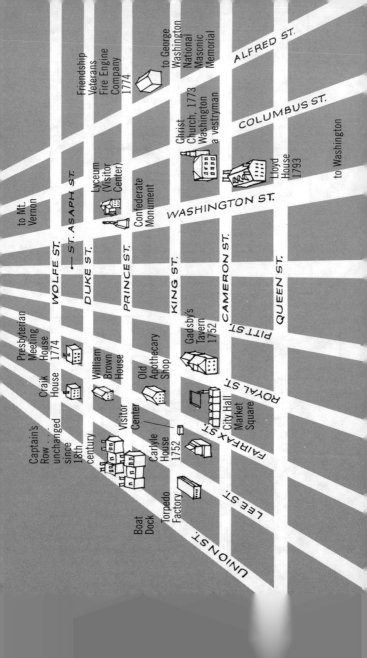

ALFRED ST.

COLUMBUS ST.

to Washington

to George Washington National Masonic Memorial

Christ Church, 1773
Washington a vestryman

Lloyd House 1793

Friendship Veterans Fire Engine Company 1774

ST. ASAPH ST.

WASHINGTON ST.

Lyceum (Visitor Center)

Confederate Monument

to Mt. Vernon

WOLFE ST.

DUKE ST.

PRINCE ST.

KING ST.

CAMERON ST.

QUEEN ST.

PITT ST.

Presbyterian Meeting House 1774

Craik House

William Brown House

Old Apothecary Shop

Gadsby's Tavern 1752

ROYAL ST.

Captain's Row unchanged since 18th century

Visitor Center

Carlyle House 1752

City Hall Market Square

FAIRFAX ST.

Boat Dock

Torpedo Factory

LEE ST.

UNION ST.

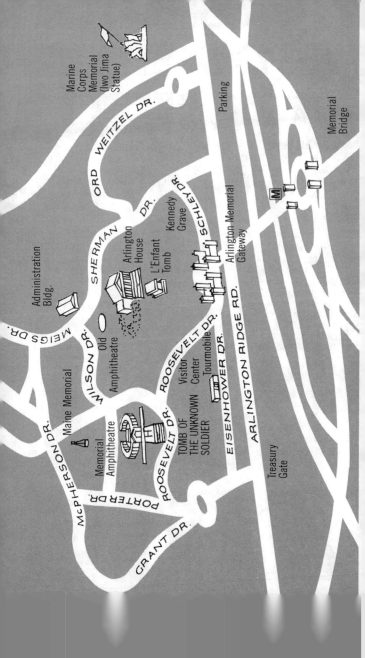

Marine Corps Memorial (Iwo Jima Statue)

WEITZEL DR.

ORD

SHERMAN DR.

Parking

Memorial Bridge

Administration Bldg.

MEIGS DR.

Arlington House

L'Enfant Tomb

Kennedy Grave

SCHLEY DR.

Arlington Memorial Gateway

WILSON DR.

Old Amphitheatre

Maine Memorial

McPHERSON DR.

Memorial Amphitheatre

ROOSEVELT DR.

ROOSEVELT DR.

Visitor Center

Tourmobile

EISENHOWER DR.

ARLINGTON RIDGE RD.

TOMB OF THE UNKNOWN SOLDIER

PORTER DR.

GRANT DR.

Treasury Gate

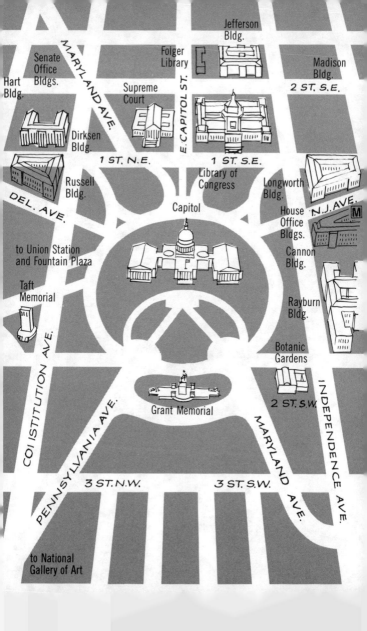

Jefferson
Bldg.

Folger
Library

Senate
Office
Bldgs.

MARYLAND AVE.

Hart
Bldg.

Supreme
Court

E. CAPITOL ST.

Madison
Bldg.

2 ST. S.E.

Dirksen
Bldg.

1 ST. N.E.

1 ST. S.E.

Russell
Bldg.

DEL. AVE.

Library of
Congress

Longworth
Bldg.

House
Office
Bldgs.

N.J. AVE.

M

Capitol

Cannon
Bldg.

to Union Station
and Fountain Plaza

Taft
Memorial

Rayburn
Bldg.

CONSTITUTION AVE.

Botanic
Gardens

PENNSYLVANIA AVE.

Grant Memorial

2 ST. S.W.

MARYLAND AVE.

INDEPENDENCE AVE.

3 ST. N.W.

3 ST. S.W.

to National
Gallery of Art

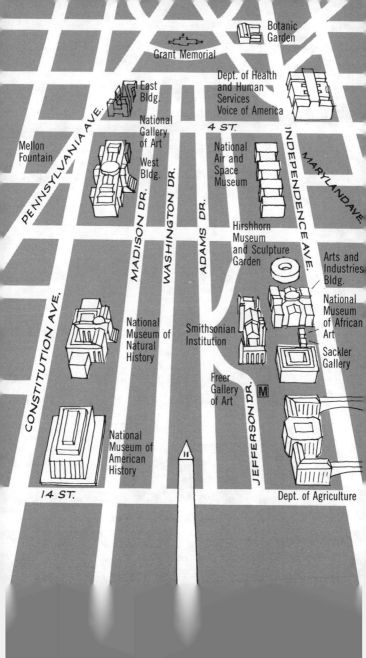

Botanic Garden

Grant Memorial

Dept. of Health and Human Services
Voice of America

East Bldg.

National Gallery of Art

West Bldg.

4 ST.

National Air and Space Museum

Mellon Fountain

Hirshhorn Museum and Sculpture Garden

Arts and Industries Bldg.

National Museum of African Art

Sackler Gallery

National Museum of Natural History

Smithsonian Institution

Freer Gallery of Art

National Museum of American History

Dept. of Agriculture

14 ST.

PENNSYLVANIA AVE.

MADISON DR.

WASHINGTON DR.

ADAMS DR.

INDEPENDENCE AVE.

MARYLAND AVE.

CONSTITUTION AVE.

JEFFERSON DR.

M

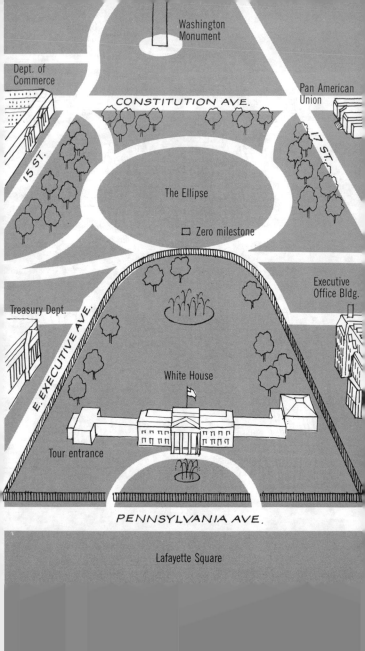

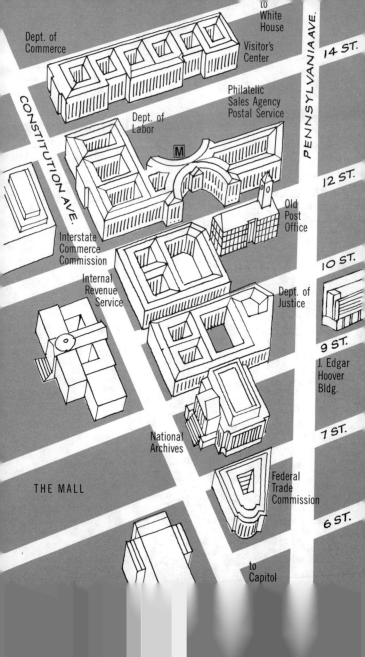

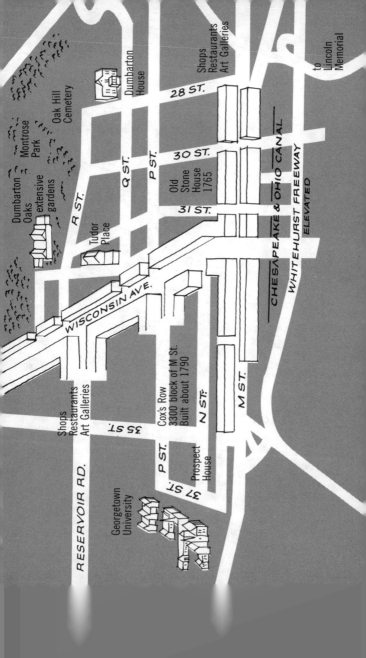

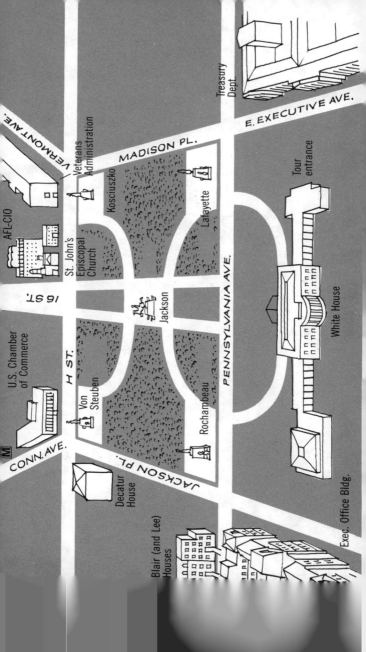

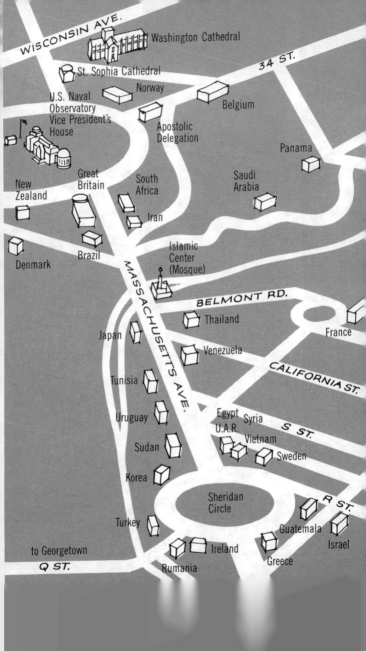

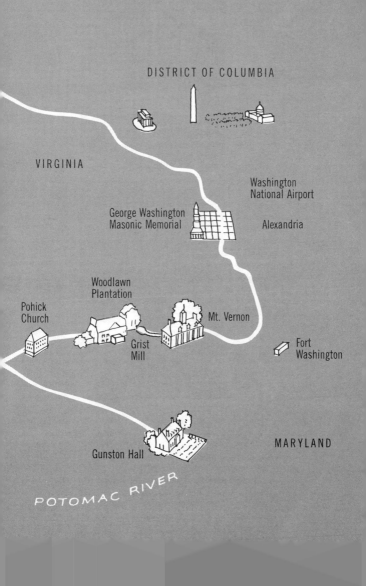

DISTRICT OF COLUMBIA

VIRGINIA

Washington
National Airport

George Washington
Masonic Memorial

Alexandria

Woodlawn
Plantation

Pohick
Church

Grist
Mill

Mt. Vernon

Fort
Washington

Gunston Hall

MARYLAND

POTOMAC RIVER

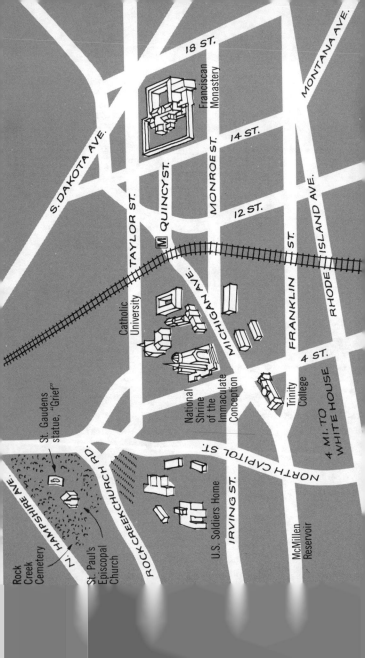

18 ST.

Franciscan Monastery

S. DAKOTA AVE.

MONTANA AVE.

14 ST.

MONROE ST.

QUINCY ST.

TAYLOR ST.

12 ST.

Ⓜ

RHODE ISLAND AVE.

Catholic University

MICHIGAN AVE.

FRANKLIN ST.

4 ST.

National Shrine of the Immaculate Conception

Trinity College

WHITE HOUSE

4 MI. TO

St. Gaudens statue, "Grief"

ROCK CREEK CHURCH RD.

NORTH CAPITOL ST.

IRVING ST.

Rock Creek Cemetery

N. HAMPSHIRE AVE.

St. Paul's Episcopal Church

U.S. Soldiers Home

McMillen Reservoir

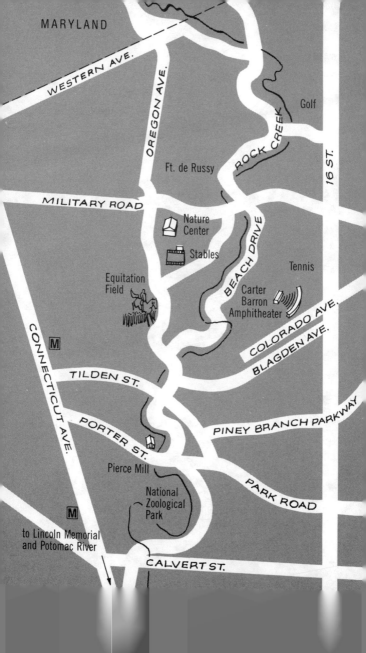

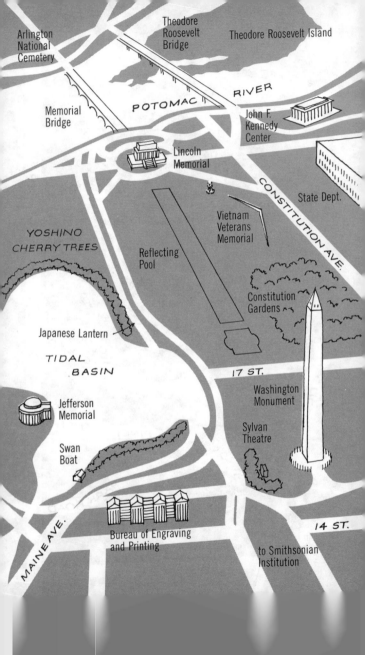

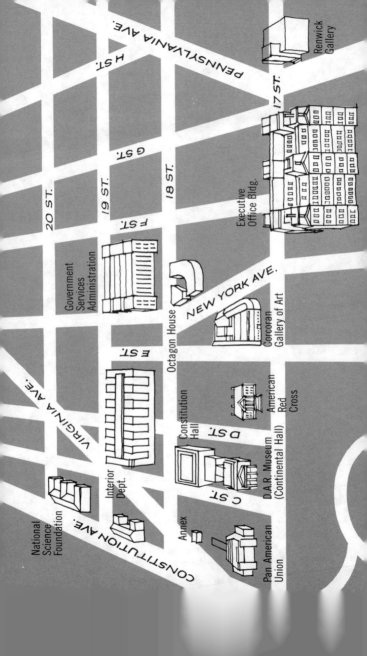

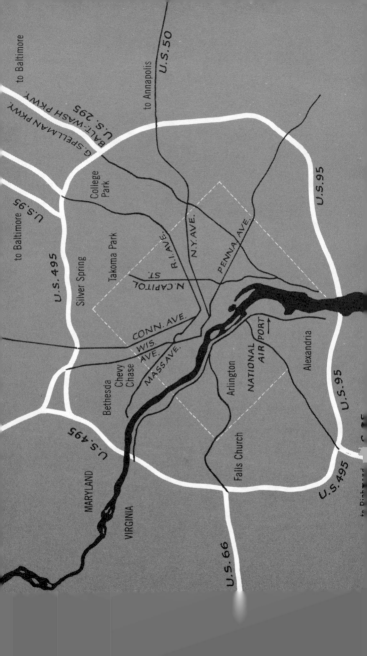

Georgetown

M Nearest stop,
Foggy Bottom

WHERE Area bet. Rock Creek Park,
Potomac River, Georgetown U. and
S St., N.W.

HOW By car (less than 10 min. from
downtown); by walking tour; or
come to browse in the Wisconsin
Ave. shops.

Georgetown retains a distinctive charm and air of individuality which sets it apart from other residential sections of the city. Historically noteworthy, physically attractive, socially and intellectually distinguished, Georgetown claims more listings in *Who's Who* than any other place of comparable size. It is home to Supreme Court Justices and lowly clerks, Cabinet members and shopkeepers. Some of its imposing estates comprise an entire city block, but more characteristic are its small narrow "row" houses. Textbook examples of Georgian and Federal architecture abound, side by side with Victorian monstrosities. Overall, however, the homes reflect civic pride and loving upkeep. Giant trees tower gracefully over the streets; postage-stamp sized gardens hide behind prim facades.

Georgetown not only exhibits the past, but the quite contemporary present. This is where the youth and the action are in the evening. Georgetown sidewalks are not rolled up at sunset. Many of the nightclubs and the singles establishments flourish here. It's not quite like New York's Greenwich Village, but the closest thing we have to it by way of ambiance, shops, pubs and entertainment.

By the late 1700s, when Washington was only a city on paper, Georgetown flourished as the greatest tobacco market in Maryland, if not in the Union. Her location at the head of navigation on the Potomac and her deep-water harbor capable of accommodating large sailing ships helped her to develop as an important seaport. Her ships sailed to Europe and the West Indies with valuable cargoes of tobacco, returning with silks, shoes, coal, tinware, tea, wines and powder for wigs. In 1800 when the federal government, comprising fewer than 150 employees, was transferred from Philadelphia to the undeveloped capital, Georgetown was looked upon as the "Court end of town." A well-established society exemplified gracious living with good schools, dancing masters, well-trained doctors, regular theatrical performances, two newspapers and even a university. Besides its own Customs House (actively in use until 1967), Georgetown could boast its own merchant marine, a textile mill, paper factory, rope walk and excellent inns, shops and counting houses.

The attitude of Georgetowners toward the Federal City shines through the opinion of Mrs. Anne Royal, who, in 1826, wrote: "The people of Georgetown are polite and hospitable; they form a striking contrast to their neighbors of Washington, their minds being generally more cultivated. It is hardly possible to conceive how towns so near each other should differ so widely as they do. One cannot behold the people of Georgetown without being struck by the disparity."

Georgetown's importance as a seaport declined in the latter part of the 19th century, with the drop in the area's water table and increasing silt deposits in the Potomac. She suffered serious financial setbacks from the failure of the Chesapeake and Ohio Canal. Her sympathetic attitude toward the Confederate cause proved politically disadvantageous to her after the South's defeat in the Civil War. The panic of 1873 spelled further doom to the town. By the 1800s, Georgetown had declined to the point where it was a cheap-rent neighborhood, and property values hit bottom.

By 1930, however, some 50 years later, the trend of buying old houses and restoring them became firmly established in Georgetown and has continued ever since. Two factors may have contributed to this new interest—the opening of the American wing of the Metropolitan Museum of Art in New York, and John D. Rockefeller Jr.'s restoration of Williamburg, VA, which reminded Americans of their early architectural heritage. Property values in Georgetown today probably exceed those in any part of town. Active citizens' groups have done a remarkable job of preserving the town's character, enforcing stringent zoning restrictions and safeguarding the architectural traditions which distinguished the old city. However, there is still much work to be done in improving the appearance of M Street and parts of Wisconsin Avenue.

These houses are open to the public:

Dumbarton House, 2715 Q St., N.W.
Dumbarton Oaks (and Gardens), 1703 32nd St., N.W.
The Old Stone House, 3051 M St., N.W.

Browse in the shops along M Street, Wisconsin Avenue, and its side streets. (See "Shopping.") If weather and season permit, take a walk in lovely Montrose Park or the adjoining

Dumbarton Gardens. See the picturesque row of houses along the towpath of the Cheapeake and Ohio Canal, south of M Street (Go down Thomas Jefferson Street). Walk or drive by these houses, distinguished for their architecture or history, but not open to the public:

Quality Hill, 3425 Prospect St., N.W. Built in 1798 by John Thomson Mason, nephew of George Mason of Gunston Hall. Fine example of a spacious, late Georgian town house.

Prospect House, 3508 Prospect St., N.W., built in 1788 by John Templeman, a prosperous shipping merchant. Note the simplicity and fine proportions of this Georgian brick house. Used for the government's "guest house" when the Trumans occupied Blair House during the White House renovation.

Cox's Row, five houses on north side of N St., east of 34th St., starting with corner house, 3339 N St. Distinctive row of brick houses in the Federal style, built about 1790 by Colonel John Cox, the first elected Mayor of Georgetown (1823). Note the graceful swags under the windows and the decorated dormer windows. General Lafayette was entertained at 3337 N St. in 1824.

Bodisco House, 3322 O St., N.W., built around 1815. Served as the Russian Legation when Baron de Bodisco came to Washington as minister in 1838. He married an American and is buried in Oak Hill Cemetery in Georgetown.

Tudor Place, 31st and Q Sts., N.W., built between 1794 and 1815. May be Georgetown's most distinguished estate; designed by Dr. Thornton, who drew up the original plans for the Capitol, for Thomas Peter and his wife, Martha Parke Custis, granddaughter of Martha Washington. It has remained in the Peter family for generations.

If you are here during the spring, check with the newspapers for tours of Georgetown's historical homes. A House Tour is usually held the last weekend in April; a Garden Tour, the third weekend in April.

Hirshhorn Museum and Sculpture Garden

M L'Enfant Plaza
Maryland Ave.
Exit

WHERE   The Mall: south side at 8th St., S.W.

WHEN   10:00 A.M.–5:30 P.M., every day except Christmas. Check for longer summer hours. Free tours at 10:30 A.M., NOON, and 1:30 P.M., Mon.–Sat.

HOW   Free.

The Hirshhorn Museum and Sculpture Garden, opened to the public in October 1974, houses an unprecedented collection of sculpture and painting of the past 125 years. Located just east of the Arts and Industries Building, the concrete cylinder stands in stark contrast to its neighboring Victorian Gothic fantasy and the glass and marble hangar for the National Air and Space Museum. In May 1966, American financier Joseph L. Hirshhorn donated to the nation his collection of some 6,000 works of art, mainly by European and American artists dating from the late 19th century to the present day; on November 7, 1966 an Act of Congress accepted the gift and authorized a site on the Mall and a building to house the collection.

When the museum opened its doors in the mid-70s, architect Gordon Bunshaft's creation was described in colorful but not always flattering terms—"The Doughnut on the Mall," "an abhorrent Fuehrer Bunker;" "a gas tank lacking only an Exxon sign;" "a relic of some long forgotten visitors from another planet." Architectural critics, self-described and otherwise, have softened their reactions since then, so there's all the more reason to make a beeline to see and enjoy this exciting addition to the Smithsonian's museums. Its offerings are dazzling. You will actually be treated to four shows—the building itself, the sculpture displayed in the surrounding plaza and adjacent sculpture garden, the three floors of paintings and sculpture arranged in a roughly chronological order indoors, and still another sculpture show charmingly displayed along with windowed walkways bordering the inside wall of the building.

The $16 million circular reinforced concrete structure, 231 feet in diameter, stands on four massive piers 14 feet above the plaza. The focal point of the inner open core, 115 feet across, is a handsome bronze fountain which, when operating at full force, can shoot water 82 feet into the air, the height of the four story building. Floor to ceiling windows open onto this court, allowing sunlight to enter the inner galleries. The exterior surface of precast concrete with pink granite aggregate is broken only by a 70-foot long balcony and window on the third floor overlooking the Mall and Sculpture Garden. A plaza area flows out and under the building; across Jefferson Drive is a multi-leveled terraced area where the stunning Sculpture Garden is located.

Rodin's *The Burghers of Calais*, Henry Moore's *Glenkiln Cross: Upright Motif* and Maillol's *Nymph* are but a few of the masterpieces which appear quite at home in their new settings. It is pleasant to walk on the brick paths amid the garden's plantings, sit on the benches and contemplate at your leisure the reflections of willow tree, sky and sculpture in the pool's quiet waters. In the introduction to the Collection's inaugural catalogue, then Secretary of the Smithsonian S. Dillon Ripley wrote: "It is hoped that the Sculpture Garden will become one of the most popular spots in Washington, a special magnet among these other magnets on the Mall, an outdoor galleria for all to enjoy and share." This suggestion has become a reality.

The building's interior is a delight. You will want to start your tour in the rectangular galleries on the lower level, which are devoted to special exhibits of exceptional quality. (Check the posters outside for titles and subjects.) As you progress by escalator to the second and third floors you will note that the paintings are arranged generally in a chronological order, with subdivision by school. Outstanding representatives of every school are to be found: 19th-century Realism and American Impressionism by Homer, Eakins and Sargent; Abstract Expressionism by DeKooning; Neoplasticism by Mondrian; Linear Art by Albers; Social Realism by the Mexican artist Siqueiros; Surrealism by Magritte and Dali; and Robert Henri's "Ashcan School." Examples of the most up-to-date art, including Op and Pop art, more recent Abstract Expressionism, Photo Realism and Mixed Media works are always on view.

For providing the springboard collection for a national museum of modern art, the nation owes a debt of gratitude to Joseph Hirshhorn, (1899–1981). The 12th of 13 children, Hirshhorn immigrated to this country from Latvia with his impoverished family when he was six years old. As a 15-year-old youth he started charting stocks on the New York Curb Market, and two years later established himself as a broker. After a successful career as a financier he became interested in mining uranium in Canada in the late 1940s. By 1955 he was operating two mines capable of producing more uranium than all of the more than 600 uranium mines in the United States. He sold his uranium interests in 1960, and began gradually to reduce his business involvements. Hirshhorn's fascination for the arts dated back to his early years when he studied reproductions on insurance calendars hung above his bed. His discriminating taste for modern painting and sculpture led him to acquire, largely on his own, a collection staggering in its size and quality. He often bought in bulk: for example, there are 52 works by Thomas Eakins, 47 by Matisse, 21 by Rodin, 22 by Degas and 47 by Picasso—the list goes on and on.

At the grand opening on October 1, 1974, Hirshhorn said: "It is an honor to have given my art collection to the people of the United States as a small repayment for what this nation has done for me and others like me who arrived here as immigrants. . .I am proud to belong to the family of Americans."

If you enjoy dining al fresco, stop for lunch at the *Plaza Café* in the Sculpture Garden. Art books, jewelry, posters and prints are for sale at the museum shop on the lower level.

Islamic Center (Mosque)

M None nearby

WHERE   2551 Massachusetts Ave., N.W.

WHEN   10:00 A.M.–6:00 P.M., daily.
Service at 12:15 P.M. Fridays.

HOW   Guide in attendance during visitors' hours; tours for groups by arrangement.

The Islamic Center provides the most dramatic illustration in the western hemisphere of the religion, art and culture of over 555 million Moslems, who constitute the second largest of religions. The graceful mosque and its slender minaret accentuate the Center's beautiful setting overlooking Rock Creek Park.

The decor of the Center is a composite of the Islamic arts. The exterior contrasts inscriptions and traceries of turquoise and white quartz with Alabama limestone. Through a Moorish colonnade you enter an open courtyard leading to the most important of the buildings, the mosque. Contrary to popular belief, the mosque does not face due east, but approximately northeast, so that it looks to Mecca, Saudi Arabia, by the shortest, or great circle, route. At each of the five prayer times during the day there is chanted in Arabic the famous Moslem call to prayer.

Inside the mosque you will marvel at the Turkish tiles, the two-ton cast bronze chandelier, inlaid with nickel, and the designs painted over the high walls and ceilings. Note the ten magnificent Iranian carpets, upon which the devout sit, kneel or prostrate themselves in prayer. The Moslem tradition permits no chairs and no music.

More than 10,000 separate pieces of wood form the Egyptian-made pulpit, or "Minbar." Each piece is joined to the whole entirely by fitting, without use of nails or other fastening material.

As you face the Moorish colonnade, the wing to the right houses administrative offices, and the wing to the left a library (destined to be the finest of its kind) and a museum. The basement contains a lecture hall, in which special programs are presented every other week during the spring, fall and winter (check for time and subject), and facilities for the mandatory ritual of ablutions before prayers.

Personnel from Al-Azhar University of Cairo, the oldest university in the world, direct the Center. Sponsors are all Islamic countries which have diplomatic representation in Washington along with some prominent American moslems. You may purchase among other interesting publications the Holy Qur'an in English and Arabic and postcards of the mosque.

Each Friday at 12:15 P.M. (wintertime) or 1:15 P.M. (daylight-saving time) a 45-minute service is held, which is open to the public. Although there are no rules other than to remove your shoes in the mosque, visiting ladies should be decently dressed.

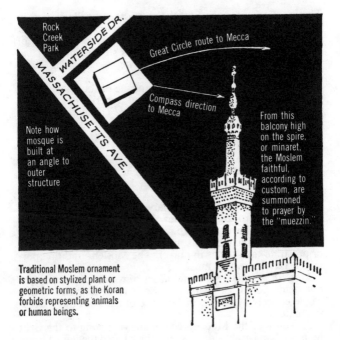

Rock Creek Park

WATERSIDE DR.

MASSACHUSETTS AVE.

Great Circle route to Mecca

Compass direction to Mecca

Note how mosque is built at an angle to outer structure

From this balcony high on the spire, or minaret, the Moslem faithful, according to custom, are summoned to prayer by the "muezzin."

Traditional Moslem ornament is based on stylized plant or geometric forms, as the Koran forbids representing animals or human beings.

Iwo Jima Statue

WHERE Virginia side of Memorial or
Arlington Bridge, bet. main
entrance to Arlington Cemetery and
Arlington Blvd. (U.S. 50).

WHEN Daily.

HOW By car or Metro and walk some
distance.

"Uncommon Valor was a Common Virtue."

—ADMIRAL CHESTER NIMITZ

The Marine Corps War Memorial translates into bronze the famous photograph by newsphotographer Joe Rosenthal of the raising of the Stars and Stripes over Mount Suribachi, Iwo Jima, February 23, 1945. The powerful group of five Marines and a sailor comprise the largest bronze statue ever cast. Note the real flag flying from the halyard.

The flag-raising on Iwo Jima, an important Japanese island base in the Pacific, followed one of the bloodiest battles of World War II, in which 5,563 Marines were killed and 17,343 others were wounded.

The statue, by Felix W. de Weldon, was dedicated in 1954 to honor all Marines who have given their lives for their country since the founding of the Corps in 1775. Three of the survivors of the flag-raising posed for the sculptor; the others who participated were killed in later battles. A Marine Corps color guard raises the flag at 8:00 A.M. and lowers it at sunset. You may attend formal ceremonies on Tuesdays between 7:00 and 8:30 P.M. mid-May to mid-October. The Marine Corps Drum and Bugle Corps, Color Guard and Ceremonial Battalion take part in the ceremony.

Every principal Marine Corps engagement is inscribed around the base of the memorial. The inscription reads: "In honor and in memory of the men of the United States Marine Corps who have given their lives to their country since November 10, 1775."

The memorial is dramatically lit at night. With a magnificent view of Washington in the distance, a visitor will be well rewarded for seeking out this statue.

Jefferson Memorial

M Smithsonian

WHERE   South shore of Tidal Basin, West Potomac Park.

WHEN   8:00 A.M.–midnight, daily.

HOW   Park guides on duty at the Memorial present talks at regular intervals. Go by car or cab, or Tourmobile. Also beautiful at night.

"I have sworn upon the altar of God eternal hostility against every form of tyranny over the mind of man."

Dedicated in 1943, the Jefferson Memorial follows the Lincoln Memorial by 21 years and the Washington Monument by 59 years. Its location and the view across the Tidal Basin toward downtown Washington are exceptional.

Thomas Jefferson was much more than George Washington's Secretary of State, the drafter of the Declaration of Independence and our third President. Reputedly, he had mastered all the learning of his time, and may be the last man to have done so. Among other pursuits he was an architect, having designed his highly original Virginia home, Monticello, and the rotunda of the University of Virginia. (He even submitted an anonymous, but unsuccessful, design for the White House!)

The Memorial features some of Jefferson's architectural motifs. It is a circular building with a low, graceful dome, surrounded by a colonnade. The main approach, facing the center of Washington, is reached through a portico eight columns wide and four columns deep. It has four open entrances, which give a feeling of airiness—indeed, if a strong wind is blowing, you may feel like a sailor on a storm-tossed craft off Cape Hatteras.

Before entering the Memorial room, stop on the steps to view the sculptural group by Adolph A. Weinman on the pediment above the portico. Jefferson stands before the committee named by the Continental Congress to write the Declaration of Independence. Familiar figures flank him—to his left, Benjamin Franklin, and seated on his right, Roger Sherman and Robert Livingston.

The Memorial centers on the bronze figure of Jefferson, shown addressing the Continental Congress. The five-ton statue by Rudolph Evans is 19 feet high and stands on a black granite pedestal six feet high. You may wonder what Jefferson is wearing. It is a fur-collared great-coat presented to him by a Polish patriot whose statue you may see in Lafayette Park just across from the White House, General Thaddeus Kosciuszko.

The four interior walls set forth excerpts from Jefferson's writings: the Declaration of Independence ("These colonies are and of right ought to be free and independent states"); the Virginia Statute for Religious Freedom and a quotation from a 1789 letter to James Madison ("I know of but one code of morality for men whether acting singly or collectively"); his view on slavery ("Nothing is more certainly written in the book of fate than that these people are to be free"); and his admonition that "laws and institutions must go hand in hand with the progress of the human mind."

The site chosen carries out an extension, proposed by the McMillan Commission of 1901, of L'Enfant's original three-point plan (i.e., Capitol, Washington Monument and White House).

The site of the Jefferson Memorial and the surrounding land which so contribute to its attractiveness have been entirely reclaimed from the Potomac. The Memorial site and the Tidal Basin, which many people think of as symbolic of Washington, are thus of quite recent origin. Note that when the city was planned the Potomac River covered most of what is now the West Mall, the Jefferson Memorial area and Hains Point (as well as land which now forms the National Airport).

The Memorial's architect, John Russell Pope, died during construction, and the work was completed by his associates, Otto R. Eggers and Daniel Higgins. Cost approximated $3 million. The dedication by President Roosevelt occurred on the 200th anniversary of Jefferson's birth, April 13, 1943.

Jefferson died July 4, 1826, aged 83. He is buried near his famous Virginia home, Monticello. He wrote the inscription on his gravestone, which lists the three achievements for which he wished to be remembered. It reads simply:

Here was buried
Thomas Jefferson
Author of the Declaration of Independence
Of the Statute of Virginia for Religious Freedom
And Father of the University of Virginia

The Memorial is at its best on soft, warm evenings, when the view of the city over the Tidal Basin is worth a special trip. During cherry blossom time, plan your visit with care. The Memorial is in the midst of the blossoms, and traffic is very difficult. At any time of year, however, the dramatic lighting of the Memorial at night provides an unforgettable experience.

John F. Kennedy Center for the Performing Arts

M Foggy Bottom

WHERE Rock Creek Parkway at New Hampshire Ave. and F St., N.W.

WHEN May be visited from 10:00 A.M. to late evening, daily.

HOW Attend a performance, join a tour, or look around on your own. Free tours are offered every morning between 10:00 A.M. and 1:00 P.M.. They leave from Motor Lobby A (last 45 min.).

The John F. Kennedy Center for the Performing Arts offers the visitor an opportunity to "tour the premises" either alone or as a member of a group tour conducted by a volunteer guide, attend a performance at one of the five facilities or enjoy a meal or light refreshment at one of three roof terrace level restaurants.

Located on the east bank of the Potomac, on the edge of Georgetown, the Kennedy Center stands on a 17-acre tract of land and was designed by the well-known architect Edward Durell Stone. The official opening took place on September 8, 1971, with the world premiere of Leonard Bernstein's *Mass* in the Opera House.

The building is imposing, measuring 630 feet in length and 300 feet in width. It is faced with Carrara marble, and offers a charming view of the Potomac River and Georgetown from the terrace outside the Grand Foyer. The three handsome theaters which occupy the main level are noted for their fine acoustics. The Opera House seats 2,200; next to it on the north side is the more intimate Eisenhower Theater seating 1,100; and on the south is the 2,750-seat Concert Hall. The red-carpeted foyer connecting the three halls and extending the length of the building is lit by 18 crystal chandeliers. A giant sculptured head in bronze of President Kennedy dominates the hall.

The American Film Institute at the Kennedy Center shows

feature films (including special shows for children on Saturday and Sunday) on a regular basis. The more intimate Terrace Theater on the second floor seats 500 and represents a great variety of theater, opera, dance, choral recitals and revues.

For Information call:

Eisenhower Theater 254-3670
Opera House 254-3770
Concert Hall 254-3776
Terrace Theater 254-9895
American Film Institute 785-4600

Tickets may be bought at the *Box office*, open Mon.–Sat., 10:00 A.M.–9:00 P.M.; Sunday, NOON to 9:00 P.M. Instant charge number is 857-0900. Tickets may be charged over the phone by credit card (AE, CC, DC, MC and Visa). Should you wish to find out "what's on" before you leave home, call the toll-free number (800)424-8504; in town, general information is 254-3600. If you are a senior citizen, a full-time student, an enlisted military personnel or handicapped, some half-price tickets are available; call 254-3774 for information.

Visitors to the Kennedy Center have a choice of three places to dine: *The Roof Terrace* (make reservations by calling 833-8870) offers elegance, a fine view and a very expensive meal; *The Curtain Call Café* is small, pleasant, with booths and a fine place for a pre- or post-performance meal or snack; *The Encore Cafeteria* features cafeteria-style food, with a large and attractive room (or balcony with a view in summer) for dining. The latter two restaurants are usually crowded both for lunch and dinner; allow 1½ hours before performance. (The Hors d'oeuvrerie, a part of the Roof Terrace, offers lighter snacks from 5:00 P.M. until midnight.)

Pay parking is available in the Center's garage; enter south from Rock Creek Parkway or E. Street Expressway.

Library of Congress

M Capitol South

WHERE   Capitol Hill, 1st St. and
Independence Ave., S.E.

WHEN   8:30 A.M.–9:30 P.M., Mon.–Fri.;
8:30 A.M.–6:00 P.M., Sat., Sun.
and holidays; closed Christmas and
New Year's Day. For information on
Library reading room hours call
287-6400.

HOW   Tours 9:00 A.M.–4:00 P.M.,
Mon.–Fri. (on the hour); or visit on
your own. Free. Guided tours for
groups by appointment.

The Library of Congress, probably the largest library in the world, serves not only as the research arm of the Congress of the United States but also as the national library. Its collections of 80 million items—books, maps, newspapers, manuscripts, prints, photographs and others—occupy 532 miles of shelves in three buildings on Capitol Hill. Several other buildings in the Washington Metropolitan area also house parts of the collection.

The Library's first responsibility is to the Congress, and it discharges this responsibility primarily through the Congressional Research Service, a department of the Library that directly responds to more than 300,000 requests from members and committees annually.

A research library, the Library of Congress does not circulate books and other materials but delivers them to readers in its own reading rooms, in 1982 providing more than 2 million items to researchers in the Library. Books were also made available to other libraries on interlibrary loan when they were necessary for research and otherwise unobtainable. The Library also extends its services to individuals throughout the country by duplication of materials in its collections; a publication program that offers guides to and facsimiles of the Library's holdings; traveling exhibits prepared for circulation to other libraries and museums; and broadcasts and recordings of concerts and literary programs.

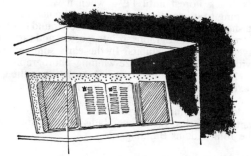

Gutenberg Bible, first great book printed from movable metal type (1455 A.D.)

The Library of Congress Building was completed at the turn of the century, before any of the other prominent buildings on the Hill except the Capitol. It was the rage of the time, and described as the "most beautiful building in the world." Whether or not the massive Italian Renaissance style and the elaborate ornamentation are to your taste, you will find, in addition to the size and scope of the Library, many points of interest.

A recent uplift of the west steps and plaza of the Library offers a charming spot for visitors to sit at tables during the summer months and enjoy a fine view of the Capitol.

The guided tour begins in the *Visitor Services Center* in the Orientation Theater near the west entrance lobby on the ground floor, and lasts about 30 to 40 minutes. An 18-minute slide/sound presentation on the Library of Congress is shown hourly from 8:45 A.M. to 8:45 P.M. weekdays and 8:45 A.M. to 5:45 P.M. weekends and holidays in the Orientation Theater. You are taken to the Visitor's Gallery above the second floor, from which you view the Main Reading Room, the heart of the Library and one of the most impressive spaces in Washington, and above it the dome, whose elaborate decorations are surmounted by a mural in the collar, *Evolution of Civilization*, and another in the lantern, *Human Understanding*.

On the main floor are some of the permanent exhibits. Do not miss the Gutenberg Bible, the first great book printed with movable metal type. The Library's copy, one of three existing perfect vellum copies probably survived because it remained in the Benedictine Abbey of Saint Blasius in Ger-

95

many's Black Forest until 1794, when it was removed for safekeeping to other abbeys during the Napoleonic Wars.

You should also visit the corridors of the ground floor where music treasures, photographs, prints, posters and cartoons are displayed in rotating exhibits. In the early summer months you will usually find the prize-winning photographs of the White House News Photographers Association in the ground floor exhibit space. Visitors not doing research are asked to stay out of the Main Reading Room.

Besides the Thomas Jefferson Building there are two supplementary libraries, the James Madison Memorial Building and the John Adams Building.

SPECIAL COLLECTIONS

The special collections exemplify the variety of the Library's stores of information. Among others:

The *Asian Division* has the largest collection of Chinese and Japanese books outside those countries.

The *European Room* boasts the largest collection in the Western hemisphere of Russian and other Slavic material.

The *Prints and Photographs Division* contains photographs, negatives, posters, caricatures and fine prints. The collection includes one of the two largest groups of glass plates made by Mathew Brady's staff recording the Civil War.

The *Rare Book and Special Collections Division* houses about 300,000 volumes. Here you find what the 1851 fire spared of the Thomas Jefferson library; Adolf Hitler's private collection; and one of the book collections of Tsar Nicholas II.

The *Music Division* contains more than six million pieces of music.

The *Motion Picture, Broadcasting and Recorded Sound Division's* Recording Laboratory on the first floor of the Madison Building sells authentic recordings of American folk music, collected throughout the country.

SPECIAL EVENTS

A *concert series* of chamber music is presented in the Coolidge Auditorium almost every week from October through April.

Some of the concerts are made possible by the Gertrude Clarke Whittall Foundation in the Library of Congress and feature, among other programs, performances by the Juilliard String Quartet, the Library's "quartet in residence," playing the Stradivari instruments given to the Library by Mrs. Whittall. (You may see them by special request.) Other concerts are presented in the Library by the Elizabeth Sprague Coolidge Foundation, the McKim Fund, the Serge Koussevitzky Foundation and others. Most concerts are on Thursday and Friday evenings. For tickets call the Music Division Concert Line on the Monday morning preceding the concert, beginning at 9:30 A.M. (287-5502).

A series of literary performances is also presented in the Coolidge Auditorium usually on Monday evenings from October through April. No tickets are required for admission to the poetry readings, dramatic readings and plays, sometimes with dance or mime, sponsored by the Whittall Poetry and Literature Fund and the Poetry Consultantship.

HISTORY

Congress established its library in 1800 with an appropriation of $5,000. Today, the Library requires more than $170 million for its yearly operations, and returns some $10 million to the Treasury from its copyright and other fee operations. From 1800 until 1897, the Library was housed in the Capitol itself. When the British burned the Capitol in 1814, the Library's

Quartet performing in Coolidge Auditorium

books were destroyed. To start the Library anew, the federal government in 1815 bought Thomas Jefferson's personal library of some 6,000 volumes. Two-thirds of these were lost on Christmas eve of 1851, in a disastrous fire which also destroyed a fine hall in the Capitol decorated by Charles Bulfinch after designs of Benjamin Latrobe. By 1879 the Library had grown to 332,000 volumes, too many for the Capitol bookshelves to display.

The cornerstone of the Library of Congress was laid in 1890. Completion required 11 years, and the services of over 50 painters, sculptors and other artists. In 1939, the Thomas Jefferson Building to the east of the Library of Congress was opened. The brand new second annex is called the James Madison Memorial Building.

A national program which provides reading materials to the blind and physically handicapped through a network of regional libraries across the United States is operated by the Library's National Library Service for the Blind and Physically Handicapped; visitors who wish information about this program may go in person to the division's office at 1291 Taylor Street, N.W. or write to that address, Washington, DC 20542.

The *Copyright Office* of the United States is a department of the Library, which became a depository for copyrights in laws of 1846, 1865 and 1870. The Library selects books and other library materials submitted for copyright registration for addition to its collections. Questions about copyright should be directed to the Copyright Offie, Crystal Mall Annex, 1921 Jefferson Davis Highway, Arlington, VA 20559.

A monthly *Calendar of Events in the Library of Congress*, which lists concerts, literary programs, exhibits and publications of a popular nature, is available free upon request to the Central Services Division, Library of Congress, Washington, DC 20540. That same office can send you a free list of *Library of Congress Publications in Print*.

Library of Congress publications, greeting cards, facsimiles and postcards are available in the *Visitor Services Center* in the west entrance ground floor lobby, open from 9:00 A.M. to 6:00 P.M. Monday through Friday, and from 9:00 A.M. to 5:00 P.M. weekends and holidays.

A fine place for breakfast or lunch is the attractive and inexpensive cafeteria in the James Madison Building, 101 Independence Ave., S.E., open weekdays from 8:30 to 10:30 A.M. for breakfast, and 11:00 A.M. to 2:00 P.M. for lunch. Next door is the Buffet Dining Room serving prix-fixe lunches from 11:30 A.M. to 2:00 P.M. in a lovely room notable for its panoramic views.

Washington is probably the greatest library center of the world. The Library of Congress serves as the focus, but others include the Folger Library, 201 East Capitol St., S.E. (world's finest collection of the 16th- and 17th-century origins of Anglo-American civilization); National Archives (see write-up below; unique material in the field of American history); National Library of Medicine, 8600 Rockville Pike, Bethesda, MD (best medical library in the world); Department of Agriculture Library (best agriculture library in the world); National Bureau of Standards Library, Gaithersburg, MD (great scientific library, particularly for physics, chemistry, engineering and mathematics); Geological Survey Library (Interior Department; best geological library in the United States); Interstate Commerce Commission, Constitution Ave. at 12th St., N.W. (best transportation library in United States); U.S. Supreme Court (see write-up below; exceptional law library); plus other specialized collections of the Departments of Health and Human Resources; Commerce and Labor; the Organization of American States and exceptional libraries at the Freer Gallery, Dumbarton Oaks, National Gallery of Art and Smithsonian Institution. Also the Martin Luther King Memorial Library, 901 G St., N.W., which serves as a community center.

Lincoln Memorial

Ⓜ Foggy Bottom

WHERE West end of Mall—on line with 23rd St., N.W.

WHEN Open 24 hours a day.

HOW Park guides on duty at Memorial present talks at regular intervals. No parking is allowed around the Memorial. All-day parking is allowed in West Potomac Park.

The Lincoln Memorial is perfection. It appeals to the eye, the mind and the heart:

> In this temple
> As in the hearts of the people
> For whom he saved the Union
> The memory of Abraham Lincoln
> Is enshrined forever.

The plan of the Memorial is of the greatest simplicity. The imposing, seated Lincoln is the focal point. The awe-inspiring statue is the work of Daniel Chester French. The 19-foot figure required 28 blocks of white marble and four years of carving.

Two rows of Ionic columns flank the statue, separating the central area from the north and south chambers. Walk behind the columns on the right and you will see inscribed Lincoln's Second Inaugural Address ("With malice toward none, with charity for all. . ."). The Jules Guerin mural above it portrays the unity of the North and South; groups on the left represent Fraternity and on the right Charity.

The Gettysburg Address is inscribed on the wall of the other chamber ("government of the people, by the people, for the people. . ."). The Guerin mural above it represents the Angel of Truth freeing a slave; groups to the right represent Immortality and to the left Justice and Law.

The architect, Henry Bacon, chose for the Memorial a classic Greek temple reminiscent of the Parthenon on the Acropolis in Athens. The 36 Doric columns forming the portico represent the 36 states in the Union when Lincoln died. Their names appear on the frieze above the colonnade. The names on the attic walls at the top of the Memorial are of the 48 states in the Union when the Memorial was dedicated.

Proportions throughout are exceptionally pleasing. The Memorial does not appear as tall as the nine-story building it is; nor does the colonnade sector appear to cover one-half of an acre, as it does. As in all Greek temples, the colonnade, the facade and the walls slant inward, each to a varying degree, and the columns are made thinner at the top than at the bottom. Otherwise, the structure would give the illusion of bulging at the top.

The Memorial was completed in 1922, 57 years after Lincoln's death, at a cost of under $3 million. The choice of the site in 1912 required foresight and courage, because at that time Potomac Park was a desolate swamp, considered by critics to be totally inappropriate for such a Memorial.

Don't miss the night view from the Lincoln Memorial down the Mall to the floodlighted Washington Monument and the Capitol—a high point of anyone's trip. Avoid rush hours, when commuter traffic around the Memorial is extremely heavy. Walk around the Memorial for a fine view of Arlington Memorial Bridge and Arlington House. A walkway to the left of the Memorial's steps leads to an elevator. See the huge concrete supports on which the marble building rests through a window near the elevator.

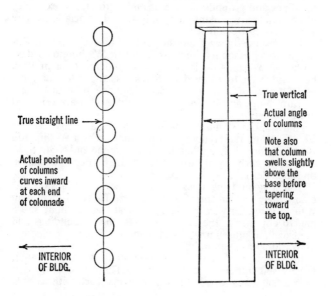

True straight line →

Actual position of columns curves inward at each end of colonnade

← INTERIOR OF BLDG.

← True vertical

Actual angle of columns

Note also that column swells slightly above the base before tapering toward the top.

INTERIOR OF BLDG. →

101

Mount Vernon

M Blue or Yellow line to Pentagon; 11P bus to Mt. Vernon

WHERE 16 miles south of Washington on Mt. Vernon Memorial Highway.

WHEN 9:00 A.M.–5:00 P.M., March 1–October 31; 9:00 A.M.–4:00 P.M., November 1–February 28.

HOW By car, by bus, or by a Washington Boat Line boat. Admission: Adults, $4.50; children under 12, $2. Information: 780-2000.

"I have no objection to any sober or orderly person's gratifying their curiosity in viewing the buildings, Gardens &ct about Mount Vernon." GEORGE WASHINGTON

Mount Vernon, George Washington's estate on the Potomac, may well be the most visited shrine in the United States. The buildings and grounds survive as one of the finest examples of an 18th-century plantation; in historical associations, they are surpassed by none.

The unspoiled view from the veranda looking over the Potomac River remains much as it did in Washington's day. Although Washington is chiefly remembered as a military hero and as the first President, his skill as one of the foremost agriculturists of his day, his discerning taste in his home and its furnishings and his love of the outdoors all are reflected in Mount Vernon.

Allow about 35 minutes to drive via the attractive Mount Vernon Memorial Highway. Or you may go by a Washington Boat Line boat leaving Pier 4, Maine Avenue and N St., S.W. daily from early April through Labor Day. (For information on schedules and rates call 554-8000.)

You may find the lines waiting to see the Mansion discouragingly long in spring and summer. To avoid them plan your visit for early in the day. Allow at least an hour and a half to enjoy fully the lovely grounds, the outbuildings and the excellent museum which contains a fascinating collection of Washington memorabilia.

In Washington's day Mount Vernon was an integrated, largely self-sufficient economic unit. The estate comprised over 8,000 acres, divided into five farms, each with its own overseer, workers (about 125 slaves worked the farms), animals and buildings. Although Washington never visited England, the estate he developed bore a remarkable resemblance to an English gentleman's country seat. As you tour the outbuildings, remember that most of the estate was highly functional. The small sections under cultivation near the Mansion were used to test new methods of growing crops and to raise vegetables and fruits for consumption. Most things used on the estate were made there. England was the nearest shopping place for many items not produced. Records exist of Washington's orders for books, furniture, wines, musical instruments, fashionable clothes and toys for his adopted grandchildren.

Your first view of the Mansion will be from the *Bowling Green*, laid out by Washington in 1785. Some of the ancient trees bordering the driveway were part of his original planting. Note the interesting "ha-has"—sunken walls which separate the formal lawns and gardens surrounding the house form the outlying fields.

The *Outbuildings* housed the means of making such necessities as shoes, material for clothing, bedding and towels. The stables suggest Washington's favorite sport of fox hunting. He took pride in breaking his own horses and in the breeding of his animals. The elaborately decorated coach in the coach house is thought to be almost identical to the one owned by Washington.

The *Mansion* itself is remarkably seeworthy for a house which accommodates as many as 10,000 visitors on some days (and well over a million each year). Throughout the house you will see exquisite examples of original 18th-century furniture (although only Washington's bedroom is completely furnished with pieces known to have been at Mount Vernon at the time of his death in 1799). Meticulous care has gone into every detail of the restoration. The original color of paint or wallpaper in each room has been found by scraping through many layers. Although the original fabrics used in curtains, draperies and bed coverings have long since disintegrated (fragments may be seen in the museum), replacements are carefully copied. Tile from the original quarry in England replaces the worn paving tile on the columned piazza. Only the fire protection is not "of the period," nor is one of two major fire hazards—falling airplanes (the other—lightning). Note the beveled siding of the Mansion's exterior, to which sand was applied when the surface was freshly painted; Washington called it "rusticated Boards." The piazza with its high columns is another distinguishing architectural feature which he may have originated in this country.

A distinctive feature of the first room you will enter, the *Banquet Room*, is the Palladian window. The agricultural implements in the stucco ceiling harmonize with the pastoral scenes in the handsome marble mantel, a gift from Washington's English friend, Samuel Vaughan.

The *Central Hall*, extending the full width of the house, with four adjoining rooms, typifies houses of this period. (Woodlawn and the Arlington House feature the same basic floor plan.) Many of the objects in the hall are original—the spyglass, model of the Bastille and its main key, barometer, clock on the landing and several of the prints. The *Little Parlor* contains the harpsichord Washington imported from London for his adopted daughter, Nellie Custis. Though he vowed he could "neither sing one of the songs, nor raise a single note on any instrument," music played a distinctive role in life at Mount Vernon.

The *West Parlor* ranks as one of the finest examples of colonial Virginia interiors because of its handsome mantel-piece (note the Washington family coat-of-arms in the pediment above it), decorated ceiling, pleasing proportions and paneled walls. Here hangs Charles Willson Peale's portrait of Washington painted during the Revolution. Note the original Chippendale card table and chairs, silver tea tray, china tea set and family pictures. The *Downstairs Bedroom* was probably used as a guest room. The *Dining Room*, though formal, was probably used by the family, but would not have been large enough to seat the ever-present guests who frequented the house after the Revolution. One notation in Washington's diary in 1774 mentions 11 guests by name who "came to Dinner and stayed all night."

The five *Bedrooms* on the second floor contain fewer original furnishings than the downstairs rooms, but each has attractive period pieces. Mrs. Washington's trunk, which accompanied her when she left Mount Vernon to join her husband at his winter army quarters during the Revolutionary War, rests at the foot of the bed in the Blue Room. *Washington's Bedroom* and dressing room were added when he enlarged the original house. The shaving table and Mrs. Washington's desk are both French pieces; the bed is the one in

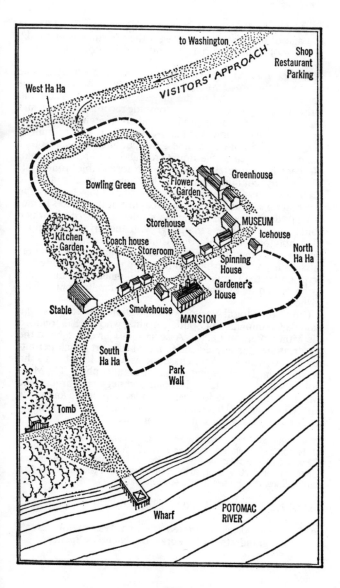

to Washington

VISITORS' APPROACH

Shop
Restaurant
Parking

West Ha Ha

Bowling Green

Greenhouse

Flower
Garden

Storehouse

MUSEUM

Icehouse

Kitchen
Garden

Coach house
Storeroom

North
Ha Ha

Spinning
House

Gardener's
House

Stable

Smokehouse

MANSION

South
Ha Ha

Park
Wall

Tomb

Wharf

POTOMAC
RIVER

which General Washington died on December 14, 1799, at the age of 67. Washington bought the "portmanteau trunk" at the foot of his bed in 1776, and used it during the war.

The *Library* on the first floor provided a sanctuary for the master of the house where he could carry on his voluminous correspondence, tend to the management of his estate and write in his diary. Many of his domestic records, accounts and published writings have survived and are contained in 37 volumes. The handsome secretary-desk, chair, globe, built-in bookcases, 75 library volumes, the hunting horn and other memorabilia such as the riding crop and gun are all original. He kept his important papers in the formidable iron chest. The *Pantry* contains pieces of the family's blue and white Canton china, a wine chest, and the small table used by the Washingtons for their wedding breakfast at the bride's home.

Walk down the hill below the stables to the *Tomb*, which contains two marble sarcophagi with the brief inscriptions "Washington" and "Martha, Consort of Washington." For many years Congress attempted unsuccessfully to obtain permission from the Washington family to remove his body to a crypt under the Capitol dome. His will made clear his desire to be buried at Mount Vernon, and his family honored his wishes.

Credit for Mount Vernon's preservation goes to Miss Ann Pamela Cunningham of South Carolina, who in 1853 founded the Mount Vernon Ladies' Association. Her efforts, and the Association's, generated the financial support which permitted the Association to purchase the estate in 1858 from John Washington, Jr., Washington's great-grandnephew. The Mansion was in a sad state of disrepair and neglect. Through the efforts of the Association, we can today appreciate and agree with Washington's statement that "No estate in United America is more pleasantly situated than This."

For an exceptional outing, combine your trip to Mount Vernon with Washington's Grist Mill (a short distance from the estate on Route 35), Woodlawn Plantation on Route 1, Pohick Church and Gunston Hall. A package of flower seeds from the unusual selection of 18th-century flowers grown in the Mount Vernon gardens makes a good souvenir of your visit. For sale at the Greenhouse Shop.

THE DEVELOPMENT OF A GREAT ESTATE

1674   5,000 acres granted to John Washington, great-grandfather of George and Nicholas Spencer.

1726	Augustine Washington, father of George, purchased Washington's half of grant then called "Hunting Creek Plantation."
1732	On February 22, George, eldest child of Augustine and Mary (Ball) Washington, born in Westmoreland County, VA.
1735	Augustine moved to Hunting Creek; stayed three years.
1740	Plantation deeded to Lawrence, George's elder half brother.
1743	Lawrence settled on estate with bride; renamed it Mount Vernon after Admiral Vernon. George's father died. George spent some time at Mount Vernon with his brother.
1754	Following Lawrence's death in 1752, title to Mount Vernon passed to George.
1754–59	George was absent, busy with French and Indian War.
1759	In January, George married Martha Dandridge Custis, wealthy widow of Daniel Parke Custis. Moved to Mount Vernon in spring with Martha's two children—John Parke and Martha Parke Custis.
1759–95	George enlarged house, developed plantation.
1775	George appointed Commander-in-Chief of Continental Army by Second Continental Congress in Philadelphia.
1775–83	George's duties as general kept him away from home for more than eight years. John Parke Custis, Martha's son, died of camp fever in siege of Yorktown. George adopted John's two youngest children—Eleanor (Nellie) Parke and George Washington Parke Custis. Lund Washington, a relative, managed estate in George's absence.

107

1783	George returned home, presumably for good, having resigned his commission as Commander-in-Chief to Congress on December 23.
1787	George went to Philadelphia as delegate from Virginia to Constitutional Convention.
1789–97	George served two terms as first President. Absent from Mount Vernon except for a few brief visits.
1797–99	George finally retired to Mount Vernon.
1799	December 14, George died. Buried in vault on estate.
1802	Martha died. Estate inherited by Bushrod Washington, George's nephew.
1829	Bushrod died. John Augustine Washington, his nephew, inherited estate, in badly deteriorated condition.
1858	Mount Vernon (200-acre tract) purchased by Mount Vernon Ladies' Association, founded by Miss Ann Pamela Cunningham of South Carolina.

National Archives

WHERE	Constitution Avenue between 7th and 9th Sts., N.W.
WHEN	Open 10:00 A.M.–9:00 P.M., daily, Apr. 1 to Labor Day; 10:00 A.M.–5:30 P.M., the day after Labor Day to March 31.
HOW	Free. Adult "behind-the-scenes" and exhibition tours. School programs by appointment. Call 523-3184.

"What is Past is Prologue"

The National Archives displays the three documents that serve as charters of our democracy—the Declaration of Independence, the Constitution and the Bill of Rights. These foundations of our government are handwritten on parchments, each the size of a newspaper page. They are dramatically displayed.

The *Declaration of Independence* is engrossed on a single sheet of parchment. Thomas Jefferson drafted much of it in a period of 2½ weeks during June 1776 ("We hold these truths to be self-evident, that all men are created equal, that they are endowed by their Creator with certain unalienable Rights, that among these are Life, Liberty and the pursuit of Happiness.") The Continental Congress adopted the text of the Declaration on July 4, 1776, and that night and the next morning it was printed. On July 19 Congress ordered that the Declaration be engrossed on parchment. The engrossed copy was signed on August 2 by the delegates present and later by others. It has faded badly from long exposure to light.

The *Constitution of the United States of America* was signed on September 17, 1787, by the delegates to the Constitutional Convention. By June 21, 1788, conventions in nine states had ratified it, and later the other states approved it. The Constitution is engrossed on four sheets of parchment of which pages one ("We the People. . .") and four (signature page) are displayed.

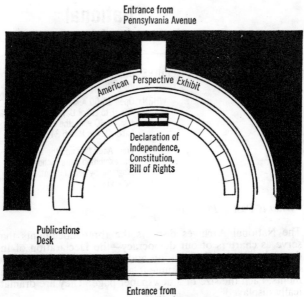

American Perspective *Exhibit*

Declaration of
Independence,
Constitution,
Bill of Rights

Publications
Desk

Entrance from
Constitution Avenue

The *Bill of Rights* was sent to the states for ratification after the First Congress passed a resolution on September 25, 1789, proposing 12 amendments to the Constitution. The Bill of Rights sprang from fears that the strong central government provided by the Constitution, if unchecked, might jeopardize individual rights. Note that in the document the First Amendment appears as the third article ("Congress shall make no law respecting an establishment of religion, or prohibiting the free exercise thereof, or abridging the freedom of speech or of the press, or the right of the people peaceably to assemble and to petition the government for a redress of grievances.") It became the First Amendment to the Constitution when the states failed to ratify the articles numbered one and two.

Helium fills the bronze and glass cases to protect the parchments from contact with the air. Special filters screen out harmful light rays. When not on display the documents are lowered into a fireproof and bombproof vault.

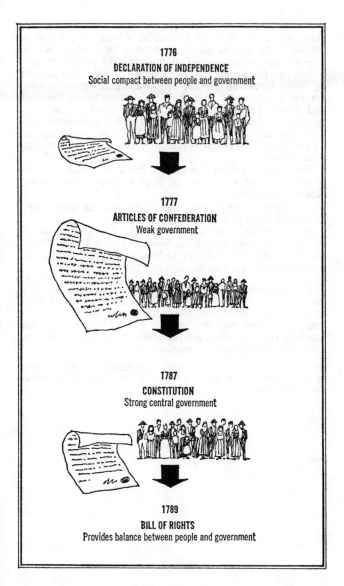

1776
DECLARATION OF INDEPENDENCE
Social compact between people and government

1777
ARTICLES OF CONFEDERATION
Weak government

1787
CONSTITUTION
Strong central government

1789
BILL OF RIGHTS
Provides balance between people and government

The exhibition cases flanking the central display tell the story in documents of the *Formation of the Union*. The documents in this exhibit mirror the doubts, the gambles and the compromises which succeeded in uniting the original states.

The two large *murals* in the Exhibition Hall were painted by Barry Faulkner. On the left you see Jefferson and his committee (Benjamin Franklin, John Adams, Roger Sherman and Robert Livingston) presenting the Declaration of Independence to John Hancock, president of the Continental Congress. On the right you see James Madison submitting the Constitution to George Washington and the Constitutional Convention.

The circular gallery behind the Exhibition Hall displays changing exhibits of documents, maps, photographs and other archival materials.

An exhibition celebrating the Bicentennial of the Constitution will open in 1987 (until March 1989).

At the Publications Desk you can buy excellent, inexpensive publications including *The Formation of the Union*, *Charters of Freedom* (reproducing in facsimile the Declaration of Independence, the Constitution and the Bill of Rights).

The *Government's Strongbox*. You will not see the 196 stack areas of the National Archives. Here, 1,300,000 cubic feet of permanently valuable records of the federal government are housed and protected by fire walls and by temperature and humidity controls. They are preserved for the use of government officials and general researchers.

For those interested in research on their family tree, extraordinary records of a personal nature—old census records, ship manifests, immigration records—may be found at the National Archives.

National Gallery of Art

WEST BUILDING

M Judiciary Square, 4th and D St. Exit

WHERE 4th through 7th Sts., and Constitution Ave., N.W.

WHEN 10:00 A.M.–5:00 P.M., Mon.–Sat.; NOON–9:00 P.M., Sun. Summer hours; call for information.

HOW All events free; Introductory Tour at 11:00 A.M., and 3:00 P.M., Mon.–Sat.; 1:00 P.M. and 5:00 P.M. Sun. (lasts 50–60 min).

Tour of the Week at 1:00 P.M., Tues.–Sat., 2:30 P.M., Sun. (lasts 50–60 min).

Tour to Painting of the Week at NOON and 2:00 P.M., Tues.–Sat.; 3:30 P.M. and 6:00 P.M., Sun. (lasts about 15 min).

Concerts by National Gallery Symphony Orchestra and other groups and artists in East Garden Court, Sun. 7:00 P.M. (no concerts during summer)—all free.

Lectures by visiting scholars and critics Sunday afternoons at 4:00 P.M. Frequent films and special exhibitions.

Information: 737-4215.

The National Gallery of Art provides the proudest jewel in Washington's crown. The collection of paintings, sculpture and the graphic arts ranks with those in the world's great museums—the Prado in Madrid, the Louvre in Paris, the Uffizi in Florence. Even if your time in Washington is limited, plan to spend some of it in this magnificent and centrally located gallery. Seeing America's only painting by Leonardo or the original of Rembrandt's *Self-Portrait*, Raphael's *Alba*

Madonna, and Fra Angelico's *Adoration of the Magi* may furnish you an unforgettable experience.

A guided tour is strongly recommended for your first visit to the Gallery. In this way you will see highlights of the vast collection and be directed to outstanding examples of leading artists representative of the schools of painting. You will absorb a great deal of information in 45 minutes, and you may even learn for the first time really to "look" at a painting. Heed the words of J. Carter Brown, the Gallery's director: "Please don't try to see everything in one visit!. . .the invariable result is what we call 'gallery fatigue.'" He suggests an hour's visit to best retain the clear memory of a few fine objects. "Plan on several short visits rather than one long one" is his advice.

There are four entrances to the Gallery. The Constitution Avenue entrance leads to the ground floor, as do the two entrances on the opposite ends of the building, one on 4th Street and one on 7th Street. The broad steps on the Mall Side lead to the main floor. The *Great Rotunda*, the heart of the museum, divides this floor into two balanced parts. A garden court at the end of each wing displays flowers grown in the museum's own greenhouses.

After you enter the museum your first stop should be at one of the information desks where you can pick up a detailed guide to the Gallery (free). Particularly helpful are the museum's floorplans showing the location of the various schools of painting starting with the earliest Italian paintings (Gallery 1) and ending with 19th-Century French paintings in Gallery 93.

As you tour the museum note these features. The building is designed to provide natural lighting to the greatest extent possible. Each gallery is relatively small in size. Wall backgrounds vary according to the period of painting displayed. For example, in the early Italian rooms, the plaster walls are painted or faced with travertine stone; in the later Italian rooms, the walls are covered with elegant damask; in the Flemish and Dutch rooms, they are of fumed oak. Painted wood paneling marks most of the galleries in the east wing, where American, British and French paintings are displayed. Air-conditioning and humidity control are scrupulously maintained for the paintings' welfare—something the visitor can cash in on in the hot summer months.

The National Gallery was a gift to the nation by Andrew W. Mellon, who served for 13 years as Secretary of the Treasury under Presidents Harding, Coolidge and Hoover. Mellon started collecting paintings in 1882 at the age of 27. His great-

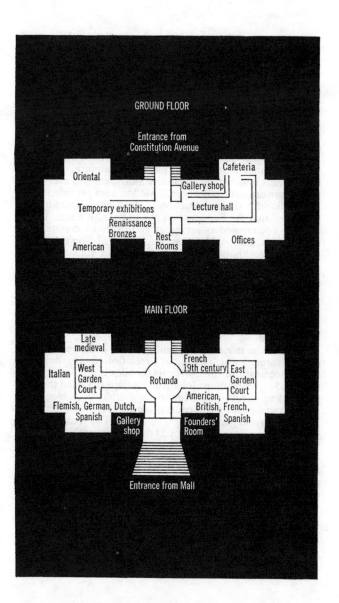

GROUND FLOOR

Entrance from
Constitution Avenue

Oriental

Cafeteria

Gallery shop

Temporary exhibitions

Lecture hall

Renaissance
Bronzes

Rest
Rooms

American

Offices

MAIN FLOOR

Late
medieval

Italian

West
Garden
Court

French
19th century

Rotunda

East
Garden
Court

Flemish, German, Dutch,
Spanish

Gallery
shop

Founders'
Room

American,
British, French,
Spanish

Entrance from Mall

115

est purchase was from the Hermitage Gallery in Leningrad, formerly the imperial gallery of the Russian Tsars. In the early 1930s his acquisition of 21 old masters for $6,500,000 helped the Russians out of a financial bind. Among these masterpieces are Raphael's *Alba Madonna,* his *St. George and the Dragon,* and Botticelli's *Adoration of the Magi.* Each picture in his collection had to meet three rigid requirements: it had to be one of the artist's great works; it had to portray a subject of outstanding interest or beauty; and it had to be in an excellent state of preservation.

To found the Gallery, his gift of 126 canvases by 70 of the world's greatest artists, and 26 pieces of sculpture, comprised the greatest endowment "that any individual had ever made to any government anywhere." Mellon also provided some $15 million for the construction of the Gallery building. He stipulated that the building was not to bear his name. In this way he encouraged other great collectors to donate their works of art. Samuel H. Kress, inspired by Mellon's example, in 1939 gave his outstanding collection of Italian art, 375 paintings and 18 sculptures. Since that time the Gallery has received important acquisitions from Rush H. Kress, Joseph E. Widener, Chester Dale, Lessing Rosenwald, Colonel and Mrs. Edgar William Garbisch and over 200 other donors. The National Gallery was opened in March 1941; in just a few decades it has probably grown faster than any other gallery in the world.

Because the museum was built "to last a thousand years" on land through which the Tiber Creek flowed in earlier days, it was necessary to drive over 6,000 piles in the soft ground to provide a foundation. John Russell Pope designed the classic building of rose-white Tennessee marble, each block gradated in shade (the lower courses are darker; the higher ones, lighter) to avoid glare in bright sunshine. The great rotunda, 100 feet across, is supported by 24 dark green marble columns. The fountain in the center features a graceful statue of Mercury by Giovanni de Bologna, which was made in Florence in 1598. The building stretches 782 feet in length, the equivalent of six city blocks, and has over a half-million square feet of floor space.

National Gallery of Art

EAST BUILDING

Ⓜ Judiciary Square,
4th and D
Street Exit

WHERE 4th St. and Constitution Ave., N.W.

WHEN Same hours as West Building.

HOW Same as West Building.

The new East Building of the National Gallery has become, since its opening in June 1978 "the biggest show in town."

Acclaimed by critics and laymen alike, "the building is proof that architecture, even monumental architecture, can have a soaring beauty as well as the ingenious use of interior space for a variety of purposes."

At first glance we are struck by several features: the building's "different" appearance; the awkward trapezoid-shaped piece of land on which the museum stands; and the beauty of the pinkish Tennessee marble matching that of the National Gallery completed 35 years earlier. The architect, I.M. Pei, was faced with the task of designing a building to serve a number of purposes: a gallery building with enclosed exhibition spaces; a covered open courtyard to correspond in function with the rotunda of the parent museum; and an office building to house the library, gallery staff and the new National Gallery Center for Advanced Studies in the Visual Arts.

Pei's masterpiece has been called "an uncompromising exercise in solid geometry." Nevertheless, it does not take a mathematical whiz-kid to understand how he solved the difficult design problem. He placed a trapezoid within a trapezoid, then sliced the pattern diagonally across from the northeast to the southwest corner. Result: two interlocking triangles, an isosceles triangle with its base facing the National Gallery and a right triangle with its base facing the Capitol.

The exhibition spaces are located in the isosceles triangle. Its points are towers, and its sides are bridges of galleries connecting the towers. The library and offices are housed in the right triangle. The pièce de résistance is the light-filled court which has been called "one of the extraordinary interior spaces in the history of 20th-century architecture."

Before entering the building note the impressive open plaza

117

between the old building and the new. Jets of water and glass triangles jutt from the stone surface. Outside the building Henry Moore's *Knife Edge Mirror Two Piece* sculpture, composed of two bronze sections roughly 17½ feet high, guard the entrance.

As you enter the court you will feel delight, surprise, awe and the certainty that you are undergoing an experience in space you have never had before. The sky is visible through the glass roof; balconies, bridges and cascades of stairways interact in a satisfying way, and yet the feeling persists that there is an underlying complexity in the design you cannot readily understand. As the sun moves, the shadows change, creating new patterns on the marble floor. You want to explore the courtyard from as many levels as possible—to stand on a balcony and look down, to stand on a staircase and look back. The people moving about in this marvelous courtyard seem part of the overall design. It is hard to take it all in, which adds to one's pleasure.

Gradually the eye falls on objects in the court. The 920-pound mobile by Alexander Calder with its balanced rods and huge red, blue and black pods hangs from the space frame. The free-floating, incrediby sensitive parts move with the air currents, adding emphasis to the interior's kinetic space. Calder, trained as an engineer, combined interests in form and motion in developing his first mobile in 1931. He did not live to see his commissioned sculpture installed in the East Building.

Hanging on the courtyard's south wall is a Miro tapestry, *Femme*, woven in Spain by Josep Royo. Fields of bright colors outlined in black convey the artist's symbol for the archetypal woman.

On a balcony underneath the upper bridge rests Anthony Caro's sculpture of welded parts which contrasts sharp welded steel parts with the smoothness of the surfaces around it. The 14-foot subtle yet vigorous vertical stone by Isamu Noguchi deserves a close-up look. It is somewhat dwarfed in its setting.

The rest of the building is full of surprises: the galleries in the three towers are skylit and beautiful; the spiral stairwells in hidden corridors await discovery; and the dozens of exhibit halls vary in size as walls are moved to accommodate different exhibitions.

Pei's superb design has been superbly executed. The workmanship throughout is meticulous. Air-conditioning, for example, circulates through unobtrusive conduits beneath the skylight and through openings in the risers of the stairs. One

118

of Pei's engineers remarked: "You have to work hard to make things look simple."

A 154,000 square foot underground link connects the old building with the new. Located here are the cafeteria of ultramodern design, the Concourse Café next to the waterfall, a book store and a gift shop.

I.M. Pei, the gallery's architect, was born in Canton, China, in 1917. Many notable buildings both in this country and abroad bear the stamp of his versatility. Examples of his designs are the John F. Kennedy Library in Boston, the National Center for Atmospheric Research in Boulder, CO, and the Industrial Credit Bank in Tehran.

This magnificent gift to the nation cost $94.4 million and was donated by Paul Mellon, the late Ailsa Mellon Bruce and the Andrew W. Mellon Foundation.

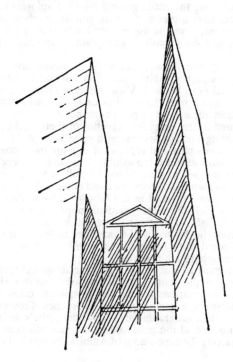

National Geographic

(EXPLORERS HALL)

M Farragut North

WHERE	17th and M St., N.W.
WHEN	9:00 A.M.–5:00 P.M., Mon.–Sat.; 10:00 A.M.–5:00 P.M., Sun. (Closed Christmas Day.)
HOW	Free; self-guided tours.

Featured in the handsome National Geographic Society building, and occupying the entire ground floor is Explorers Hall. This is no ordinary museum, for here you share adventures, past and present, from the many varied achievements in the National Geographic's continuing program of exploration and research.

This exciting tour through the world of exploration, represented by modern exhibits, takes you into far corners of the world, and even beyond. View the huge maps of exploration, then move into the reaches of man's most distant past—the dramatic exhibit of prehistoric people, life-size figures presented in the everyday activities of their worlds, including painting hunting scenes on a cave wall. A film on discovering man's past and replicas of dug-up archeological relics and skulls introduce the exhibit. Unique is a fiberglass cast of footprints left in East Africa 3.6 million years ago by two of modern man's ancestors or extinct cousins. In contrast, the early cultures advanced in the New World—be they Olmec, Maya or Cliff-Dwellers—suddenly appear in an almost contemporary light. The great Olmec stone head and the treasures from the Mayan well of sacrifice indicate some of the archeological work being done as the ancient secrets of our own hemisphere are revealed.

A huge illuminated globe, slowly rotating above a glistening pool, dominates the central north wing of Explorers Hall. Dramatic demonstrations for visiting groups are often featured in the mornings, comparing sizes and shapes of countries by projecting their geographic areas onto the globe's surface.

Proceeding around the pool and globe, you will come to exhibits depicting the expeditions of Admiral Robert E. Peary to the North Pole and Admiral Richard E. Byrd to the South Pole. Included are Peary's flag and sled. Other exhibits portray exploration under the oceans, and include a cannon from a sunken Spanish treasure ship.

The gallery of transparencies flanks the east entrance to the Hall, with large, lighted photographs from the Society's files of eight million pictures.

Nearby are video presentations of how the National Geographic Society makes and prints its maps and globes.

A souvenir from outer space on exhibit is a moon rock retrieved by astronauts Alan Bean and Charles Conrad on the Apollo 12 lunar mission. A space curiosity is a fragment of Skylab, which disintegrated as it fell to earth. The astronomy exhibits are striking. Paths of the planets are presented in an abstract manner, with orbits traced in tiny blinking lights, all timed in ratio, as each planet pursues its course. Note the exceptional color photographs of galaxies taken through the Palomar telescope, and the telescope models displayed.

Current activities of the Society are reflected in the changing exhibit area of Explorers Hall. The ten-story building, designed by Edward Durell Stone, contrasts white marble with black granite. This magnificent building and Explorers Hall are highlights of a visit to the nation's capital.

For sale are the superb maps, globes and richly illustrated texts for which the National Geographic Society has become justly famous.

For daily information on changing exhibits, phone: 857-7588 Mon.–Fri., 857-7000 Weekends.

National Museum of American Art

M Gallery Place

WHERE G and 8th Sts., N.W.
WHEN   10:00 A.M.–5:30 P.M., daily.
HOW   Free.

One of Washington's handsomest buildings, and most historical, is the "Old Patent Office Building," located between the Capitol and the White House. Since 1968 the National Museum of American Art and the National Portrait Gallery have shared these commodious quarters, both of them a part of the Smithsonian Institution. The architect for this largest and in some ways finest of the Greek Revival buildings in this country was William Elliot; construction was begun in 1836 and completely finished only in 1867. At that time it was the largest building in the United States, and occupied a major site in Major Pierre Charles L'Enfant's great plan for Washington—at the cross-axis of the Mall. Although his plans for erecting a Pantheon to honor those who had given their best in the service of their country never materialized, the building has served its nation well.

During the Civil War it was used as barracks, hospital and morgue. After the Battle of Antietam in the fall of 1862 more than 2,000 wounded and dying soldiers were brought into the new wing of what was then the Patent Office; beds were laid on the marble floors between the display cases crowded with models in miniature "of every kind of utensil, machine or invention." Poet Walt Whitman visited the soldiers "to soothe and relieve" their suffering, and Clara Barton also cared for the wounded. A happier event took place on the evening of March 6, 1865, when President Lincon's second inaugural ball and banquet took place in what is now the Lincoln Gallery, and the elegant north Salon.

The Patent Office occupied the building for 92 years until 1932. We owe a debt of gratitude to David Finley, Commissioner of Fine Arts in 1953, who brought to the attention of President Eisenhower the fact that the building was authorized to be razed for a parking lot. Through his efforts and those of a group of Senators and Congressmen, the building was saved and consequently renovated for its present purpose.

The National Museum of American Art is a center for the enjoyment and understanding of American art. The museum produces about 15 outstanding exhibitions a year, accompanied by definitive publications, treating various, often less well-known aspects of American art; it also circulates exhibitions of American arts across the country. Work in crafts and design is presented in its Renwick Gallery.

The museum's holdings of some 32,000 works of art have all been registered on computer and are available to scholars for study. You will see a significant portion of them on display in the museum.

The first major refurbishment of the museum since its opening in the Old Patent Office makes it easy to trace and compare the history of 250 years of American art.

In the new installation you will find:

First floor	graphic arts, early American art, art of the West, American portraits, miniature paintings
Second floor	mid and late 19th-century art, Hiram Powers Gallery, Homer/Ryder/Inness, American Impressionists, turn-of-the-century paintings
Third floor	early 20th-century art, art of the 1930s and 1940s, modern art (in the Lincoln Gallery)

During the warmer months you may enjoy having lunch or a snack in the handsome central court graced by two Civil War era elms. This is one of the pleasantest spots in the whole downtown area for rest and relaxation.

National Portrait Gallery

M Gallery Place

WHERE	F and 8th Sts., N.W.
WHEN	10:00 A.M.–5:30 P.M. , daily.
HOW	Free. Walk-in tours, 10:00 A.M.–3:00 P.M., Mon.–Fri.; NOON–3:00 P.M., Sat. and Sun.

The National Portrait Gallery, the National Museum of American Art and the Archives of American Art are all housed in the magnificent "Old Patent Office Building" described in the write-up on The National Museum of American Art. Only the White House and the Capitol building are older and comparable in beauty.

Starting back in 1857 Congress made its first official gesture toward creating a national portrait gallery when G.P.A. Healy was commissioned to paint a series of Presidential portraits for the White House. Several of them hang there today, including the portrait of Lincoln over the fireplace in the State Dining Room. However, it was more than a hundred years later, in 1962, that Congress officially established the National Portrait Gallery of the United States. It is the fourth such gallery in the world and the first in the Western Hemisphere.

Its purpose is "to exhibit portraits and statuary of men and women who have made significant contributions to the history, development and culture of the people of the United States." Also honored by the museum are the artists who created these works.

The Gallery aims to form a permanent collection of portraits of notable figures; whenever possible they should be taken from life or be contemporary with the subject. The subject must have been dead at least ten years before his or her portrait can be admitted to the permanent collection.

To the left of the main entrance you will find galleries for special, temporary exhibits. Note the gracefully curved double staircase leading to the second floor; the portrait of Pocahontas at its foot was painted by an unknown English artist in 1616.

You will undoubtedly recognize the full-length portrait of George Washington by Gilbert Stuart, painted in 1796 and known as the "Lansdowne" portrait, which hangs in the second floor vestibule. The "Athenaeum" portraits of George and Martha Washington are here on a part-time basis, as they are owned jointly with the Boston Museum of Fine Arts. Of great interest is the Presidential Corridor with its portraits of the Presidents; a special alcove at the eastern end, under the Presidential Seal, is reserved for the present occupant of the White House. The intimate galleries to the right and left of the Presidential Gallery display portraits from the permanent collection in chronological order. Such famous portraitists as John Singleton Copley, Charles Willson Peale, Thomas Sully, John Singer Sargent and Augustus Saint-Gaudens are represented.

Not to be missed is the Meserve Gallery (number 212), containing photographs by the famous Civil War photographer, Mathew Brady. The modern prints of well-known personalities of mid-19th century (Longfellow, Samuel Morse and Jefferson Davis, amongst others) were made from glass-plate negatives. Brady's studio still stands not too many blocks away between 6th and 7th Streets and Pennsylvania Avenue.

An extraordinary sight awaits you on the third floor. The Great Hall, which once displayed thousands of patent models in glass cases, epitomizes the flamboyant American Renaissance style with its colorful tiles, stained-glass windows and carved friezes on the wall. Once the largest room in America, the Great Hall suffered a terrible fire in 1877. The decor you see reflects the exuberance of the 1880s.

Because of the off-the-beaten-track location, the Museum of American Art and the Portrait Gallery do not attract the large number of visitors enjoyed by other Smithsonian museums on the Mall. All the more reason for you to head over to F and 8th Strets for a fascinating day of exploration. Both of the museums have fine gift shops.

National Shrine of the Immaculate Conception

M Brookland-CUA

WHERE   Michigan Ave. at 4th St., N.E.

WHEN   7:00 A.M.–6:00 P.M., daily (winter schedule) 7:00 A.M.–7:00 P.M., daily (summer schedule).

HOW   Guided tours every half hour from Memorial Hall (allow 45 min.) 9:00 A.M.–4:00 P.M., Mon.–Sat.; 1:30–4:00 P.M., Sun. (check for schedule).

Huge in concept and size, the National Shrine of the Immaculate Conception is the newest of Washington's national shrines, the largest Catholic Church in the country and the seventh largest religious structure in the world. Impressive and beautiful are the huge mosaics around the main altar and in the Dome; they are amongst the largest in the world. The Shrine was dedicated in November 1959 to the Virgin Mary.

Because "even steel wears out," the Shrine is built entirely of stone and masonry. The architecture may be classified in general terms as Romanesque and Byzantine. However, its architect, E.F. Kennedy, Jr., describes the styles as "reminiscent of no other building in the world."

The exterior has 180 pieces of sculpture, life-size and heroic. The bell tower, rising 329 feet from the ground (three-fifths the height of the Washington Monument), contrasts with the horizontal lines of the church. The length of the Shrine is half again that of a football field—459 feet; at the nave the width is 157 feet. A bird's-eye view would show you that the Shrine has the shape of a Latin cross.

You will be overawed by the immensity of the Shrine's interior, in which 3,000 may be seated and 6,000 accommodated. Around the main altar of the upper church are 15 side chapels dedicated to the mysteries of the Rosary. Above these chapels are three huge mosaics of Christ in Majesty, Mary Immaculate and St. Joseph the Worker. In the Dome above the altar another mosaic shows the Triumph of the Lamb.

On a lower level is a crypt church completed in 1927, but beautifully accommodated to the new liturgy. In this church there are also 15 side chapels with marble altars and mosaic backgrounds. The great Moller organ and the chancel organ were dedicated on April 25, 1965. The 56-bell carillon in the Knight's Tower was dedicated in 1963.

An air-conditioned cafeteria, open from 7:30 A.M. to 7:00 P.M., serves breakfast, lunch and dinner. A trip to the Shrine may be combined with one to the Franciscan Monastery.

Outstanding musical events presented by the National Shrine Music Guild take place throughout the fall, winter and spring.

National Zoological Park

Ⓜ Cleveland Park
  or Woodley Park

WHERE   Entrances in the 3000 block of Connecticut Ave., N.W., and Harvard St., N.W.

WHEN   Buildings:
9:00 A.M.–6:00 P.M., Apr. 1–Oct. 15. 10:00–4:30 P.M., rest of the year.
Grounds:
8:00 A.M.–8:00 P.M., Apr. 1–Oct. 15. 8:00 A.M.–6:00 P.M., rest of the year.

HOW   Free admission; parking, $3.00.

The National Zoological Park occupies 163 acres within Rock Creek Park in northwest Washington. Its animal population totals nearly 3,000 specimens. Perhaps its best known residents are the Giant Pandas, Ling-Ling and Hsing-Hsing, gifts from the People's Republic of China. You can see them fed at 11:00 A.M. and 3:00 P.M. in their handsome, specially-designed Panda House.

Your first stop at the zoo should be the Education Building, near the Connecticut Avenue entrance. There you can pick up a map (be prepared; the distances are vast); see an orientation slide show in the Auditorium, 10:00 A.M.–4:30 P.M. daily, Memorial Day to Labor Day, weekends only the rest of the year; and pick up tickets to the Zoo Lab, where children will enjoy peering through a microscope or handling objects such as nests and elephant tusks.

Snacks are available at the *Panda Cafe* (outdoors), and the *Mane Restaurant/Cafeteria* near the Beach Drive entrance. Or better still, bring your own picnic.

The Zoo is a bureau of the Smithsonian Institution. In the 1880s taxidermists working on animal exhibits for the Smithsonian kept many animals on the Mall for models. Among them were nine American bison, survivors of the millions killed during the 19th century. They served to focus attention on the demise of the once beautiful herds and resulted in adoption of federal laws to protect the few remaining animals.

The Zoo was established by an act of Congress in 1889 largely through the efforts of the then Secretary of the Smithsonian, Samuel Pierpont Langley. In 1890, the first keeper, William H. Blackburne, of Barnum and Bailey's Circus, borrowed a wagon and trundled 185 animals from the Mall pens to their new home. This is the one zoo in the United States owned by all Americans.

Be sure to visit the Great Outdoor Flight Cage, connected to the Bird House. This remarkable structure, outlined on six slender parabolic arches of steel, is covered with vinyl-coated mesh wire, forming a hemisphere 130 feet in diameter. Here visitors walk among waterfalls and boulders, with no physical barriers between them and the birds.

You may wonder what the sign—a bovine skull with VAN-ISHING ANIMAL superimposed on it—means. It marks those animals in the Zoo's collection whose numbers are diminishing in the wild. The National Zoological Park, like most zoos, is dedicated to the preservation of rare and endangered species.

Since 1975 the Zoo has renovated all its animal exhibits. The modern facilities offer visitors excellent animal viewing. The hilly site requires a great deal of hiking, so "ground grippers" should be the uniform of the day.

Organization of American States

(PAN AMERICAN UNION)

M Farragut West	WHERE	17th St. and Constitution Ave., N.W.
	WHEN	9:00 A.M.–5:00 P.M., Mon.–Fri.; closed weekends.
	HOW	Tours 9:30 A.M.–4:00 P.M., or visit on your own.

This handsome building serves as the headquarters of the Organization of American States, the oldest international organization of nations in the world and the embodiment of almost a century of peaceful cooperation between the independent nations of the Americas.

The OAS building, formerly known as the Pan American Union, is intended to represent a "House of the Americas;" its design and decor were chosen to be representative. The house and grounds are of unusual beauty.

The OAS building is worth visiting whether or not you take the instructive tour. Tours leave from the Tropical Patio at frequent intervals, last about 40 minutes, and are free, by reservation only. (Call 789-3751.)

The *Tropical Patio* combines exotic planting and pre-Columbian ornamentation. You will see banana, rubber, yerba-mate, palm and coffee trees. There are usually birds in the patio. The fountain of pink marble in the center features fine carvings in Aztec and Mayan style. Note also the designs on the patio floor, surrounding the fountain, copied from Mayan and Inca ruins. Coats-of-arms of the 21 original member nations hang high on the stucco walls.

Of general interest is the *Museum of Modern Art of Latin America*, just behind the Aztec Garden at 201 18th St., N.W. On view are more than 200 paintings, sculptures, drawings and prints. (Open 10:00 A.M.–5:00 P.M., Tues.–Sat.; free.)

The *Hall of Heroes and Flags* on the second floor overlooking the patio leads to the *Hall of the Americas*, an ornate room designed for inter-American activities. Meetings of the

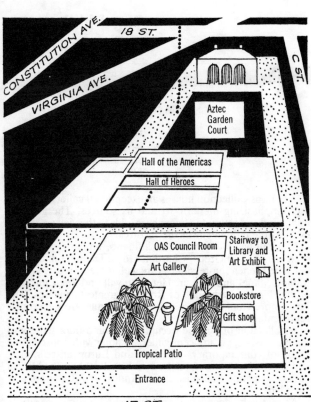

CONSTITUTION AVE.

VIRGINIA AVE.

18 ST.

C ST.

Aztec Garden Court

Hall of the Americas

Hall of Heroes

OAS Council Room

Stairway to Library and Art Exhibit

Art Gallery

Bookstore

Gift shop

Tropical Patio

Entrance

17 ST.

Council of the OAS take place in the *New Council Chamber* on the first floor. Don't miss the Aztec Garden at the back of the building. There a statue of Xochipilli, the Aztec God of Flowers, presides over a blue-tiled pool, surrounded by well-kept plants and flowers which follow the seasons.

The OAS is the regional organization of the Western Hemisphere created to maintain peace and security, and promote the economic and social welfare of all Americans.

The Phillips Collection

M Dupont Circle

WHERE 1600 and 1612 21st St., N.W.
(just north of Massachusetts Ave.).

WHEN 10:00 A.M.–5:00 P.M.,
Tues.–Sat.; 2:00 P.M.–7:00 P.M.,
Sun.; closed Mon.

HOW No charge; concert (free) 5:00 P.M.
Sun. Tour: Wed. and Sat., 2:00
P.M.

The Phillips Collection houses an exceptional gallery of paintings emphasizing modern art and its sources. The gallery's unhurried and intimate atmosphere adds to the viewers' greatest possible enjoyment of the pictures.

You will be able to trace the influence on later painters of such artists as El Greco, Chardin, Goya, Daumier and Courbet. The French Impressionists are well represented by Degas, Monet, Manet and Renoir. Here you will find *The Luncheon of the Boating Party,* one of Renoir's greatest canvases. The Post-Impressionists Van Gogh and Cézanne are generously represented.

A collection of Braque occupies a ground-floor gallery of the New Wing; an adjacent gallery is hung with a fascinating group of contemporary American and European paintings, and there is a room of works by Mark Rothko. Traditional American painters such as Eakins, Inness and Ryder are also included.

Attractively decorated and furnished rooms, carefully lighted pictures, and comfortable chairs invitingly placed for you to contemplate the paintings at your leisure characterize the Phillips. Museum feet and gallery fatigue are unheard of here. The gallery is the four-story red brick residence which was the former home of the late Director and Mrs. Duncan Phillips, and the New Wing (1960) is at 1612 21st St.

A special treat are the Sunday afternoon at five concerts presented in the gracious living room. Seating is limited, so plan to arrive early. Homemade gourmet food is available at *Suzanne's Café* on the lower level. This is a pleasant place for lunch or afternoon tea; it is open Tuesday to Saturday, 10:00 A.M. to 4:30 P.M.; Sunday, 2:00 P.M. to 4:00 P.M.

Renwick Gallery

M Farragut West
or North

WHERE   Pennsylvania Ave. at 17th St.,
N.W.

WHEN   10:00 A.M.–5:30 P.M., daily
except Christmas.

HOW   Free.

The distinctive red brick building with sandstone trim standing at the corner of Pennsylvania Ave. and 17th St. houses the *Renwick Gallery* of the Smithsonian Institution. It is well worth a visit, if only to savor the beautifully restored *Second Empire Grand Salon* of the 1870s on the second floor. With its red velvet banquettes, heavy draperies, paintings which hung there almost a century ago, and air of dignified formality, this room is one of the handsomest in Washington. See, too, the *Octagon Room*, another period piece notable for its lovely proportions and rich furnishings. In the first floor galleries you will be treated to special exhibitions on American design and crafts, and works from abroad. Quilts, Shaker boxes, mirrors, textiles and furniture, 19th-century Western saddles, and 200 years of Royal Copenhagen Porcelain are some of the beautifully mounted exhibitions of the past few years.

In 1859 William Wilson Corcoran, a Washington banker and philanthropist, commissioned James Renwick, Jr., to design a building in the Second Empire style for his art collection. Before the museum was completed the Civil War broke out, and the federal government seized it for a temporary hospital, later using it as headquarters of the Quartermaster General's Corps. In 1869 the building was returned to Corcoran who spent the next five years repairing damage and furnishing the rooms. For the next 25 years it served as Washington's first extensive art museum; in 1897 the collection was moved to the larger Corcoran Gallery a few blocks away. The United States Court of Claims used the building from 1899 to 1964, when the Smithsonian acquired it. Renamed the *Renwick Gallery*, it was opened to the public in January 1972.

Take a few moments to admire the building's exterior. Note especially the wealth of architectural sculpture devices such as the wreaths of finely carved foliage, Corcoran's monogram and a profile portrait with the motto "Dedicated to Art." The second-story niches originally contained seven-foot high marble statues of "the greatest artists and sculptors of all time." Unfortunately they are empty today except for two which were installed in Feburary 1974—the reproductions are of Murillo and Rubens and appear in niches on the 17th Street facade.

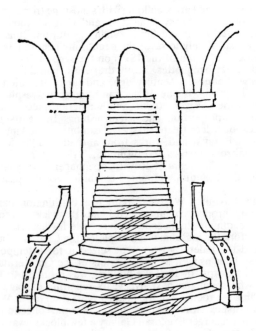

Smithsonian Institution

M Three stops serve the Mall. Consult map.

WHERE Nine museums and galleries on the Mall, bet. 4th and 14th Sts.; five more (including the Zoo) in other parts of Washington and one in New York City.

WHEN 10:00 A.M.–5:30 P.M., every day except Christmas. Extended spring and summer hours are determined annually. National Zoo and Anacostia Neighborhood Museum hours differ.

HOW Generally, on your own. Smithsonian volunteers man information desks, give diverse orientation lectures and some tour guidance. Telephone the Smithsonian switchboard, 357-2700, to see what services are available to you. **Dial-A-Museum** may be dialed direct—357-2020—for information on new museum exhibits and highlights of permanent exhibits and special events, such as lectures, concerts, and motion picture and other theatrical performances. **Dial-A-Satellite** 737-8855 for daily satellite and astronomical data.

"Men have searched the earth, the air, even the sun and stars, in their never-ending quest for knowledge."

The Smithsonian Institution organizes and displays public exhibits in the fields of natural history, art, history, technology and science. It sponsors programs and lectures throughout the year on scientific, technological and cultural subjects as well as classical and folk music concerts, and performances of national and international traditional and contemporary mime, dance and theater.

The 24 million visitors a year to the Smithsonian Institution will probably try to see as many buildings on the Mall as time

135

and energy allow. They are: the Museum of American History, the Museum of Natural History, the Arts and Industries Building, the Hirshhorn, the new Air and Space Building, the Freer Gallery and the original Smithsonian Building, but don't plan to see it all in one visit. If you were to spend one minute day and night looking at each object on exhibit, at the end of ten years you would have seen only 10 percent of the whole. Even so you will see on exhibit at any one time only a small fraction of the more than 100 million catalogued objects in the collection—and they are increasing at a rate of about a million items each year.

Here are highlights of the many activities of the Smithsonian Institution. Remember that exhibits frequently change as part of the program to make the displays interesting and to bring the collections and activities to the public:

NATIONAL MUSEUM OF AMERICAN HISTORY

This museum at 12th St. and Constitution Ave., N.W. on the Mall presents permanent and special exhibits in the fields of United States history and its technological progress. For example:

Hall of Graphic Arts contains exhibits of printing processes, hand printing methods, photo-mechanical printing processes, the derivation of the modern alphabet and materials used for writing and drawing.

Hall of Transportation exhibits examples of the many forms of transportation and traces the development of each throughout our history. The largest exhibit is a steam engine which carried President Franklin D. Roosevelt's body from Warm Springs, GA to the capital. A record of the sounds of the locomotive starting, traveling and stopping also qualifies this exhibit as the noisiest.

Hall of Underwater Exploration demonstrates this increasingly important phase of exploration and features a most lifelike exhibit of a diver going down for visible treasure.

A great favorite with visitors is the *First Ladies Hall* in which models in suitable settings are clothed with actual gowns worn by the wives and hostesses of American Presidents from our earliest days up to and including Nancy Reagan. Nearby is the *Bradford Doll House*, a replica of an American home of the early 1900s, completely furnished, even to a piano.

The *National Postage Stamp Collection* contains examples of every conceivable aspect of philately and postal history, including postal stationery, pre-stamp materials and three-dimensional objects used in the mail service.

In *Flag Hall*, you will find the actual Star Spangled Banner which, as it flew over Fort McHenry during the British attack in 1814, inspired Francis Scott Key to compose our national anthem.

NATIONAL MUSEUM OF NATURAL HISTORY

At 10th St. and Constitution Ave., N.W. on the Mall, this museum of natural history houses a diversity of fascinating permanent exhibits, as well as many rotating special or loan exhibits.

As you enter the large Rotunda notice the colorful banners that indicate the location of the exhibit halls on this floor and the one above. Start with *Fossils: The History of Life*, where you will learn how living things have evolved during the billions of years since the earth was formed, and continue in a right to left sequence starting from the Mall entrance. Especially popular is the *Dinosaur-Fossil Hall*, where skeletons of these great reptiles that dominated the earth for 140 million years may be seen.

The *Hall of Birds* (Gallery 8) has mounted exhibits of birds found in each of the major land and sea areas of the world, including the now extinct passenger pigeon. You will learn about bird migration, courtship, feeding habits and many other aspects of bird life.

The largest elephant ever recorded in modern times is mounted in the Rotunda of the Natural History Building. This is the *Fénykövi Elephant*, estimated to have weighed eight tons when alive and standing 13 feet 2 inches at the shoulder.

In the *Halls of Native Peoples of the Americas*, well reproduced exhibits explain the history, surrounding, habitat, tools, painting, weaving, hunting and other phases of the culture of the North American Indian and Eskimos.

For children a visit to the *Insect Zoo* (Gallery 20) is a must. Keepers feed and handle the live insects and answer your questions about the world of "bugs." Also popular with children is the *Discovery Room* (Gallery 5) where hundreds of natural history objects may be touched, tasted and smelled.

In the *Hall of Gems and Minerals* (Gallery 31) the softly lighted and elegant exhibit cases display one of the world's greatest gem collections. Among the gems is the priceless 45-carat blue Hope Diamond, the largest blue diamond known. Since it was smuggled out of India in the 1640s the Hope Diamond's owners have been the victims of a series of tragedies. New York jeweler Harry Winston presented it to the Smithsonian. Be sure also to see the fabulously beautiful Star of Asia, a star sapphire weighing 330 carats. In nearby areas maps and special exhibits explain the composition of meteorites and the areas of the United States most commonly visited by this natural phenomenon. The structure of the Earth is

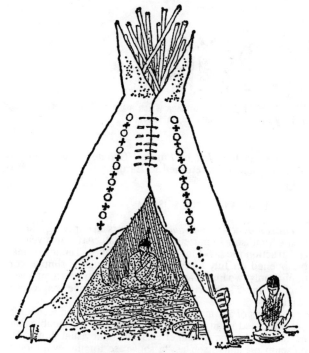

Full-size tepee and family of Indians

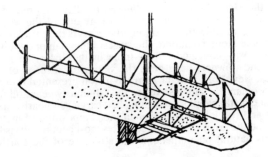

Original Wright Brothers airplane which made first successful air flight at Kitty Hawk, North Carolina, in 1903.

examined in the *Hall of Physical Geology*. Next door are several moon rocks returned to Earth by the Apollo astronauts.

NATIONAL AIR AND SPACE MUSEUM

The National Air and Space Museum is an imposing addition to the Smithsonian museums on the Mall. After five years of construction the 680-foot building of pinkish Tennessee marble opened on July 4, 1976. Its basic design is simple, containing only two lines of galleries on each of two exhibit levels. Each of the 23 galleries is accessible from one long central corridor.

The facts of aeronautical and space science and technology are presented in an uncomplicated and understandable manner, using objects, special effects and audiovisual shows. The museum presents itself as "a showcase for the evolution of aviation and space technology as well as a celebration of flight."

Favorite history makers are: Lindbergh's *Spirit of St. Louis* (1927); the Wright Brothers' *Flyer* (1903); John Glenn's *Friendship 7*; and the *Apollo 11* command module. Few resist the temptation to touch a moon rock and to enter the Skylab Orbital Workshop.

Visitors of all ages flock to the special films on flight, projected onto a five-story movie screen in the museum theater. Tickets to the movies are issued for a specific time, cost $1.50 for adults, 75 cents for children, and should be picked up immediately on entering the museum.

The museum also has a first-rate gift shop and a cafeteria.

SMITHSONIAN BUILDING

No visitor should leave the Smithsonian complex of buildings and museums on the Washington Mall without at least a brief visit to the original *Smithsonian Building*, at 1000 Jefferson Dr., S.W., sometimes casually referred to as "the Castle." James Renwick designed this architectually distinctive red sandstone edifice, begun in 1846 and completed in 1855, in Romanesque style somewhat reminiscent of an old Norman

castle. It is noteworthy for its beautiful exterior and its elegant and impressive interior Great Hall.

Just inside the main entrance is the *Tomb of James Smithson*, whose remains were disinterred from an Italian cemetery and brought to America. He was an Englishman who never visited the United States. He died in 1829 bequeathing a fortune of $550,000 "to found at Washington, under the name of the Smithsonian Institution, an establishment for the increase and diffusion of knowledge among men." The Institution was officially established by an Act of Congress in 1846.

The Institution takes James Smithson's injunction seriously and has contributed to the increase of knowledge through original scientific investigations in many fields, including art, geology, history, anthropology and ecology. It has sent out thousands of expeditions to all parts of the world. Over 19 years ago it established a museum, the *Anacostia Neighborhood Museum* in southeast Washington, to serve the community in a manner similar to a branch public library. The *Festival of American Folklife* with traditional American music and dances and craftsmen assembled from widely separated areas of the United States is sponsored by the Smithsonian each year, and is held on the Mall.

In addition, the Smithsonian administers:

On the Mall

> Arts and Industries Building
> Freer Gallery of Art
> Hirshhorn Museum and Sculpture Garden
> National Gallery of Art
> The Quadrangle (open May 1987)

Off the Mall

> National Museum of American Art
> National Portrait Gallery
> Renwick Gallery
> Museum of African Art

A short distance away

> National Zoological Park
> Anacostia Neighborhood Museum

(See individual write-ups of these attractions.)

In the *National Museum of American History*, you will find the following:

A *Cafeteria and Snack Bar* at the west end of the basement level. Open daily, 10:00 A.M.–5:00 P.M. (longer hours in summer).

Museum Shops to the left and right inside the Mall entrance; on the lower level, the principal shop with an outstanding selection of books, toys, craft items, records and jewelry.

Smithsonian Station—a 19th-century post office operated by the U.S. Postal Service next to the Constitution Ave. entrance.

The Smithsonian Associates affords individuals and families an opportunity to support the many worthwhile activities of the Smithsonian by becoming either a *National* or a *Resident* member. Dues are nominal, and benefits extraordinary. They include: eligibility to subscribe to Foreign and Domestic Study Tours; a discount on books published by the Smithsonian Institution Press and a 10 percent discount on books and purchases at nine museum shops; the opportunity to enjoy lunch any day or brunch on weekends at the Associate Court in the Natural History Building; a year's subscription to *Smithsonian*, a monthly magazine of the sciences, arts and history (not sold on news stands); *The Associate*, a monthly newsletter listing lectures, special events, tours and classes for Resident Associates of all ages. For additional information, write: The Smithsonian Associates, The Great Hall, Smithsonian Institution, Washington, DC 20560. Tel: 357-2700.

Ice skating on the Mall is available at the Sculpture Garden Outdoor Rink during the winter months. It is located between the National Gallery of Art and the Natural History Museum on Constitution Ave., N.W., just across from the National Archives.

Supreme Court of the United States

M Capitol South
or Union Station

WHERE Capitol Hill; E. Capitol and 1st
Sts., N.E.

WHEN 9:00 A.M.–4:30 P.M., Mon-Fri.;
closed Sat., Sun. and holidays.

HOW See the Court in session; hear a
courtroom lecture and take a self-
guided tour. Information Office
479-3000.

"Equal Justice under Law"

The Supreme Court of the United States, the highest court
in the nation, provides a unique vantage point from which an
observer may learn about the judicial branch of our federal
government. The building alone merits a visit. Some find it
a sterile, cold marble palace, but most people consider it a
magnificent temple of justice. It is of classic Greek style, faced
with the whitest marble.

How you plan your visit will depend a great deal on whether
the Court is sitting. Since the lectures are suspended during
the hearings, you can time your visit during sessions to see
the Justices on the bench or to hear the lecture. The Supreme
Court hears cases in about half the weeks from October to
June, Mondays through Wednesdays, from 10:00 A.M. until
3:00 P.M., with a lunch recess from NOON to 1:00 P.M. To be
sure of the court schedule on the day you visit, you can telephone the information office. The best time to observe is at
the start of the daily session at 10:00 A.M. Be early! Court
convenes on the second and there are only 100 or so seats for
the public.

Sessions of Court are opened by the Crier. The nine Justices
enter by threes, wearing black robes. The Chief Justice sits
at the center, flanked by Associate Justices right and left in
order of appointment. The first order of business is the brief
but pleasant ceremony of admitting new attorneys to practice.
If opinions are to be issued, they are then announced from
the Bench. Occasionally a Justice will give a brief oral pres-

SUPREME COURT BENCH,
1987

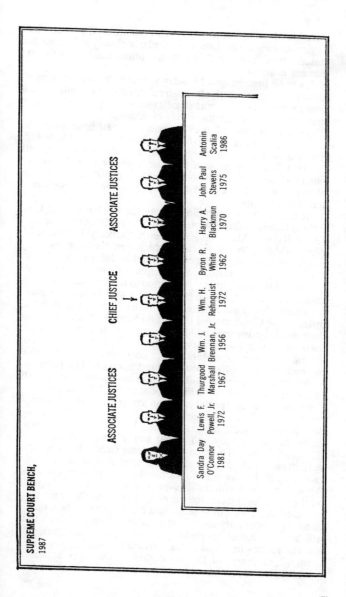

ASSOCIATE JUSTICES

CHIEF JUSTICE

ASSOCIATE JUSTICES

Sandra Day
O'Connor
1981

Lewis F.
Powell, Jr.
1972

Thurgood
Marshall
1967

Wm. J.
Brennan, Jr.
1956

Wm. H.
Rehnquist
1972

Byron R.
White
1962

Harry A.
Blackmun
1970

John Paul
Stevens
1975

Antonin
Scalia
1986

entation of his or her longer written opinion. The Court then begins hearing cases. Listen particularly closely at first for the statement of facts, so that you can understand what the argument is about.

Try to be present on a Monday as that is the day when most actions are announced, although rulings may be handed down now on any day the Court sits. "Decision days" are the most dramatic times to see the Court in action.

Lectures are provided every hour and half hour when the Court is not sitting. They start at 9:30 A.M.; the last is at 4:00 P.M. and runs for about ten minutes. You are then free to tour the first floor and ground floor on your own. A 30-minute film in which the Chief Justice and others explain the workings of the Court may be seen on the ground floor, as well as a series of exhibits.

At the front of the building note the double row of Corinthian columns three stories high. The pediment was sculpted by Robert Aiken and represents "Liberty Enthroned." The two sliding leaves of bronze which form the front doorway weigh 6½ tons each and were sculpted by John Donnelly, Jr.

For most of its history, the Supreme Court was the poor relation of the government, relegated to the low vaulted crypts under the Capitol, where it competed with boxes and bales for room. When the Senate wing of the Capitol was finished in 1860, the Court moved to the Old Senate Chamber. From then until the present building was completed in 1935 it sat there in crowded and cramped dignity. The Justices did not even have private quarters to put on their robes. They hid themselves as best they could behind a screen. The principal architect of the present building was Cass Gilbert; total costs of construction and furnishings were under $10 million.

Except for a few special cases, an aggrieved person bringing his case before the Supreme Court has no "right" that will permit him to have his case argued before the Court. Normally, he has already had a trial and at least one appeal in the courts below. To reach the Supreme Court, he must persuade the Court that his case is of special significance. For example, if the decision in a case decided by one Court of Appeals conflicts with the deision of another Court of Appeals on the same legal issue, the Supreme Court may hear the case to establish a controlling precedent on the point. The Court's most important duty in reviewing cases is to settle those that will have a wide effect on the lives of many Americans, not just the parties involved in the particular case.

In recent years, of the more than 5,000 cases appealed annually, the Court has granted petitions for only about five percent. Each year it hands down between 100 and 175 full-length printed decisions.

Average Business in One Term of Supreme Court

About 2,800	Lower Court decisions acted upon
About 150	Cases heard
About 100–175	Cases ruled on by written opinions

The effect of the decisions in cases that are taken, however, may be enormous. For example, in the "public school desegregation" cases the Supreme Court held in 1954 that "separate but equal" school facilities provided for blacks were contrary to the Constitution. The decision is of daily national significance. Some aspects of these cases involved state laws and some rights under the Constitution. Therefore, the cases represent good examples of how the Supreme Court reviews decisions of a state court.

The Supreme Court is an institution of traditionally long service by its members. In all our history there have been but 101 men to serve on its bench, 15 Chief Justices and 86 Associate Justices. Once they have been appointed by the President and confirmed by the Senate they hold office for life (the Justices and lower federal judges are the only federal officers who have life tenure).

The cafeteria on the ground floor is open to the public for breakfast and lunch—crowded in the spring at lunch hours, but good. Look for the fine view of the Capitol from the top of the entrance steps. Don't forget how easy it is to combine your visit with ones to the Capitol, the Library of Congress and the Folger Library.

Textile Museum

M Dupont Circle

WHERE   2320 S St., N.W.

WHEN   10:00 A.M.–5:00 P.M.,
Tues.–Sat.; 1:00 –5:00 P.M., Sun.
Closed all holidays.

HOW   Free. (Donation welcome.)

The Textile Museum provides a most unusual experience for the scholar, student and casual visitor interested in ancient fabrics and Oriental rugs. Of particular value in our machine age, the museum preserves the fine craftsmanship and art traditions of the past in textiles. George Hewitt Myers founded the museum in 1925 to make his extensive collection available to the public and to provide a center to carry on technical and artistic studies in the textile field.

Almost every cultural area of the world is represented except for Europe and areas of dominant European influence. The three most important groups of materials are Oriental rugs, Near and Middle Eastern textiles and Peruvian textiles. Smaller but significant weavings come from the Near East, Indonesia, the Far East, Central America, the American Southwest and Africa.

The rare and beautiful Oriental rug collection emphasizes the many styles of carpets which originated in the broad area stretching from Spain through North Africa, the Middle East, Central Asia and China. Of unrivaled importance are the Spanish rugs (Hispano-Moresque) and carpets from the great Mamluk period in Egypt. Many unique textile items have been preserved from Egypt, Greco-Roman, Coptic and Islamic periods, thus displaying in this outstanding collection a vast historic panorama of the textile arts of these countries.

Visitors will be intrigued with the group of Tiahuanaco tapestry with its bold, abstract design and daring color scheme, appealing directly to the modern taste as well as to the connoisseur of Peruvian artifacts. The Peruvian collection, the most important of its kind in the world today, was built by the Myers who became intrigued with the Spanish-Colonial period of Peru. Their splendid holdings of this period established a connecting link between their New and Old World

S Street, N.W., between 23rd and 24th Streets, showing
Textile Museum and Netherlands and Pakistan Embassies

collections in which ancient Peruvian traditions mingled with those of Islam, filtered through Spain.

Because of the museum's limited gallery space, only a fraction of its textiles and rugs collection can be exhibited at one time. The museum's extensive research and reference library on technical, historic and artistic aspects of rugs and textiles, is available to students and visitors.

Visitors to the museum will find themselves in a delightful section of Washington with its elegant town houses, diplomatic residences and chanceries. The Textile Museum is part of the Dupont-Kalorama Museum Consortium, an unincorporated association of seven geographically related, but culturally diverse institutions. (See page 208.)

Allow time to browse in the Museum Shop housed in the elegant wood-paneled library of the museum's founder, George Hewitt Myers. A wide selection of books relating to the fiber arts will please the visitor interested in needlepoint, embroidery, knitting, crochet, weaving and macramé. High quality yarns, a careful selection of handwoven textiles and tapestries, fabric dolls, neckties, scarves and other gift items are for sale. A Museum Shop Catalogue for those who wish to shop by mail is available for $1. Call 667-0441 for information.

Vietnam Veterans Memorial

M Foggy Bottom

WHERE	21st and Constitution Ave., N.W. between the Washington Monument and the Lincoln Memorial.
WHEN	Open daily, 24 hours.
HOW	Meter parking is permitted on Constitution Ave. All-day parking is allowed in West Potomac Park.

"In honor of the men and women of the Armed Forces of the United States who served in the Vietnam War. The names of those who remain missing are inscribed in the order they were taken from us."

The Vietnam Veterans Memorial is unlike any other in Washington. Located in a place of honor on the Mall between the Lincoln Memorial and the Washington Monument, the simple 492-foot wall of black granite from Bangalore, India evokes complex feelings in those who recall the longest war in our nation's history (1959–1975).

To some, the wall is stark and foreboding—to others, eloquent and magnificent. As you journey along the wall you will pass by the names of almost 60,000 men and women who gave their lives or are still missing. According to the season and the weather, reflections of blue sky, billowy clouds, brightly colored leaves, white snow and the dramatic silhouettes of the neighboring monuments play upon the polished surface of the wall. Though severe and uncompromising in its rigidity, the wall's surface is ever-changing and responsive to the daily tributes left by friends and families.

The two walls contain 140 separate panels; the largest at the vertex are 10.1 feet high and contain 137 names, five to a line; the shortest are but a few inches high. At the bottom of each panel you will see a number from 1 (at the vertex) to 70 (at the extreme end of each wall). Below the date 1959 on the first line of panel one on the east wall appear the names of the first casualties. They are inscribed in chronological order of the date of death. At the tip of the west wall the names resume, ending at the wall's vertex above the date 1975.

Credit for the founding in 1979 of the Vietnam Veterans Memorial Fund goes to Jan Scruggs, a former infantry corporal during the war. The group of veterans in Washington wanted to have a tangible symbol of recognition from American society. The design to be chosen had to meet four basic criteria: 1) that it be reflective and contemplative in character; 2) that it harmonize with its surroundings; 3) that it contain the names of all who died or remain missing; and 4) that it make no political statement about the war.

A national design competition in 1980 brought forth 1,421 entries. First prize was awarded to 21-year-old Maya Ying Lin of Athens, Ohio, who was at that time a senior at Yale University. The memorial was dedicated November 13, 1982.

Some distance from the wall stand a flagstaff and figurative sculpture, forming an entrance plaza. Washington sculptor Frederick Hart describes his bronze, life-sized group of servicemen as follows: "The contrast between the innocence of their youth and the weapons of war underscores the poignancy of their sacrifice. . .Their strength and their vulnerability are both evident."

Contributions from private and public organizations and from 275,000 individual Americans totalled $7,000,000, the cost of establishing the memorial. The National Park Service administers the memorial.

Washington Cathedral

M Cleveland Park

	WHERE	Mt. St. Alban, Wisconsin Ave. and Woodley Rd., N.W.
	WHEN	10:00 A.M.–4:30 P.M., Monday–Saturday. 8:00 A.M.–5:00 P.M., Sundays.
	HOW	Free conducted tours between 10:00 A.M. and 3:15 P.M. from Crossing inside Cathedral; Sun. after 11:00 A.M. service, at 1:00 and 2:00 P.M.; or tour on your own with a guidebook. (Free will offering.)

The Washington Cathedral (Cathedral Church of St. Peter and St. Paul) towers over the northwest section of Washington. It serves as a national church and a "House of Prayer for all People." Although administered by the Protestant Episcopal Cathedral Foundation, many services are ecumenical, and people of all faiths are welcome.

The Cathedral creates in 20th-century Washington a religious structure based on the 14th-century French and English characteristics of the Gothic style. Nevertheless, it is an original architectural design with the decorative work done by native artists using modern methods.

The Cathedral's completed nave opened in 1976. Only the twin west towers, now under construction, remain to be completed, probably before the end of this decade (1988–89). It will one day stand as the sixth largest religious structure in the world; in this country only New York's Cathedral of St. John the Divine is larger. Work progresses as money becomes available. The cornerstone was laid in 1907. George Bodley of London and Henry Vaughan of Boston drew the original plans for the Cathedral; before his death in 1972 the late Philip H. Frohman completed all the plans for the finished Cathedral. He is considered *the* architect of the structure.

You cannot make the most of your visit unless you take the guided tour or use a guidebook to the Cathedral; tours take about 45 minutes. You may purchase a complete and beautifully illustrated guide in the Cathedral Museum Shop. This outstanding booklet will give you full details on the points of interest in the Cathedral, fascinating bits of information on its construction, and other places of interest on the Cathedral Close.

The intricately carved *Canterbury Pulpit* at the Crossing was made of stone from Canterbury Cathedral. Bas-reliefs around the 10-foot-high sides recount the history of the English Bible.

The great *Rose Window* in the *North Transept* shows a life-sized Christ at the center of the Last Judgment. At dusk, the blues and reds blend into a beautiful purple. Lawrence B. Saint designed the 27-foot windows, which uses more than 9,000 pieces of stained glass. On the south side of the Cathedral you may see the *Space Window*; embedded in it is a piece of moon rock brought back to earth by the astronauts of Apollo 11. The west *Rose Window*, almost 26 feet in diameter, has ten petals and is abstract in design. Rowan LeCompte is the artist, and the window is his meditation on the theme of creation.

The *South Transept* contains a 24-foot *Rose Window* representing "The Church Triumphant" (the life of the world to come) by Joseph G. Reynolds and Wilbur H. Burnham.

The *Nave*, with its 102-foot vaulted ceiling, is 518 feet long. You will wish to see the memorials to Andrew W. Mellon, former Secretary of the Treasury and founder of the National Gallery of Art; Frank B. Kellogg, co-author of the Kellogg-Briand Peace Pact; Robert E. Lee-Stonewall Jackson; Mabel Boardman of the American Red Cross and the tomb of Woodrow Wilson. Dedicated in 1956, the Wilson Memorial Bay contains intricate carvings relevant to the former President's life.

The *Choir* and *Sanctuary* (Chancel) disclose the full richness and nobility of the Gothic architecture. Above the Jerusalem Altar the stone screen contains 96 statues of oustanding men and women who represent the "company of Heaven." A life-size figure of "Christ in Majesty" dominates the central panel. The altar cross, nearly six feet high, is so large that you can see it from the furthermost end of the Cathedral nave.

In the *Communion Rail* before the Altar you will see carved figures of the 12 Apostles. The uncarved block of wood at the extreme left represents Judas, the "unfinished Character." Do not overlook the elaborate carving of the oak choir stalls, and look above to the keystones, or bosses, which

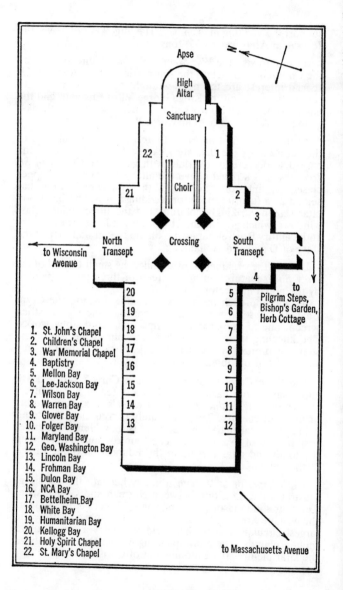

Apse

High
Altar

Sanctuary

22   1

Choir

21   2

3

North   Crossing   South
Transept   Transept

← to Wisconsin
Avenue

to
Pilgrim Steps,
Bishop's Garden,
Herb Cottage

4

20   5
19   6
18   7
17   8
16   9
15   10
14   11
13   12

1. St. John's Chapel
2. Children's Chapel
3. War Memorial Chapel
4. Baptistry
5. Mellon Bay
6. Lee-Jackson Bay
7. Wilson Bay
8. Warren Bay
9. Glover Bay
10. Folger Bay
11. Maryland Bay
12. Geo. Washington Bay
13. Lincoln Bay
14. Frohman Bay
15. Dulon Bay
16. NCA Bay
17. Bettelheim Bay
18. White Bay
19. Humanitarian Bay
20. Kellogg Bay
21. Holy Spirit Chapel
22. St. Mary's Chapel

to Massachusetts Avenue

support the vaulting in each bay. The huge keystone over the Jerusalem Altar weighs 5½ tons.

Be sure to visit the *War Memorial Chapel*, directly beyond the Children's Chapel on the south side of the Cathedral. Of special interest are the hand-wrought silver altar cross and candlesticks, the gift of King George VI of England, and the needlepoint kneelers, worked by English women in thanksgiving for American help in World War II.

At the delightful *Children's Chapel* note the small scale of the furnishings, the delicately carved fan vaulting, and the carved wood reredos overlaid with gold. The *Chapel of St. John* displays a panel above the altar with The Last Supper chiseled in limestone. Since 1932 the *Chapel of St. Mary* has served as a favorite place for weddings. Note the basswood altar screen, strikingly colored, and the three stained-glass windows, which portray the 21 Parables of Jesus. The six huge 16th-century Brussels tapestries on the chapel walls depict the story of David and Goliath.

Beyond the ornamental iron grille, the small *Chapel of the Holy Spirit* features an altar screen of three panels painted by the noted illustrator N.C. Wyeth.

As you approach the stairway leading down to the Crypt Chapels, pause to admire at the entrance the Gothic stone screen, one of the Cathedral's fine sculptured stone works. The kneeling figure of Abraham Lincoln at the top of the steps, in bronze by Herbert Houck, is said to be the only statue of Lincoln in an attitude of prayer.

The three Crypt Chapels symbolize Christ's birth, death and resurrection; each exemplifies a different period of architecture. The *Bethlehem Chapel* reveals decorated Gothic of the 14th century. The elaborately carved alabaster tomb behind the altar marks the grave of Bishop Henry Satterlee, first Bishop of Washington. The four columns surrounding the tomb and altar rest upon the Foundation Stone of the Cathedral.

The *Chapel of St. Joseph*, directly beneath the Crossing, illustrates the transition between Norman and Gothic style. The four solid masonry pillars, some 27 feet across, support the weight of the central tower. They probably constitute the largest circular piers in the world and carry a weight of 15 million pounds. The mural painting by Jan De Rosen above the altar pictures the Entombment of Christ.

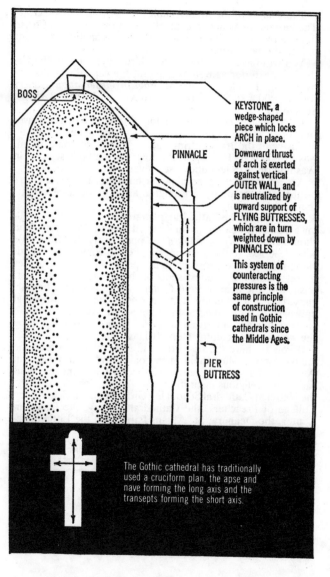

BOSS

KEYSTONE, a wedge-shaped piece which locks ARCH in place.

Downward thrust of arch is exerted against vertical OUTER WALL, and is neutralized by upward support of FLYING BUTTRESSES, which are in turn weighted down by PINNACLES

This system of counteracting pressures is the same principle of construction used in Gothic cathedrals since the Middle Ages.

PINNACLE

PIER BUTTRESS

The Gothic cathedral has traditionally used a cruciform plan, the apse and nave forming the long axis and the transepts forming the short axis.

157

The *Chapel of the Resurrection* is of Norman architecture. The mosaics of Venetian enamel glass show the Risen Christ, flanked by two dozing Roman soldiers and an angel kneeling before the open tomb.

You will have an unforgettable bird's eye view of the Cathedral's exterior as well as many of the capital's landmarks by taking the elevator to the *Pilgrim Observation Gallery* (open 10:00 A.M. to 3:15 P.M. weekdays, and 12:30 to 3:15 P.M. Sundays).

As you leave, notice the 301-foot Gloria in Excelsis Tower (not open to the public). Total cost of the tower assembly, exclusive of the 10-bell "ring" and a 53-bell, 60-ton carillon, was $1,800,000. The top of the tower is the highest point in Washington, 676 feet above sea level.

Art critics and the general public have praised the sculpture on the west facade by Washington artist Frederick Hart. Its theme is Creation.

After visiting the Cathedral, plan to spend some time strolling around the beautifully landscaped grounds (57 acres). You should see the *Bishop's Gardens*, open every day from 9:00 A.M.–5:30 P.M. (6:00 in summer). The old English boxwood, stone-paved walks, rose gardens, pools and carved arches make one of the loveliest spots in the city to stop and rest. Visit, too, the nearby *Herb Cottage* where gifts may be purchased. Stop for a moment at the Pilgrim Steps, the principal approach to the Cathedral from the South. At the foot of the steps stands an equestrian statue of George Washington by the well-known sculptor Herbert Haseltine.

If you are here the first Friday in May, plan to attend the annual Flower Mart, held in the oak grove near Wisconsin Avenue. The grounds on the Cathedral Close include education and religious institutions: St. Albans School for Boys, the National Cathedral School for Girls, Beauvoir School, the College of Preachers, the Cathedral Library, the Diocesan Center, the Deanery, St. Albans Parish and the Little Sanctuary.

A delightful new skill may be acquired by adults and older children at the London Brass Rubbing Centre near the Cathedral Museum Shop. In just an hour a wallhanging of a knight or lady, a king or merchant of medieval England may be made from a facsimile of an old English church brass.

Washington Monument

M Smithsonian

WHERE Center of Mall, Constitution Ave.,
at 15th St., N.W.

WHEN 8:00 A.M.–MIDNIGHT, first Sun. in
April–Labor Day; 9:00 A.M.–5:00
P.M. every day remainder of year;
closed Christmas.

HOW Free.

*"First in war, first in peace,
first in the hearts of his countrymen."*

The capital's best known monument is also its most promi-
nent. The marble and granite obelisk commemorating George
Washington points 555 feet skyward from the center of the
Mall, midway between the Capitol and the Lincoln Memorial.

The top of the Monument provides your best panorama of
the city. To get there you must ascend by elevator; the steps
are closed to climbers. En route you will spend an instructive
minute listening to a recorded commentary on the structure
and what it symbolizes. To descend you have the option of
going by elevator or walking down the 898 steps and reviewing
the 190 memorial stones set into the wall. There are no windows on the stairs, but inscriptions on memorial stones offer
diversion. You can see stones donated by "The Citizens of
the U.S. Residing in Foo Chow Foo, China," "Otter's Sum-
mit, Virginia's Loftiest Peak," "The American Whig Society," "The Islands of Paros and Naxos, Grecian
Archipelago," "The Alexandrian Library in Egypt" and "The
Cherokee Nation, 1850" among many others.

The windows in the cap provide a vista in all four directions.
Sketches above the windows are of some help in identifying
places of interest, but a map in hand is also a good idea.

Don't be nervous about taking the elevator or standing at
the top. Although the Monument may be the tallest stone
and masonry structure in the world, it is very stable. In a 30-
mile wind it sways only one-eighth of an inch. In the last 30
years it has settled a mere two inches. Walls 18 inches in
thickness at the top broaden to 15 feet at the bottom.

Look carefully and you will see a change in the color of the marble facing of the shaft about 150 feet from the base. The difference in hue is due to the fact that the marble comes from a different strata (rather than from weathering). This line indicates the height of the shaft when work was stopped on the Monument due to lack of funds, the impending Civil War and an incident which occurred in 1854. Pope Pius IX had sent over from the Temple of Concord at Rome with the inscription "Rome to America," a block of Africa marble for inclusion in the Memorial. The block was stolen on the night of March 15, 1854, and public opinion blamed a political and antireligious group known as the "Know Nothings." The event discouraged further contributions, which had been meager from the beginning, and the project ran out of funds.

Work was not resumed until the federal government took it over in 1876. Upon review of the project, enlarged and strengthened foundations were found to be necessary before proceeding with the shaft. Work was finally completed in 1884 at a cost of $1,187,710. The Monument was first opened to the public on October 9, 1888.

Your map is accurate in showing that the Monument is several hundred feet southeast of the cross-axis of the Mall and the White House and Ellipse. L'Enfant had planned for a memorial to George Washington at the exact intersection, but that location was considered too marshy. The Monument was designed by Robert Mills, who also was the architect for the neighboring Treasury Department. Fortunately, those portions of Mills's plans calling for Victorian elaboration at the base of the Monument were not carried out.

Parking near the Monument is difficult. Crowds usually are enormous, but the line moves rapidly. Plan your visit early in the day, if possible.

During the peak tourist season it is necessary to get a number at a tent on the Ellipse for a specific time to enter the Monument.

"Down the Steps" tours are given daily in summer at 10:00 A.M. and 2:00 P.M.. You will learn about the Monument's construction and see the carved stones mentioned above.

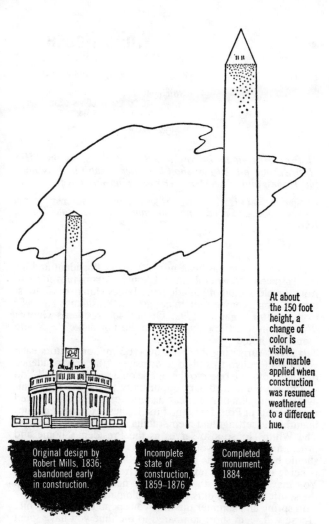

At about
the 150 foot
height, a
change of
color is
visible.
New marble
applied when
construction
was resumed
weathered
to a different
hue.

Original design by
Robert Mills, 1836;
abandoned early
in construction.

Incomplete
state of
construction,
1859–1876

Completed
monument,
1884.

CONSTRUCTION OF THE WASHINGTON MONUMENT

161

White House

M McPherson Square

WHERE   1600 Pennsylvania Ave., N.W.

WHEN   10:00 A.M.–NOON, Tues.–Sat.;
10:00 A.M.–2:00 P.M., Sat. during
summer. Closed Mon.

HOW   Free.

"I Pray Heaven to Bestow the Best of Blessings on THIS HOUSE and on All that shall hereafter Inhabit it. May none but Honest and Wise Men ever rule under this Roof."

INSCRIPTION FROM A LETTER WRITTEN BY JOHN ADAMS ON HIS SECOND NIGHT IN THE WHITE HOUSE. (*Carved into the mantel in the State Dining Room.*)

The White House has been home to every President and his family since 1800, when John and Abigail Adams moved there from the old capital of Philadelphia. James Hoban of Charleston, SC won a competition to design the "President's Palace." Construction began in 1792. Of our 40 presidents George Washington was the only one who did not make the White House his home.

It is not surprising that well over 1.5 million visitors each year pass through this historic mansion, "the only residence of a head of state open to the public on a regular basis." You will have an extraordinary opportunity to see the finest imaginable museum of American history, for here are assembled the portraits of Presidents and First Ladies, exquisite antiques in authentic settings and memorabilia of historic significance. The White House also serves as the President's home and office, and although you will see only five State rooms, you should be aware of the fact that the business of government is being conducted a few feet away from the tourists' path. You may even catch the President's helicopter alighting on the south lawn, just outside the Diplomatic Entrance.

In spring and summer the time you spend inside the White House will seem short compared to the time you have spent in line. You will not have a guided tour; time elapsed between entrance and exit may be as short as ten minutes. We therefore urge you to read through this section before you go in. On an average day about 6,000 persons take the tour (9,000 during July and August). Presidents are active hosts; in 1978 President and Mrs. Carter had 297 functions to which 47,797 guests were invited!

EAST WING

Most visitors will enter the White House through the *East Wing Lobby*. As you pass through note the portraits of Presidents and First Ladies hanging on each side of the wood-paneled hall. The next point of interest is the *Garden Room*, redecorated in 1971; the delicate furniture gives it the appearance of an English garden room during the Regency period, 1811–20. As you look outdoors you will see the *Jacqueline Kennedy Garden*, used as an informal reception area by the President's wife. On the walls are portraits of former Presidents—Millard Fillmore, Chester Arthur, Grover Cleveland and Calvin Coolidge. The *Ground Floor Corridor* with its handsome vaulted ceiling, walls and floors of marble, antique furniture and works of art bears no resemblance to the way it looked before 1902 and the major renovation of the White House. In 1861 an aide to Abraham Lincoln remarked that the basement had "the air of an old and unsuccessful hotel." On either side of the Diplomatic Reception Room entrance are the portraits of "Lady Bird" Johnson and Jacqueline Kennedy Onassis. A Sheraton-style breakfront bookcase displays pieces of White House china.

EAST ROOM

The great *East Room*, used for receptions, balls, concerts, plays, weddings, funerals, press conferences, bill-signing ceremonies and church services, remains essentially as it was after the 1902 renovation. As you enter this rather sparsely furnished room you may have that "déja vu" feeling. Thanks to television most Americans have visited in this room on many dramatic occasions. In October 1973, President Nixon presented Gerald Ford as his Vice-Presidential nominee to an after-dinner group of government officials; on August 9, 1974, you witnessed President Nixon's farewell to his staff, and a few hours later, Mr. Ford taking the oath of office as 38th President of the United States.

It was in this room that Abigail Adams hung her clothes to dry when she moved to the unfinished White House in 1800. The "Public Audience Room" remained undecorated until President Jackson's day; he spent nearly $10,000 on draperies, chandeliers, mirrors and chairs. The famous portrait of George Washington, painted in 1796 by Gilbert Stuart, is the oldest original possession in the White House; Dolley Madison rescued it when the British set fire to the building in August 1814. E.F. Andrews painted the companion portrait of Martha Washington in 1878.

The parquetry oak floor, bronze electric light standards, upholstered benches and three Bohemian cut-glass chandeliers date back to the 1902 renovation when the room was restored to the early 19th-century classical style. The room has been used six times for funeral services for six Presidents who died in office—Harrison, Taylor, Lincoln, Harding, Franklin Roosevelt and John F. Kennedy. Four Presidents' daughters were married here—Nellie Grant, Alice Roosevelt, Jessie Wilson and Lynda Bird Johnson. After State dinners guests gather in The East Room for a musical or theatrical presentation, or a twirl around the dance floor.

GREEN ROOM

Known as the *Green Drawing Room* since President John Adams's day, this charming and elegantly furnished room has traditionally served as a parlor for small teas and receptions. Thomas Jefferson, the second occupant of the White House, however, used it as a dining room. On the floor was a "canvass floor cloth, painted Green," and history books tell us that it was in this room that Mr. Jefferson introduced his guests to such novelties as macaroni, waffles and ice cream.

The green watered-silk fabric you see on the walls today is the same as that chosen originally by Mrs. Kennedy in 1962, although the room was completely refurbished in 1971. The stunning draperies of striped beige, green and coral satin were designed from a document of the Federal period. The pair of handcarved American eagles above the curtains' cornices remind us that the eagle, patriotic symbol of the United States, was a common and favorite motif of this period; as you glance about the room you will see it in many forms.

The English cut-glass chandelier was made about 1790 and was a gift to the White House during Hoover's administration. Most of the furnishings date from 1800–1815, and are outstanding examples of the Sheraton style. Many pieces are attributed to the New York workshop of Duncan Phyfe, a Scottish-born cabinet-maker. A pair of his benches made about 1810 stand in the window niches. Another well-known cabinetmaker of this time was George Hepplewhite, an Eng-

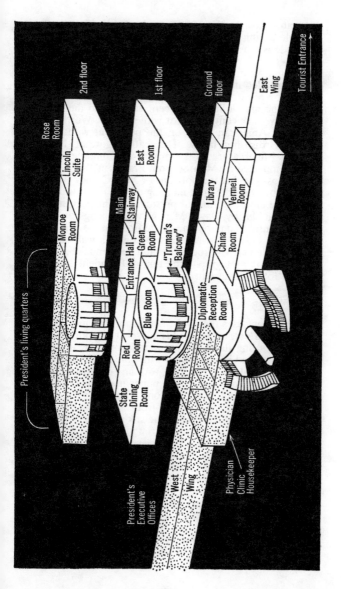

2nd floor
Rose Room
Lincoln Suite
Monroe Room
Entrance Hall
Main Stairway
Blue Room
Red Room
State Dining Room
President's living quarters

1st floor
East Room
Green Room
"Truman's Balcony"

Ground floor
Library
Vermeil Room
China Room
Diplomatic Reception Room

East Wing
Tourist Entrance

President's Executive Offices
West Wing

Physician
Clinic
Housekeeper

165

lishman, whose book of furniture designs had great influence on style during the Federal period. An excellent example of this style is the tall secretary-desk standing between the two windows.

The marble mantle on the east wall was one of a pair originally installed in the State Dining Room and ordered from France by Monroe. You will see its mate in the Red Room. Above the mantle hangs a recent addition to the room, the 1820 New York convex mirror with sconces. Worth noting is the large American eagle on the pediment with the much smaller British lion below. The seated figure of the Roman goddess Minerva graces the bronze-doré mantle clock, one of two imported by Monroe from France in 1817.

It is possible that the portraits of John Quincy Adams and his wife by Gilbert Stuart hanging on the north wall hung in the White House during his presidency. The portrait of Benjamin Franklin by David Martin, which hangs on the west wall, is considered to be one of the finest in the White House collection. Other portraits of note on this wall are that of President James Monroe attributed to Samuel F.B. Morse, inventor of the telegraph, and that of President James Madison by John Vanderlyn.

BLUE ROOM

The President uses the oval *Blue Room*, the most formal of the three parlors, to receive his guests at receptions and state dinners. During its most recent redecoration, in 1972, the walls, which had been covered with blue fabrics during much of the 20th century, were hung with an American silk-screen wallpaper copied from French paper made in 1800. A blue frieze borders the top and bottom. The blue satin draperies with gold valances are copied from an early 19th century document, and the patterned blue silk upholstery reproduces the original fabric of Monroe's time, recorded in a portrait of James Monroe by John Vanderlyn.

Hoban's plans for the elliptical-shaped saloon (and the oval rooms above and below it) demonstrate one of the most elegant features of his plans for the White House. Monroe, in redecorating the oval room after the fire of 1814, ordered a suite of French mahogany furniture; instead the firm took it upon themselves to ship gilded furniture, suggested that it was more appropriate for a "Saloon." However, it was not until 1837 that the tradition of a "blue room" was started by President Van Buren. President Buchanan sold the French

Bellangé chairs and sofas at auction, though some of Monroe's other purchases were retained. Four of the original chairs have returned to the White House; additional copies have been made. In 1902 the empire decor was restored.

Several Presidents' portraits grace the walls. That of President Tyler by George P.S. Healy hangs to the left of the white Carrara marble mantel; on the west wall to the right of the windows is a portrait of John Adams by John Trumbull, painted from life in 1800. Two other well known American painters are represented. John Wesley Jarvis painted Andrew Jackson in uniform (to the left of the center window) and Rembrandt Peale's 1800 portrait of Thomas Jefferson as Vice President hangs to the window's right.

RED ROOM

The *Red Room* will impress you as much with its priceless antiques as with its vivid color. In 1962, during the Kennedy Administration, the American Empire style was chosen for this charming parlor or sitting room; its most recent redecoration was in 1972. Most of the furniture dates from about 1810 to 1830, and reflects many of the motifs similar to those you saw in the French Empire pieces in the Blue Room.

Several of the room's most notable pieces are attributed to the French-born Charles Honore Lannuier, whose New York workshop produced some of the period's finest furniture. "The most important piece of American Empire furniture in the White House collection" is the small round table of mahogany and fruitwoods opposite the fireplace. With its trompe-l'oeil marble top, bronze-doré female heads surmounting the carved and fluted legs and delicate inlays, this table represents the acme of the American Empire style. The graceful sofa to the right of the fireplace has the distinctive curved back rail and scrolled arms of this period, and its gilded dolphin feet add a note of whimsy.

The red twill satin covering the walls and the furniture upholstery of red damask were woven in this country from French Empire designs. The white marble mantel with caryatid figures matches the one in the Green Room. Above it hangs the romantic portrait of Angelica Van Buren painted by Henry Inman in 1842. She served as the official hostess for her father-in-law President Van Buren; his bust, one of three sculpted by Hiram Powers, appears in the picture's background. One of them can be seen displayed above the secretary-desk.

STATE DINING ROOM

You will be struck by the more subdued appearance of the *State Dining Room* after strolling through the colorful opulence of the Green, Blue and Red Rooms. At one time this room was a great deal smaller, measuring only 30 feet by 50 feet. During the 1902 renovation the room was enlarged to its present dimensions; at present 140 guests can be seated comfortably for a luncheon or dinner. The architecture was molded on that of neoclassical English houses of the late 18th century. Natural oak paneling with Corinthian pilasters and a beautifully carved frieze were installed; in 1961 the room was painted antique ivory, and so it remains today. Gold cut velvet on the Queen Anne-style chairs, and silk-damask drapes of the same color lend elegance to this pleasantly proportioned room. A focal point is the marble buffalo-head mantel, carved with an inscription from a letter written by John Adams on his second night in the White House.

The only picture hanging in this room is the portrait of President Abraham Lincoln by George P.S. Healy, painted in 1869. It hangs above the mantel and was acquired in 1939 as a bequest of the widow of Lincoln's son, Robert Todd Lincoln.

NORTH ENTRANCE

Your exit from the White House will be through the *Cross Hall*, impressive with its red carpet covering the marble floors, and the *North Entrance Hall*. You will pass the main stairway, which leads to the First Family's living quarters on the second floor. (The public is never allowed to proceed beyond the State Rooms on the tour.) Before leaving see the pictures of Lyndon B. Johnson painted by Elizabeth Shoumatoff in 1968, and the youthful John F. Kennedy by Aaron Shikler.

By planning your trip well in advance you may be able to obtain tickets for the VIP early morning tour of the White House. Write your Senator or Congressman stating the dates you will be here, and how many tickets you require. In the "high" season this is a long shot, as each Senator is limited to 15 tickets a week for distribution, each Representative, 10. The 8:00 A.M. tour ensures your entrance and provides a slightly more extensive visit accompanied by a guide. (Other sights offering early morning special tours before the general public is admitted are: the FBI, the Capitol and the Kennedy Center.)

Part III
Special Features

Areas of Special Interest

We have included write-ups of Georgetown and Alexandria in Part II, but want to bring to your attention several smaller areas of the city you might enjoy visiting.

CAPITOL HILL AREA

The area east of the Capitol is an old one—it was in this direction that the residential portion of the city was originally expected to grow. There are no exceptionally old structures, because houses erected in the 18th century, for example, would have been farm houses. However, there are a number of residences dating from the mid-1800s that provide an atmosphere of this time. See, for example, residences immediately east of the Capitol and "Philadelphia Row" on 11th St., S.E., between Lincoln Park and Independence Ave.

After seeing the *Capitol, Botanic Gardens, Library of Congress, Supreme Court,* and *Folger Shakespeare Library* you may want to wander down Pennsylvania Avenue to view the antique stores, boutiques and unusual small restaurants. *The Eastern Market*, 7th St. between North Carolina Ave. and C St., S.E. (open Tues.–Sat.) is a delight. You will find an extraordinary array of fresh poultry, seafood, imported cheeses, fresh fruits and vegetables. Summer weekends offer "a bit of the old country" with the stalls of farmers selling produce and flowers—a colorful sight.

SOUTHWEST REDEVELOPMENT AREA

In contrast to the older, imitative forms, the *Southwest Redevelopment Area* has become a showcase for contemporary architecture, which includes apartment complexes, townhouses, shopping centers, a variety of unusual churches and a picturesque marina. Here, too, are many fine seafood restaurants, perfect for pre-theater dining. They are just a short stroll away from the Arena and Kreeger Theaters.

L'Enfant Plaza, an office and shopping center in the area along the 10th Street Mall, has been hailed for its magnificent architecture ("a setting as thrilling as the Place de la Concorde in Paris, but more human and intimate"). The complex includes two glass and steel office buildings, the elegant *L'Enfant Plaza Hotel*, an extensive shopping mall and a small theater. Architect I.M. Pei and his partners have done justice to L'Enfant's original concepts of combining efficient urban function with impressive grandeur.

PENNSYLVANIA AVENUE

In 1972 Congress created the Pennsylvania Avenue Development Corporation to guide the redevelopment of *Pennsylvania Avenue* and its environs. Although the plan is not slated for completion until 1990, the results to date are stunning, an indication of how the public sector and private industry can cooperate toward restoring the Avenue to its role of the "Nation's Main Street."

The renovation of three important buildings—the *National Theatre*, the *Old Post Office* and the *Willard Hotel* has been completed. The delightful and imaginative Western Plaza between 13th and 14th Streets features a paving design based on Pierre L'Enfant's 1791 plan for the Capital City. Quotations about the life of the capital have been carved into the granite surface of the Plaza. Adjacent to the Plaza sits *Pershing Park*, with its ice skating rink and café, an informal oasis in a formal setting. The elegant flagship *Marriott Hotel* and the *National Place Shopping Mall* have enhanced an area which was run down and shabby a few short years ago.

EMBASSY ROW

More than 140 foreign governments have diplomatic missions in Washington. Be on the lookout for the coats of arms and flags identifying their embassies and chanceries.

To see a concentration of embassies, start at Sheridan Circle and go to Observatory Circle on Massachusetts Avenue. Note the well-modeled Indian elephants flanking the entrance of the Indian Chancery at 2107 Massachusetts Ave.; the huge and impressive British Embassy at 3100 Massachusetts Ave. with its modern chancery next door; and the spectacular Iranian Chancery at 3005 Massachusetts Ave. faced in blue and white native Persian ceramics (closed since the 1980–81 hostage crisis). Most of the embassies are well marked on the outside so you can identify them easily. The flag of the country is usually flying outside (or above) the building. At 1225 16th St., N.W., you may also see the tightly shuttered and forbidding exterior of the Russian Embassy.

The foreign representation accords a special flavor to the capital. Do not be surprised to see graceful Indian saris or distinctive native African robes on the streets. Embassy parties provide diplomatic Washington with a social circle all its own. The June birthday of the Queen of England is celebrated by strawberries and Devonshire cream in the gardens of the British Embassy. The Dutch have a tulip festival at the height of the tulip season. The tea ritual is faithfully followed in the teahouse on the grounds of the Japanese Chancery.

Virtually all the delegations are headed by ambassadors, and thus qualify as embassies. Those headed by ministers are termed legations. Most have small staffs, who work in house-sized buildings. Some maintain specialized commercial, military, scientific and cultural staffs that occupy large office buildings. "Embassy" refers to the ambassadorial residence and to the diplomatic mission in general. "Chancery" refers to the diplomatic office or office building.

Each spring—usually the second weekend in April—half a dozen embassies hold open house for the benefit of a local charity. If you are in the city during the embassy tour, you can gain a firsthand view of a distinctive part of Washington life.

See Massachusetts Avenue (Embassy Area) Map 9.

Children, Especially for

Washington with children can prove a delight or a disaster. Don't attempt too much—a child's interest span is short, the same length, approximately, as the parents' patience. We present a brief list of suggestions of places to go and things to do, and entitle it "The ABCs of Washington for Kids."

★ Attend Discovery Theater at the *Smithsonian* (357-1500).
★ Buy a coin or a medal at the Exhibit Room, *U.S. Treasury Building*.
★ Cruise to *Mount Vernon* with the Washington Boat Line, Pier #4, 6th and Water Sts., S.W. (554-8000).
★ Drool at the greenbacks printed at the *Bureau of Engraving and Printing*.
★ Explore *Theodore Roosevelt Island*.
★ Flock to the *Tidal Basin* for a paddle-boat ride.
★ Gawk at the fish at the Commerce Department *Aquarium*.
★ Hike along the *C&O Canal* (or rent a canoe or bike at *Thompson's Boat Center*, Virginia Ave. at Rock Creek Pkwy., N.W. (333-4861).
★ Ice skate on the *Reflecting Pool* if it's a cold winter's day.
★ Jump at the chance to go aboard the U.S. Destroyer *Barry* at Pier 2, Washington Navy Yard, 9th and M Sts., S.E.
★ Keep track of the U.S. population with the Census Clock at *Commerce*.
★ Lunch at a cafeteria in one of the Smithsonian Museums on the Mall.
★ Marvel at the falls at *Great Falls, MD*.
★ Nod in the sun at the *Hirshhorn Sculpture Garden*.
★ Observe colonial crafts at the *Old Stone House* (3051 M St., N.W.).
★ Pack a snack to nibble when spirits lag and feet drag.
★ Queue up for the *Washington Monument* elevator ascent—then walk down.
★ Ride the *Tourmobile*; save time, shoeleather and learn while sitting.
★ Smell the flowers at the *Botanic Garden*.
★ Take the FBI tour.
★ Uplift yourself at the *National Archives* with the "three charters of freedom."
★ Visit the Children's Chapel at the *Washington Cathedral*.

★ Watch the Changing of the Guard at the *Tomb of the Unknown Soldier*.
★ Examine the dinosaurs (and the world's biggest elephant) at the *Smithsonian Natural History Museum*.
★ Yield to the temptation to climb on Beasley the Dinosaur on the Mall.
★ Zero in on *DAR Children's Museum (1776 D St., N.W.)*.

Other activities for children might include the following:

The movies *To Fly*, *The Dream is Alive* (astronauts in outer space), *Flyers* and *Living Planet* at the *Air and Space Museum*.

Claude Moore Colonial Farm at Turkey Run, 6310 Georgetown Pike, McLean, VA (442-7557). Life on a colonial farm.

The *Capital Children's Museum*, 800 3rd St., N.E., a "hands-on" museum. (548-8600).

Washington Dolls' House and Toy Museum, 5236 44th St., N.W., adjacent to Lord and Taylor, a delightful collection of antique dolls, doll houses and games. (244-0024).

Glen Echo Park *Carousel*, Goldsboro Rd. and MacArthur Blvd., Glen Echo, MD; open weekends May–Oct. (492-6252).

Adventure Theatre, at Glen Echo Park. Children's plays presented by professional group in small theater. Call between 10:00 A.M. and 2:00 P.M. for reservations (320-5331).

The National Capital Trolley Museum, Northwest Branch Regional Park, Wheaton, MD. Tours and special programs. (384-9797).

Dial-a-Story (638-5717); the D.C. Public Library records a new story on the line every week.

Highly recommended is *Going Places With Children*, an imaginative guide to Washington published by the parents of Green Acres School.

Churches

A separate and sizeable book could be devoted to Washington's exceptional churches. The most recent is the striking *Temple of the Church of Jesus Christ of Latter-Day Saints* in Kensington, MD. This Temple cannot be visited by non-Mormons, but is one of the most visible landmarks in the city. Multi-media tours are given at the Washington *Temple Visitors Center*, 9900 Stoney Brook Dr., on the grounds of the Temple. The tour is given seven days a week, 10:00 A.M.–9:00 P.M. and is free.

Well over 20 denominations have chosen Washington as the site for a national church. Three outstanding examples—the Washington National Cathedral, the National Shrine of the Immaculate Conception and the Islamic Center—are described in some detail in the preceding section.

ST. JOHN'S CHURCH

Of enduring interest is *St. John's Church*, at the corner of 16th and H Sts., N.W., directly across from the White House on Lafayette Square. St. John's qualifies as the "church of the Presidents" because every President since James Madison has attended occasional services here and many were members.

The mellowed yellow walls, classic columned portico and graceful tower make St. John's a landmark of distinction. In continuous use since 1816, this Church was the first building

to be constructed in the vicinity of the White House. Substantial changes have been made in the original design by Benjamin Henry Latrobe (architect of the neighboring Decatur House and much of the Capitol interior). To the initial form of a Greek cross with a flat dome and lantern cupola, an extended west end has been added, as well as a gallery, Doric portico, side vestibule and tower with cupola. The present seating arrangement replaced the original enclosed boxes in 1842. James Renwick supervised the redesign of the altar and interior in 1883.

Two "Presidents Windows" in the north gallery honor six Presidents who were communicants of the Church—James Madison, James Monroe and Martin Van Buren; and William Henry Harrison, John Tyler and Zachary Taylor. Another large window was given by President Chester Arthur as a memorial to his wife who was a choir singer at St. John's when he met and married her. At his request the window was placed in the south transept so that he could look across Lafayette Square at night from the White House and see the light of the Church shining through.

FRANCISCAN MONASTERY

Also of special interest is the *Franciscan Monastery* at 14th and Quincy Sts., N.E. While the Franciscan Monastery has sacred shrines of special significance to Catholics, visitors of all faiths will enjoy the exquisite rose gardens (late May to early June) and a chance to see the Holy Land Commissariat of the Franciscan order in the United States.

The interior of the Memorial Church contains reproductions of the sacred shrines of the Holy Land. Here you will see: the Stone of Anointing, which stands in front of the Holy

Sepulchre; the Altar of Calvary; the Grotto of Nazareth; and the Grotto of Bethlehem. Beneath the church you will wander through a short, narrow passageway copied from the Roman catacombs where the early Christians worshiped to escape persecution. This passageway will give you only a limited idea of those in Rome, which have been estimated to be 600 to 900 miles long.

Not included on your guided tour, but well worth seeing, is Portiuncula Chapel, a reproduction of the one near Assisi, Italy, where St. Francis established the Franciscan Order in 1209.

The Rosary portico near the main entrance leads to "Gethsemane Valley." In this outdoor setting you will find: The Grotto of Gethsemane; the Tomb of the Blessed Virgin; the Grotto of Lourdes; the Chapel of St. Anne; and the Chapel of the Ascension.

The Monastery comprises 44 acres, part of an original grant from George Calvert, First Lord Baltimore, to an early colonist. Father Godfrey Schilling founded the Monastery in 1899 to interest Catholics in the work of the Franciscan Order in the Holy Land. Tours are conducted every hour on the hour (526-6800).

The Monastery is only a short distance from Catholic University and the Shrine of the Immaculate Conception. You can easily combine your visit to both. Saint-Gaudens's famous statue of "Grief" in Rock Creek Cemetery is only a few minutes away by car.

Washington has an unusual balance in religious affiliations. The absence of dominating sects has contributed to a remarkable degree of interfaith and interdenomination cooperation. The following are among the many other churches of special interest.

BAPTIST

The Luther Place Memorial Church at 1226 Vermont Ave., N.W. and the National Baptist Memorial Church at 16th St. and Columbia Rd., N.W. were erected in Washington by the Northern and Southern branches of the Baptist church as a means of healing the wounds caused by the Civil War.

The First Baptist Church, now at 16th and O Sts., N.W. was founded in 1802. The new sanctuary containing stained glass windows of some of the great Christians of history is a most unusual and special feature of this church.

CATHOLIC

Washington seeks to place second only to Rome as head-quarters for Catholicism, having two universities (George-town and Catholic), two hospitals (Georgetown and Providence), 34 theological seminaries, the seat of the Catholic Welfare Conference and the National Shrine:

National Shrine of the Immaculate Conception, Michigan Ave. and 4th St., N.E.; the newest national shrine (dedicated 1959), the largest Catholic Church in the United States and the seventh largest religious structure in the world.

St. Matthew's, 1725 Rhode Island Ave., N.W.; considered "too far out" when the site was acquired in 1893, now the centrally located Cathedral of Washington. Funeral services for President John F. Kennedy were held here on November 25, 1963. Pope John Paul II performed mass here on Saturday, October 6, 1979, during his Washington visit.

EPISCOPAL

St. John's Church, Lafayette Square, B.H. Latrobe, architect. See write-up p. 75.

Washington Cathedral, Mt. St. Alban, Wisconsin and Mas-sachusetts Aves., N.W.; of interdenominational interest. Seat of the Presiding Bishop of the Protestant Episcopal Church. See write-up p. 53.

Christ Church (Alexandria), 118 N. Washington St., Al-exandria; built 1773, the church of George Washington and General Robert E. Lee, and a structure of exceptional charm. Washington's pew is preserved. In his day adults faced the pulpit, and children faced the adults; the center of the pew was used for hot coals or other heating devices. A marker on the communion rail records the confirmation in 1853 of Gen-eral Lee. In April 1861, Lee left Christ Church and walked one block north to the Lloyd House, 220 N. Washington St., to accept command of the Army of Virginia. Silver plates commemorate the attendance of President Roosevelt and Prime Minister Churchill on the National Day of Prayer, Jan-uary 1942. Presidents have worshiped here for many years on the Sunday nearest to Washington's birthday.

ETHICAL CULTURE

Washington Ethical Society, Meeting House and Administra-tion Building, 7750 16th St., N.W., where liberal religious, educational and community service activities are held. Stress is placed on the educational functions of Ethical Culture for adults and children in the character of its Sunday meetings and platform addresses, as well as its work for enlightened and humane social attitudes.

JEWISH

Washington Hebrew Congregation, Macomb St. at Massachusetts Ave., N.W.; the oldest of the Hebrew congregations in Washington, specially chartered by the Congress in 1855. In 1857, the congregation returned the favor. Congress had been unable to choose a Speaker of the House after two months of wrangling. At this point, the acting Speaker approached the president of the congregation and asked that a prayer be offered to break the deadlock. Following a prayer for harmony by a rabbi visiting the congregation, balloting was resumed and a Speaker chosen. The present modern temple succeeds the former one at 816 8th St., N.W.

LUTHERAN

Georgetown Lutheran Church, Wisconsin Ave. and Volta Pl., N.W. Tradition has it that George Washington attended several services at the log building that was the forerunner of this church on the same site. Note the 100-year-old bell in the stone setting before the church.

METHODIST

Metropolitan Memorial Methodist Church, Nebraska and New Mexico Aves., N.W.; the national Methodist church, the first of the national churches in Washington, completed 1869.

The Metropolitan African Methodist Episcopal Church, 1518 M St., N.W., is 122 years old, but did not take its present name until 1872. This is the church of Frederick Douglass, abolitionist and U.S. Minister to Haiti from 1889 to 1891.

PRESBYTERIAN

National Presbyterian Church and Center, 4125 Nebraska Ave., N.W. (at corner of Van Ness St., just east of Ward Circle). Harold E. Wagoner of Philadelphia designed this streamlined modern edifice with Gothic overtones. The 173-foot-high semi-detached tower makes the complex visible for miles around. Notable are the 42 semi-abstract stained glass windows in the sanctuary.

SEVENTH-DAY ADVENTISTS

General Conference of Seventh-Day Adventists, the world headquarters are located at 6840 Eastern Ave., Takoma Park, MD. The principal publishing house, a college, seminary, sanitarium and other institutions are centered there.

SOCIETY OF FRIENDS (QUAKERS)

Friends Meeting of Washington, 2111 Florida Ave., N.W. President and Mrs. Herbert Hoover's names headed the membership list. The reaction of the Friends against ritual is observed in the simplicity of the meeting house, and in its services. Silent meditation is the basis of worship. Services are conducted without a minister, with everyone present responsible for the meeting, and each privileged to speak "When the Spirit Moves You."

UNITARIAN

All Soul's Church, 16th and Harvard Sts., N.W., the successor to the church attended by Presidents John Quincy Adams, Millard Fillmore and William H. Taft. The present structure is modeled after St. Martin-in-the-Fields, Sir Christopher Wren's design in Trafalgar Square, London.

Foreign Visitors

THE INTERNATIONAL VISITORS INFORMATION SERVICE (IVIS)

A special service is offered for visitors from abroad by the International Visitors Information Service (IVIS). You will be welcomed at their office at 733 15th St., N.W., Suite 300, Washington, DC 20005. Office hours are Mon.–Fri., 9:00 A.M.–5:00 P.M. (783-6540). This organization has been formed specifically to help you as a foreign visitor get the most out of your stay in Washington. No matter what your request may be, IVIS will do its best to solve your problem, fulfill your need or answer your questions.

Here you may obtain up-to-the-minute bilingual information on cultural or sports events, sightseeing, accommodations, places to eat, local transportation, etc. (IVIS has volunteer language assistants to aid those who have difficulty speaking the English language.)

IVIS booths at Dulles International Airport and at the Tourist Information Center, Department of Commerce (Great Hall), 14th St. and Pennsylvania Ave., N.W. (789-7000), open Mon.–Sat., 9:00 A.M.–5:00 P.M.; Sunday, 9:00 A.M.–5:00 P.M. (April–end of Sept.) are manned by volunteers.

Seventy-eight Washington area organizations that serve foreign visitors are also members of IVIS. A non-profit, nongovernmental organization, IVIS is financed and administered by Meridian House International.

A FEW COMMENTS

The capital's broad, tree-lined streets are reminiscent of major cities in other countries, and cause the foreign guest to feel at home. Nonetheless, the foreign visitor must make substantial adjustments. He must depend entirely on his English, with rare exceptions; American customs may be new and strange to him; he cannot avoid the high cost of living.

To those of you who come to visit Washington from other countries, this *Guide* makes the following comments. Remember that Washingtonians are generally friendly, and you need not hesitate to ask questions at your hotel or on the street.

Hotels. Washington hotels quote their rates in advance and their prices by law are posted in each room. Be sure to note the checkout time so that you will not have to pay for an extra day. On rare occasions you may find a hotel, usually a resort hotel, offering the "American Plan," which means that meals are included in the price quoted for the room. Most hotels do *not* include any meals with their room rates. Should you stay at a "Bed and Breakfast" place, however, your breakfast (but no other meals) is included. A bellboy will carry your bags and show you to your room; make sure that he explains any special equipment in the room, such as heating and air-conditioning and the hotel telephone. You should tip him at least $1. The custom of leaving shoes to be shined outside your room is not followed in the United States. Most hotels provide a safe where you may leave your valuables in custody without charge. Never leave valuables in your room.

Meals. The typical American breakfast, served from about 7:00–10:00 A.M., consists of a juice or fruit, toast and coffee, and frequently includes a cereal and eggs. Lunch, served from about 12:00–1:30 P.M., and dinner, served from about 6:00–9:00 P.M., may be obtained from a great variety of sources, from the inexpensive counter of a drugstore to a cafeteria or a fine restaurant. See the "Restaurant" section for suggestions. All food is completely safe, and is prepared in accordance with the highest standards of hygiene.

Beverages. Ice water is usually served with a meal. All water—including water for your bath—is purified. Milk is a popular beverage; all milk is pasteurized and thus safe. Coffee is probably the most popular drink (sometimes served with the meal unless you request that it be served afterwards), but tea is also served. Beer and wine are available at many restaurants. Typical alcoholic drinks served before dinner include American whiskey (bourbon), Scotch whiskey and such cocktails as the martini (gin and dry vermouth) or the manhattan (bourbon and sweet vermouth).

Tipping. Tip about 15 percent of your total bill at meals; checking your coat and hat calls for a tip of about 50¢–$1. Cab drivers expect a 10–15 percent tip. You NEVER tip government employees, bus drivers, policemen, theater ushers, store or hotel clerks. Your spoken thanks will suffice.

Telephone. Use the telephone to save yourself steps and time. For example, you can telephone to find out when places you want to visit are open; whether stores have for sale what you want to buy. You may make reservatons by telephone. For weather information, dial 936-1212; for the time, dial 844-2525. If you are at your hotel you may ask the hotel telephone operator for assistance. You will find much useful information in the front of the DC *Yellow Pages*—emergency numbers, maps and a section called "Welcome Visitors" with current telephone numbers of the most popular sights. At public pay telephones, look up the number in the white or the *Yellow Pages* telephone book, deposit 25¢, wait for the dial tone (a steady hum), and dial the number, which will consist of seven numbers. The number you are calling may already be in use; if so, you will hear a series of interrupted buzzes. Hang up the receiver and your coins will be returned. For help, deposit a quarter and dial "O"—the telephone operator. For assistance in locating a number that you cannot find in the telephone book deposit the required coins and dial 411—"Information".

Letters. You may buy stamps at the hotel, most drugstores and at post offices. Stamps from machines cost more than their face value. You will find blue mail boxes on many streets. Mark all air-mail letters "Air Mail" or "Par Avion." Post offices are usually open from 8:00 A.M. to 5:00 P.M., Monday through Friday, from 8:00 A.M. to NOON on Saturday, and closed Sunday.

What to wear. Your native costume is always appropriate. If you wear Western dress, men should wear jackets and preferably ties for most occasions. Sport shirts may be worn for informal occasions. Slacks can be worn by ladies.

Embassies. Your embassy (consult "Embassies and Legations" in the D.C. "Yellow Pages") will prove a source of advice in emergencies, particularly for those inquiring for doctors and dentists.

Transportation. See "Transportation" in Part IV.

Banks. The hours of banks vary, but almost all are open Monday through Friday in the mornings through 2:00 or 3:00 P.M. Some banks have longer hours on Friday. Banks are the preferred place to cash your travelers checks, because many hotels, restaurants and stores do not accept them. You will get a better rate of exchange at a bank than at a hotel or restaurant.

Gardens and Parks

Springtime in Washington is justifiably famous. Unless the Great Rain God has overstayed his visit, or a late cold snap has nipped the tender buds, you will find the city at its most luxuriant between mid-April and mid-May. It is true that the forsythia lights up the town in March, and the cherry blossoms grace the Tidal Basin around the first week of April, but these spectaculars are mere warm-ups for the Big Production. The beds of daffodils, jonquils, tulips, hyacinths and azaleas along the parkways, in mini-parks, formal parks and city parks, and in clusters around the government buidings, create a patchwork of color and beauty bright enough to cheer the soul of even the most harried civil servant. Thanks for much of this floral extravaganza is due Lady Bird Johnson, who, during her years as First Lady, carried out on home territory her mandate to "Keep America Beautiful." An opportunity to view the Tulip Library with roughly 250,000 tulips in 95 beds at the edge of the Tidal Basin, is worth a trip to Washington in the springtime.

If you love gardens, here are a few special ones we suggest you visit:

BOTANIC GARDEN, foot of Capitol Hill, Maryland Ave. and 1st St., S.W.; 9:00 A.M.–5:00 P.M., until 9:00 P.M. June–Aug., daily (225-8333). Daily tours; free.

Don't pass the Botanic Garden by; it provides a fine antidote to the facts, figures, historical highlights and hard floors of sightseeing.

Perhaps most famous is its American-developed azalea collection, which rates as one of the best. If you are visiting Washington during March and early April don't miss this beautiful display. Seasonal exhibits include chrysanthemums, acacias, cinerarias, Easter lilies, hyacinths, tulips, narcissi, gladioli, primrose and poinsettias. The orchid display, drawn from more than 500 varieties, should not be overlooked. The permanent collection of tropical and sub-tropical plants (over 8,000 species and varieties) contains representative plants from all over the world.

Although the Botanic Garden is not operated as a scientific institution, students, botanists and floriculturists have an unparalleled opportunity to study many rare and unusual botanical specimens at the Conservatory.

Don't miss the outdoor display garden featuring a fountain by Frederic Auguste Bartholdi, creator of the Statue of Liberty, just across from the Botanic Garden.

DUMBARTON OAKS GARDENS, 1703 32nd St., N.W. (338-8278) in Georgetown. Entrance to the gardens is on R St.; Open 2:00–5:00 P.M. daily; until 6:00 P.M., early March–late Oct.

Dumbarton Oaks Gardens are amongst the loveliest you will ever see, particularly in the spring. The extensive gardens, covering about ten acres, are basically formal, with strong accent on design. The many evergreens and shrubs form a

Paved pot garden, a portion of the extensive gardens at Dumbarton Oaks.

frame for the tremendous variety of flowers. Reflecting pools, winding paths, broad terraces leading down to the more informal lower gardens and judiciously placed decorative ornaments lend distinction and originality to the gardens at every season of the year. Spring finds the magnolias, forsythia, Japanese cherries and crab apples in superb flower. Chrysanthemums in an extraordinary range of color and variety enliven the gardens in the autumn. Mrs. Robert Woods Bliss, the late owner, and the landscape architect Beatrix Farrand planned the gardens.

HILLWOOD GARDENS, 4155 Linnean Ave., N.W. on the estate of Mrs. Marjorie Merriweather Post, are open between 11:00 A.M. and 4:00 P.M.; reservations not required. $2.00 per person. (See write up of Hillwood, under "Historic Homes" below.)

KENILWORTH AQUATIC GARDENS, Kenilworth Ave. and Douglas St., N.E., near Eastern Ave.; 7:30 A.M.–8:00 P.M., Memorial Day–Labor Day; 7:30 A.M.–6:00 P.M. the rest of the year. (Tours by park naturalists during summer, or walk about on your own.)

The Kenilworth Aquatic Gardens contain water lilies of every imaginable color, many varieties of lotuses, water hyacinths, bamboo and some 40 species of pond and marginal plants. Native trees—willow oaks, red maples, elms, ashes, magnolias, river birch, sycamores and sweet and black gums—frame the 14 acres of ponds. The glorious displays occur in mid-June (hardy day-blooming lilies) and in July and August (day-blooming and night-blooming tropical water lilies).

Plan your visit for early in the morning, since many of the night-blooming tropicals close for the day once the sun is high.

Bird watchers will want to visit the gardens during the spring migration (waterfowl begin to migrate in early February; the last of the warblers in early June). Children may see frogs, turtles, toads, beetles, small fish and insects. Raccoon, opossum and muskrat inhabit the area, but do not present themselves too frequently.

W.B. Shaw, a government employee, started the gardens in 1882 with water lilies brought from his native state of Maine. His hobby turned into a vocation. The federal government acquired the property in 1938. Today the National Park Service administers the gardens.

NATIONAL ARBORETUM, Maryland Ave. and M St., N.E. (475-4815). 8:00 A.M.–5:00 P.M., Mon.–Fri.; 10:00 A.M.–5:00 P.M., weekends. *Bonsai collection and Japanese garden,* daily 10:00 A.M.–2:30 P.M.

A visit to the 444-acre National Arboretum in springtime is an experience you will long remember. Of unusual interest are the azalea plantings, among the most extensive in the nation; the collection of Oriental plants in the Cryptomeria Valley; the dogwood planting; and Fern Valley. Nine miles of paved roads provide access to the principal plant groups. However, you will want to park your car and enjoy these lovely gardens on foot.

Not to be missed is the charming collection of Bonsai trees, more than 50 in number, and beautifully displayed. This collection was Japan's bicentennial gift to the people of the United States.

CONSTITUTION GARDENS, between the Washington Monument and the Lincoln Memorial on Constitution Ave., N.W., now a pleasant park, was once the location for "temporary" government buildings (from World War I). Opened in 1976, the park contains a six-acre lake with a landscaped island, walks and bike paths. In the western part of Constitution Gardens is the Vietnam Veterans Memorial.

THEODORE ROOSEVELT ISLAND, south of Key Bridge in the Potomac River; 9:30 A.M. to dark, daily (285-2601). (Pedestrian Causeway from parking lot off the northbound lane of the George Washington Memorial Parkway—Virginia shore—one-fourth mile north of Theodore Roosevelt Bridge.)

Theodore Roosevelt Island, a living memorial to the great conservationist President, provides a unique natural sanctuary within the environs of the nation's capital.

Dedicated in 1967, a 17-foot bronze statue of Theodore Roosevelt by the late Paul Manship shows the President with his hand upraised in a characteristic speaking pose. The statue stands in front of a 30-foot granite shaft and overlooks a handsomely landscaped oval terrace. The visitor approaches the memorial via footbridges which cross a water-filled moat. Four large granite slabs at the back of the monument are inscribed with quotations from Roosevelt's speeches and reflect his philosophy of citizenship.

Georgetown University　　　　　Georgetown

Key Bridge

View from Roosevelt Island,
looking northwest.

Two and one-half miles of foot trails wind through and
around the island and allow good hiking and first-hand observation of bird and animal life. Interpretive markers along
the trails further reveal the fascinating human and natural
history of the island. The land was granted originally by
Charles II to Lord Baltimore in 1631. Later, the George Mason family of Virginia maintained an estate here for 125 years.
Subsequent owners used the island as a resort until 1931 when
the Theodore Roosevelt Memorial Association bought it and
donated it to the federal government to form a living memorial
to President Roosevelt.

A park naturalist conducts interpretive walks during spring
and summer, weather permitting. The walks originate at the
memorial. For tour information call 426-6922.

Historic Homes

A visit to Washington's historic homes affords you the opportunity to appreciate many of the area's handsomest buildings notable for their architecture, furnishings and the people who lived in them. We suggest the following, all open to the public except for the Blair-Lee Houses:

THE BLAIR-LEE HOUSES, at 1651–53 Pennsylvania Ave., N.W. (diagonally across from the White House) have served as the guest houses of the nation since 1942. Unless you are an important and official guest of the United States you may see them only from the outside.

These houses date back to the 1820s. The government acquired them in the early 1940s. President Truman lived here from 1948–52 when it was discovered that the White House was "standing up purely from habit," and a $5,800,000 complete renovation was undertaken. Two Puerto Rican nationalists attempted the assassination of President Truman here on November 1, 1950. On the iron railing at the front entrance you will see the plaque commemorating Leslie Coffelt, the White House guard killed resisting the attempt.

If you are lucky in the timing of your visit, you may see a cavalcade of large, black limousines drawn up before the Blair-Lee Houses, waiting to whisk a visiting dignitary to his next appointment.

The houses are superbly furnished with American antiques. In historical association and in style, these houses are worthy representatives of the United States.

DECATUR HOUSE is located at 748 Jackson Place, N.W., (673-4210), overlooking Lafayette Square. Metro: Farragut West. It is open from 10:00 A.M. to 2:00 P.M., Tues.–Fri., and NOON–4:00 P.M. Sat. and Sun. Admission: adults, $2.50; students, military, senior citizens, $1.25.

Decatur House boasts notable lines, lineage and associations. Designed in 1818 by one of the early capital's most distinguished architects, Benjamin H. Latrobe, it stands today as a fine example of an elegant Federal-style town house.

Before entering the house note the forthright simplicity and

Decatur House

lack of ornamentation of the red brick exterior. As you pass into the classic hall you will see a curving staircase through two archways. On the second floor two drawing rooms of imposing proportion suggest the use the builder had in mind for the house—a center for Washington society.

Commodore Stephen Decatur, a dashing naval hero who achieved wealth and notoriety through his daring exploits in the Barbary Wars, commissioned Latrobe to design the house. Latrobe is well known for his designs of nearby St. John's Church, the portico of the White House and much of the interior of the Capitol. Decatur and his wife entertained lavishly in their new home for but one brief season. Early in the morning of March 22, 1820, Commodore James Barron fatally wounded Decatur in a duel at Bladensburg, MD.

Mrs. Truxtun Beale restored Decatur House in 1944 in accordance with 11 of Latrobe's original drawings. The National Trust for Historic Preservation has owned the house since Mrs. Beale's death in 1956. In 1967, the National Trust continued the restoration and today, the ground floor looks much as it did in Stephen Decatur's time. The second floor, appearing as it did during the residency of General Edward F. Beale, is furnished with pieces of the Victorian period. In contrast, the two give us an idea of the transition in domestic life over a period of 50 years.

After visiting Decatur House be sure to stop by the bookstore and gift shop of the National Trust for Historic Preservation located in the building next door.

DUMBARTON HOUSE, at 2715 Q St., N.W., is open 9:30 A.M.–12:30 P.M., Mon. to Sat., and closed Sun. and holidays. Check for summer hours (337-2288).

Dumbarton House is one of Georgetown's finest early Federal houses—and one of the few open to the public. Since 1932 it has served as Headquarters for the National Society of Colonial Dames of America, who have done an outstanding job of restoring and furnishing the red brick mansion with authentic pieces of the period 1780–1815. You will find the collection of silver and china noteworthy. The terraced garden in the back suggests a Georgetown garden of 1800.

The house is thought to have been built about 1799 by Samuel Jackson. No record remains of the architect. Dolley Madison stopped here briefly when forced by the British in 1814 to flee from the White House. In 1915 the house was jacked up, put on rollers and moved 100 yards north of its original site to its present location in order to make way for Q Street.

DUMBARTON OAKS MUSEUM (AND GARDENS), 1703 32nd St., N.W., is open 2:00–5:00 P.M., Tues.–Sun. Gardens are open 2:00–5:00 P.M. daily; to 6:00 P.M., early March–late Oct., weather conditions permitting, (342-3200).

Dumbarton Oaks offers you two unusual features in juxtaposition—formal gardens that rank with the most beautiful in the country, and choice collections dedicated primarily to the minor arts of the Early Christian and Byzantine periods, and to pre-Columbian art. The latter is housed in a strikingly styled building designed by Phillip C. Johnson. In the other collection you will see jewelry, ivory, silver, metalwork and textiles from ancient Greece and Rome, the ancient Near East, Christian Egypt and the Medieval West, in addition to the pre-Columbian collection of sculpture, jades, jewelry and textiles.

Mr. and Mrs. Robert Woods Bliss acquired the property in 1920, remodeled the house and added to the grounds. The objects of art assembled by Mr. and Mrs. Bliss form the nucleus of the collections and have been increased extensively during the last 27 years. In 1940 the property was conveyed to the Trustees for Harvard University to serve as a research center for the study of Byzantine and medieval humanities. Dumbarton Oaks maintains both an administrative and scholarly staff.

Queen Anne granted the original tract of land known as The Rock of Dumbarton to Ninian Beall in 1702. However, William Hammond Dorsey did not build the house until 1801. Though greatly enlarged and adapted for its present use, the house maintains the overall character of the original building. (See "Gardens".)

THE FREDERICK DOUGLASS HOME (Cedar Hill) is located at 1411 W St., S.E., and open 9:00 A.M.–5:00 P.M., Apr. through Oct.; 9:00 A.M.–4:00 P.M., Nov. through Mar. (426-5960). Admission is free. This home of the noted black orator, writer and editor, Frederick Douglass, was completed in 1854, and contains many of his personal effects. You will enjoy the impressive view of Washington. A guided tour is available.

Frederick Douglass was born a slave in 1818 in Talbot County, MD. Although Douglass never went to school he became one of the most commanding figures in America's battle for civil rights through his writings and lectures. Douglass lived at Cedar Hill from 1877 until his death in 1895. Through the efforts of his second wife, Helen Pitts Douglass, Cedar Hill has been preserved intact as a memorial to him. This Victorian house has a wonderful view across the Anacostia River of the Capitol and the city. Most of the furnishings in the house are original. Mementos on display cover periods in his life when he served in important posts: as U.S. Marshal of the District of Columbia (1877); as recorder of deeds of the District (1881); and as consul-general to Haiti. The Douglass Home is administered by the National Park Service. Tourmobile service is available from the Mall: call 554-5100.

GUNSTON HALL, four miles east of U.S. Route 1 on Virginia Route 242, is open 9:30 A.M.–5:00 P.M., daily. Admission fee for adults is $3; for children, $1; (703)550-9220.

Gunston Hall provides an outstanding example of an early colonial mansion, with gardens comparable to those at the Governor's Palace at Williamsburg. It was the home of George Mason (1725–92), whom Thomas Jefferson called the "wisest man of his generation." Of the original 5,000 acre estate, 550 remain today.

A pair of tall chimneys and a steep roof dominate the story-and-a-half, square brick house. It is pleasingly simple from the outside; the interior is one of the richest of its time. The dining room was the first in the colonies to be done in the

Chinese Chippendale style. The carved woodwork in the Palladian drawing room, the work of the English carpenter William Buckland, is unsurpassed in this country. Note here the portrait of Ann Eilbeck, first wife of George Mason, and mother of his nine children. A companion portrait of Mason hangs above the fireplace in the dining room. The study contains the table on which Mason wrote the Virginia "Declaration of Rights." Be sure to go to the second floor where you may obtain a fine view of the hedges and formal gardens. George Washington was a frequent visitor to Gunston Hall, arriving by barge from Mount Vernon.

The gardens are superb. They are divided by a boxwood walk, 14 feet high and 250 feet long, planted by Mason himself. The view of the Potomac framed by this boxwood hedge is rightfully considered "one of the great sights of Virginia." The elaborate 18th-century gardens on either side have been restored by the Garden Club of Virginia.

You will be delighted with the restored schoolhouse, a pleasant stroll from the main house. Here George Mason's nine children received their early education from a professor who lived in a loft above the schoolroom. Eighteenth-century wood from a house in Charlotte County, VA, was used in reconstructing the schoolhouse on its original foundations. The kitchen, laundry, dairy, smokehouse, well and kitchen yard area have been reconstructed to complete the interpretation of domestic activities on George Mason's plantation.

Many furnishings are original, gifts of Mason descendants and of the National Society of the Colonial Dames of America. The estate has been open to the public since 1952, after Mr. Louis Hertle left it to the Commonwealth of Virginia. It is administered by a Board of Regents appointed from the National Society of the Colonial Dames in America. You will find the gift shop attractive and stocked with superior souvenirs.

George Mason was the principal author of the Virginia "Declaration of Rights," the forerunner of the Bill of Rights. He refused to sign the Constitution because it contained inadequate safeguards for individual liberty and failed to provide for the abolition of slavery. Mason lived to see his first objection corrected: the federal Bill of Rights was adopted in 1791, the year before his death.

The National Park Service made Gunston Hall a National Historic Landmark in June 1962, the 185th anniversary of the adoption in Virginia of Mason's "Declaration of Rights."

HILLWOOD MUSEUM, located at 4155 Linnean Ave., N.W.. is the home of the late Mrs. Marjorie Merriweather Post (1887–1973). Tours, by advance reservation only, are given every day except Tuesdays and Sundays at 9:00 and 10:30 A.M., NOON and 1:30 P.M. (686-5807). Both individuals and groups can be accommodated, but only 25 people can be scheduled for any one tour. The tour lasts about two hours and costs $7. Children and pets are not allowed. Admission to the gardens only (open from 11:00 A.M. to 4:00 P.M. is $2. Parking is free. To reach Hillwood from downtown Washington, go north on Connecticut Ave., right on Tilden St., and left on Linnean Ave. to 4155.

Hillwood is not an "historic home" in the literal sense. However, visitors to Hillwood will see what has been termed "the most representative Russian collection outside Russia." This 40-room mansion of red brick was built in 1926 in the Georgian style. The house is located on 25 acres bordering Rock Creek Park, and was acquired by Mrs. Post in 1955. She completely remodeled the interior and added a third floor and a wing.

Rooms on display downstairs include: the Porcelain Room, where dinner services used by Catherine the Great are exhibited; the Icon Room, where gold and silver chalices, icons and jeweled Easter eggs by Carl Fabergé may be seen; and the Drawing Room, which contains an exceptional collection of 18th-century French furniture and rare tapestries.

Upstairs the visitor will see Mrs. Post's bedroom and dressing room, the Adam Room with its fine collection of Wedgewood, the Russian Folk Art Room, the Empire Room and the English library.

The elaborately landscaped grounds include a formal French parterre and an authentic Japanese garden. A greenhouse contains many unusual species of orchids and cutting flowers for the house. The picturesque Dacha, a one-room adaptation of a Russian country house, lends a special charm to the gardens. An Adirondack-style lodge houses Mrs. Post's collection of North American Indian art.

A new café is open Mon., Wed. and Sat. from 10:00 A.M.–4:00 P.M. Call 686-8893 for reservations.

THE OCTAGON, located at 1799 New York Ave., N.W. is open from 10:00 A.M.–4:00 P.M., Tues.–Fri.; 1:00–4:00 P.M., Sat. and Sun. Closed Mon.; tour guides are on duty at all times. Admission: Adults, $2; children, 50 cents. (638-3105) Metro:

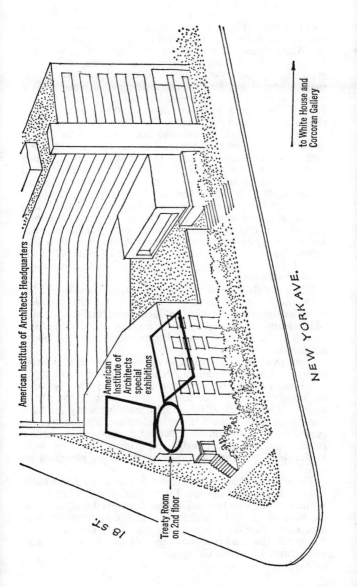

American Institute of Architects Headquarters

American Institute of Architects special exhibitions

Treaty Room on 2nd floor

18 ST.

NEW YORK AVE.

to White House and Corcoran Gallery

Farragut West. The Octagon ("eight-sided") is an early town residence of unusual architectural interest two blocks west of the White House, with which its early history is entwined.

The graceful Federal style structure was designed by Dr. William Thornton, the architect of the Capitol. To fit the sharply angled lot, Dr. Thornton designed a house with a semicircle as the front facade and by normal count, six sides. From the beginning, however, Colonel and Mrs. John Tayloe, the owners, called it the "Octagon" and their name prevailed.

Most furnishings date from the early period of the house. In the circular room just over the entrance President Madison ratified, on February 17, 1815, the Treaty of Ghent, which terminated the War of 1812, the last war between the United States and Great Britain. At the center of the room you can see the table he is said to have used at the treaty's signing.

The Octagon was completed in 1800, just before the White House, at a time when the city amounted to little more than a paper plan. The house immediately became a center of social activity; every early President (except Washington, who died before the house was finished), as well as Decatur, Webster, Clay, Lafayette, Calhoun, Randolph and Van Rensselaer was familiar with the house.

When the British burned the White House on August 24, 1814, the French Minister was staying at the Octagon. His presence—signaled by his flag—may have saved it from a similar burning. Two weeks later, President and Mrs. Madison moved to the Octagon, which became their home for about six months.

Since 1898 the building has served as national headquarters for the American Institute of Architects. In 1968 the Octagon was bought by the AIA Foundation. The AIA has restored the house and the smoke house and has adapted the site to its use by adding an administration building along the back line of the plot. Before the rehabilitation, ten families occupied the Octagon, rubbish filled the drawing room, window panes were smashed, and dirt and grime covered the walls and ceilings. Structurally, however, the house remained intact.

The circular table in the Treaty Room has a remarkable history. It passed from the Tayloe family in 1897 to a San Francisco lady who rescued it from threatened destruction at the time of the 1906 earthquake and fire by wrapping it in sheets and wheeling it through the streets to a place of safety. Eventually the San Francisco chapter of AIA bought the table and returned it to the Octagon.

In 1961 the Octagon was designated a registered National Historic Landmark. The second floor galleries, formerly the bedrooms of the Octagon, house changing architectural exhibitions.

The OLD STONE HOUSE, 3051 M St., N.W. is open 9:30 A.M.–5:00 P.M., Wed.–Sun.; (426-6551). The Old Stone House survives as the only pre-Revolutionary house in Georgetown open to the public. It dates from 1765, 14 years after Georgetown was founded. Originally a small and humble home, it has been enlarged and remodeled by subsequent tenants.

You will tour five rooms—kitchen, parlor, dining room and a bedroom, each furnished with items typical of the period between 1765 and 1810. In the shop room, the story of the house is told, and craft demonstrations are given. The homey

and unpretentious atmosphere provides a welcome antidote to many of the more famous mansions. You will find it easy to visualize Christopher Layhman, who is thought to have built the house, working at his cabinet-making in the downstairs room. The house and gardens are built on the original lot, number 3, of the 80 included in the original 1752 survey of Georgetown. One old story, not proven, has it that Washington and L'Enfant used the Old Stone House as headquarters for the planning of the Federal City. The National Park Service, which administers the house, acquired the property in 1950 and began restoration in 1955.

THE SOCIETY OF THE CINCINNATI (Anderson House),
2118 Massachusetts Ave., N.W., is open 2:00 P.M.–4:00 P.M.,
Tues.–Sat.; closed Mon. and holidays. Metro: Dupont Circle.
(785-0540). Anderson House, Headquarters and Museum of
The Society of the Cincinnati, is one of the few remaining
palatial residences that welcomes the public. It was built in
1902–1905. As you admire the elaborate marble floors, the
ornate ceilings and the Brussels tapestries which date from
1650, in the dining room, you will understand why official
Washington has used Anderson House for many formal receptions.

You will enjoy visiting the art collections, including fine
Far Eastern works of art, and the Society's Museum of Revolutionary War relics. Among numerous noteworthy objects
are portraits, historic swords and firearms and the only complete portrayal of the uniforms of all French regiments and
naval units participating in the Revolution.

The Society was founded in 1783, near the close of the
Revolutionary War to perpetuate the ideals of the Revolution.
Its first President General was George Washington. Mem-
bership consists of about 2,650 descendants of both military
and naval officers commissioned by the Congress in the
United States and some 175 such descendants in France.

Concerts are given on Saturday afternoons at 3:00 P.M. Call
for schedule and program information.

"A most beautiful site for a Gentleman's Seat."
—GEORGE WASHINGTON

WOODLAWN, on Route 1, 13 miles south of Washington,
and 3 miles south of Mount Vernon, is open from 9:30
A.M.–4:30 P.M., daily. Adult admission is $4; students, military
and senior citizens, $3.50. A combination ticket for Woodlawn
and the Pope Leighey House is $7. (703/557-7881).

Architecturally and historically, Woodlawn is one of the
most interesting Virginia homes of the early 19th century. Its
close ties to Mount Vernon stem from two sources: Dr. William Thornton, an intimate friend of the Washington family
and architect of the Capitol, designed it; Eleanor (Nellie) and
Lawrence Lewis, members of the Washington family and
household, were its original owners. Visitors to Mount Vernon will be well rewarded by driving the three short miles
south to include Woodlawn in their itinerary.

Dr. Thornton's late Georgian design features a central unit with flanking wings. The wide central hall with doors at each end, separating two large rooms on either side, characterizes the Virginia house plan of the period.

To the right of the central hall as you enter are the dining and music rooms; to the left, the parlor and master bedroom, entered through the parlor. The second floor, almost identical in plan to the ground floor, has four bedrooms. The largest, the Lafayette bedroom, commemorates the great French general's visit to the Lewises in 1824.

The winding staircase with walnut handrail is a handsome feature. See also the fine view toward the Potomac River from the marble-tiled portico on the east facade.

The large, well-proportioned room, high ceilings and big windows give the mansion an air of quiet elegance, serenity and dignity. Many of the furnishings came originally from Mount Vernon; others are typical of the period. Ladies will admire the beautiful examples of Nellie's skill as a needle-woman. Much of the woodwork throughout the house has been "grained" or painted to imitate various kinds of wood—in the dining room, mahogany; in the hall, walnut. Your visit will be incomplete without a walk around the grounds and gardens, authentically restored by the Garden Club of Virginia. Much of the boxwood was probably "slipped" from the gardens at Mount Vernon.

The mistress of Woodlawn, Eleanor Custis Lewis, was adopted at the age of three by the Washingtons after her father, John Parke Custis, Martha Washington's son by her first marriage, died of camp fever following the siege of York-town. In 1797, Major Lawrence Lewis, Washington's nephew, was invited to live at Mount Vernon as his uncle's secretary. Washington's diary of February 22, 1799, his last birthday, noted: "Miss Custis was married abt. Candle light to Mr. Lawe. Lewis." As his wedding gift to the couple he set aside 2,000 acres of his 8,000-acre estate. Following his death in December 1799, the Lewises continued to live at Mount Vernon until 1802, when Martha Washington died. They first occupied a wing of the new house, not completed until 1805.

Nellie Lewis continued at Woodlawn the Mount Vernon traditions of Virginia hospitality until 1839, by which time her husband and six of her eight children had died. She then moved to Audley Plantation in Clarke County, Virginia, developed by her son, Lorenzo.

The National Trust for Historic Preservation has administered Woodlawn since 1951. If you are here in March, plan to attend the Needlework Show, nationally recognized as one of the finest in the country.

THE POPE-LEIGHEY HOUSE, located on the grounds of Woodlawn, is open weekends, Mar.–Nov., from 9:30 A.M.–4:30 P.M. Call (703)557-7881 for information.

Visitors to Woodlawn Plantation should allow time to visit the nearby Pope-Leighey House, which provides provocative contrast between an early 19th-century Georgian mansion and modest suburban living in the mid-20th century. (Same hours as Woodlawn Plantation.)

The Pope-Leighey House is the only structure open to the public in the Washington area designed by Frank Lloyd Wright. It was moved to its present site as a result of the activities of preservationists when the house was threatened by demolition at its original location.

This house of cypress, brick and glass is one of several Wright designed for individuals of modest means during the 1940s. Known as "Usonian" houses, they contain several significant features now common in our contemporary houses. Wright eliminated the steep-pitched roof, considered too expensive, too difficult to build and unnecessary in the Usonian house: the flat roof was born. The carport replaced the garage, the basement was eliminated and radiant heating through coils laid in the floor replaced former methods.

THE WOODROW WILSON HOUSE, at 2340 S St., N.W., is open from 10:00 A.M.–4:00 P.M., Tues.–Sun.; closed January. Admission: adults, $3.50; students, military, senior citizens, $2. Metro: Dupont Circle. (387-4062). This is the house where President Woodrow Wilson lived after his retirement at the end of his second term. He died here three years later on February 3, 1924, and is buried in the Washington Cathedral. His second wife, Edith Bolling (Galt) Wilson, who lived in the house until her death on December 28, 1961, left the house to the National Trust in memory of her husband.

Filled with memorabilia from the Wilson era, this red brick house of Georgian style reflects the mode of life of Wilson's last year. His own personal library, which numbered more than 8,000 books, was presented by Mrs. Wilson to the Library of Congress, where it is housed in a special room.

The Wilsons, like many people of the day, enjoyed playing games. Mr. Wilson liked Canfield, a form of solitaire; Mrs.

Wilson was an avid bridge player. From the many games still in the house you will see one displayed on the little rolling cart Mr. Wilson used as both a dining and game table. In all the Wilsons' fun is an edge of desperation as Mrs. Wilson wracked her brain to think of amusing diversions for her husband. Their house was filled with clutter, and an unusual number of photographs and familiar objects were liberally scattered about. After the President's death, Mrs. Wilson dabbled in the occult to try to reach him. In the house are a Ouija board and typed transcripts of séance sessions in the sewing room.

Museums, Galleries, and Special Exhibits

During the past few years Washington's museums have increased at an outstanding rate. We have become one of the great museum centers in the entire world, and almost without exception these museums are free to the public.

To the museums described in greater detail in Part II we add here galleries and special exhibits, some of them devoted to a specific discipline or subject matter, which merit the visitor's attention.

B'NAI B'RITH INTERNATIONAL CENTER AND KLUTZNICK MUSEUM, 1640 Rhode Island Ave., N.W. (857-6583); the Museum and Shop are open 10:00 A.M.–5:30 P.M., Sun.–Fri. Metro: Farragut North. B'nai B'rith members number almost half a million in 45 countries. The Museum is Washington's largest institution devoted to Jewish art, history and culture. It houses a permanent collection of Jewish ceremonial and folk art and maintains a regular schedule of exhibitions, tours, lectures and films. In addition, there is a gallery of B'nai B'rith history and another that contains antiquities and an ancient Judaic coin collection. The National Jewish Visitors' Center, located near the Museum Shop and Bookstore, provides visitors with information on sights of Jewish interest in Washington.

THE COLUMBIA HISTORICAL SOCIETY (The Heurich Mansion), 1307 New Hampshire Ave., N.W. (785-2068); open 10:00 A.M.–4:00 P.M., Wed., Fri. and Sat. Garden open 10:30 A.M.–5:00 P.M.; Mon.–Fri. Admission to mansion, $2. Metro: Dupont Circle. Guided tours NOON–4:00 P.M., Wed., Fri. and Sat. This extraordinary house, built in 1892–94, serves two purposes: as headquarters of the Columbia Historical Society, and as a museum reflecting the Victorian tastes of a highly successful immigrant German brewer and businessman, Christian Heurich. The four-story brownstone and brick mansion contains 34 rooms, 15 carved mantlepieces, elaborately painted, plastered and carved walls, ceilings and woodwork. The furnishings are original. During the summer the garden is open to the public, and serves as an oasis for nearby office workers to dine al fresco. Membership in the Columbia Historical Society ($30 a year) offers rich and varied opportunities to slide lectures, walking tours and visits to little-known sites in the Washington area.

THE DAR MUSEUM, 1776 D St., N.W. (879-3242); open 9:00 A.M.–4:00 P.M., Mon.–Fri.; 1:00 P.M.–5:00 P.M., Sun.; closed Congress week—the week in which April 19 falls. Metro: Farragut West. The museum is housed in Memorial Continental Hall of the National Society of the Daughters of the American Revolution; the spacious Museum Gallery is in the connecting Administration Building. Of great interest to antique lovers and historians are the four floors of Continental Hall where the 33 period rooms maintained by state organizations are located. A few examples showing the great difference in styles are: the Tennessee State Room, with its elegant furniture from President Monroe's White House, and the famous portrait of President Andrew Jackson; the Missouri Parlor, a mid-19th century interior straight out of the steamboat era; the Oklahoma Room featuring an early American kitchen and huge fireplace; and the New Hampshire Society's Children's Attic, with a delightful collection of old dolls, toys and banks.

An excellent geneaological library allows DAR members to trace their ancestry (open to the public at a small daily charge). A fascinating collection of Revolutionary War period artifacts may be seen in the Museum. Of special interest is the silver made by Paul Revere and the collection of Chinese export porcelain. The Museum staff offers a special touch program which allows children to experience at first hand the look and "feel" of life in Colonial America.

The DAR was founded in 1890 to "perpetuate the memory and spirit of the men and women who achieved American independence." Members must prove through geneaological research direct lineal descent from ancestors who "with unfailing loyalty" served in a military or civil capacity in the cause of American independence.

AMERICAN INSTITUTE OF ARCHITECTS, (The Octagon), 1799 New York Ave., N.W. (638-3105). Open 10:00 A.M.–4:00 P.M., Tues.–Fri.; 1:00 P.M.–4:00 P.M., weekends; closed Mon. and holidays. Metro: Farragut West. Special exhibits. See "The Octagon."

ANACOSTIA NEIGHBORHOOD MUSEUM, 2405 Martin Luther King, Jr., Ave., S.E. (287-3369). Open 10:00 A.M.–6:00 P.M., Mon.–Fri.; 1:00–6:00 P.M., weekends. Exhibit and educational center responsive to needs of local community.

BARNEY STUDIO HOUSE, 2306 Massachusetts Ave., N.W. (357-3111). Informal guided tours at 11:00 A.M. and 1:00 P.M. Wed. and Thurs. and at 1:00 P.M. the second and fourth Sunday of each month by reservation only. Metro: Dupont Circle.

This small gem of a house, now owned by the Smithsonian Institution, was the second house built on Sheridan Circle, N.W. The architect, Waddy B. Wood, designed this unusual studio-house for his client Alice Pike Barney as a "meeting place for wit and wisdom, genius and talent." It reflects the varied interests and talent of this colorful woman who lived here off and on from 1903 to 1924. Wealthy and independent, she became a painter of accomplishment, a writer of plays and pageants, a designer of costumes and sets, a hostess of unusual social events, a friend and financial supporter of needy artists and above all the founder of a settlement house which still exists and bears her name.

DUMBARTON OAKS MUSEUM, 1703 32nd St., N.W. (338-8278). Open 2:00–5:00 P.M., Tues.–Sun.; closed Mon. Collection dedicated primarily to minor arts of Early Christian and Byzantine periods, and to pre-Columbian art. This small museum is perfection. See write-up under "Historic Homes."

FONDO DEL SOL Visual Art and Media Center, 2112 R St., N.W. (483-2777). Open 12:30–5:30 P.M., Wed.–Sat. Metro: Dupont Circle, Q St. Exit. The Center was founded in 1973 to increase, promote and encourage an appreciation of artists of Hispanic, Caribbean, Afro-American and Native American heritage. The Center offers exhibitions of contemporary artists and craftsmen, educational programs, lectures, concerts and festivals. Especially noteworthy is the Caribbeana Arts Festival held each summer on the third Sunday in June where visitors flock to the 2100 block of R St. to enjoy music, food, crafts and dance of the Caribbean.

INTERIOR DEPARTMENT MUSEUM, C St. between 18th and 19th Sts., N.W., 1st floor (343-5016). Open 8:00 A.M.–4:00 P.M., Mon.–Fri. Metro: Farragut West. Work of Interior Department explained and dramatized in ten exhibit galleries. Dioramas and paintings of historic events, Indian exhibits of past and present. The Indian Crafts Shop is opposite the museum entrance in Room 1023. Indian jewelry, some of it of prize-winning quality, pottery, rugs, baskets, dolls and other crafts are for sale from 8:30 A.M.–4:30 P.M., weekdays.

LIBRARY OF CONGRESS, Capitol Hill, 1st St. and Independence Ave., S.E. (287-5000). Open 8:30 A.M.–5:30 P.M., Mon–Fri.; 1:00–5:00 P.M., Sun. Metro: Capitol South. The building itself is a museum. Don't miss the view from the balcony looking down on the Main Reading room. On main floor, permanent exhibits include Gutenberg Bible; rotating exhibits on ground floor. See "Library of Congress."

MEDICAL MUSEUM of the Armed Forces Institute of Pathology, 6825 16th St., N.W. (Bldg. 54, on grounds of Walter Reed Army Medical Center). (576-2418). Open 9:30 A.M.–5:30 P.M., Mon.–Fri.; NOON–5:00 P.M., Sat. and Sun. Exhibits of man and animal diseases.

MUSEUM OF MODERN ART OF LATIN AMERICA, 18th St. and Constitution Ave., N.W. (789-3000). Open 10:00 A.M.–4:00 P.M., Tues.–Sat. Metro: Farragut West. Displayed in five galleries are many styles of Latin-American art, including primitive or naive art from Central America, and paintings of Japanese-Brazilian artists whose works display vivid Brazilian colors and Oriental themes.

MUSEUM OF AFRICAN ART is moving to the Mall.

NATIONAL BUILDING MUSEUM, Judiciary Square; F and G Sts., between 4th and 5th Sts., N.W. (272-2448). Open 10:00 A.M.–4:00 P.M., Mon.–Fri., NOON–4:00 P.M., Sat. and Sun. This extraordinary building, with its breath-taking interior is a must. Tours: 11:00 A.M. Tues., 12:15 P.M. Thurs. and 1:00 P.M. Sat. Civil War General Montgomery C. Meigs designed the building to house the Pension Bureau whose 1,500 employees issued pension checks to war veterans. Today the National Building Museum, opened in 1985, commemorates and encourages the building arts. Permanent exhibitions and temporary exhibits may be seen. Don't miss the audiovisual program "Meet the Architect: General Montgomery C. Meigs." The restoration of this architectural gem was an enormous challenge, as it had been severely altered and badly neglected over the years.

PIERCE MILL, Beach Dr. and Tilden St., N.W. in Rock Creek Park, (426-6908). Open 9:00 P.M.–5:00 P.M., Wed.–Sun. This typical grist mill of the early 19th century was powered by a water wheel. A great place for children to see how wheat was ground into flour.

ROCK CREEK NATURE CENTER, Glover Rd. in Rock Creek Park, ⅛ mi. south of intersection of Military Rd. and Oregon Ave., N.W. (426-6829). Open 9:30 A.M.–5:00 P.M.,

Mon.–Fri.; 10:00 A.M.–5:00 P.M., weekends. Nature activities exhibits, especially for children; planetarium.

U.S. NAVY MEMORIAL MUSEUM (Building 76), 9th and M Sts., S.E. (main gate of Washington Navy Yard). Open 9:00 A.M.–4:00 P.M., Mon.–Fri.; 10:00 A.M.–5:00 P.M., weekends and holidays. More than 4,000 objects on display in museum building and outdoors in waterfront park. History of naval service from Revolutionary War to space age. Visit the Submarine Annex with Civil War and World War II midget submarines. The U.S. Navy destroyer *John Barry* is moored permanently and may be boarded.

Silver sword, awarded by Continental Congress to Capt. John Hazelwood for valorous acts during American Revolution; on display at Navy Memorial Museum

---

THE DUPONT KALORAMA MUSEUM WALK. A varied and culturally rich experience awaits visitors whose curiosity and stamina allow them to explore the neighborhoods and museums in the Dupont-Kalorama area. The seven museums within this area have been described elsewhere in the *Guide* (see Index). They are The Phillips Collection, the Textile Museum, the Woodrow Wilson House, Anderson House, the Columbia Historical Society, Barney Studio House and Fondo del Sol (visual Art and Media Center). All are within walking distance of the Dupont Circle Metro at Q St., N.W.

The Dupont-Kalorama neighborhood contains a variety of architectural styles, including Victorian, Georgian Revival, Spanish and Beaux Arts. During the 1920s this neighborhood became known for its embassies and private mansions. An attractive pamphlet containing full descriptions of the museums, a map and a list of neighborhood galleries (many of them listed below) may be obtained free of charge. Write to: Dupont-Kalorama Museums Consortium, 1600 21st St., N.W., Washington, DC 20009. Be sure to enclose a stamped, self-addressed envelope.

There are many commercial art galleries in Washington where original paintings and works of art may be purchased. Most of them have monthly shows. For list of current exhibits see "Gallery Art" in the front of the *Washingtonian* magazine. Here are some of them:

Aaron Gallery, 1717 Connecticut Ave., N.W.
Aberdeen Gallery, 3236 P St., N.W.
Addison/Ripley Gallery, 9 Hillyer Ct., N.W.
Affrica, 2010 R St., N.W.
Andreas Galleries, 2904 M St., N.W.
Anton Gallery, 2108 R St., N.W.
Art Barn, 2401 Tilden St., N.W. (in Rock Creek Park)
Bethesda Art Gallery, 7950 Norfolk Ave., Bethesda, MD
Brody's Gallery, 1706 21st St., N.W.
David Adamson Gallery, 406 7th St., N.W.
Dimock Gallery, 21st and H Sts., N.W. (Lisner Auditorium)
Fendrick Gallery, 3059 M St., N.W.
Fisher Galleries, 1511 Connecticut Ave., N.W.
Foundry Gallery, 9 Hillyer Ct., N.W.
Foxhall Gallery, 3301 New Mexico Ave., N.W.
Franz Bader, 1701 Pennsylvania Ave., N.W.
Gallery K, 2010 R St., N.W.
Gallery 10, 1519 Connecticut Ave., N.W.
Glass Gallery, 4931 Elm St., N.W.
Henri, 1500 21st St., N.W.
Hom Gallery, 2103 O St., N.W.
Jackie Chalkley, 3301 New Mexico Ave., N.W.
Jane Haslem Gallery, 406 7th St., N.W.
McIntosh/Drysdale Gallery, 406 7th St., N.W.
Middendorf Gallery, 2009 Columbia Rd., N.W.
Shogun Gallery, 1083 Wisconsin Ave., N.W.
Spectrum Gallery, 1132 29th St., N.W.
Touchstone Gallery, 2130 P St., N.W.
Venable Neslage Rosen Galleries, 1803 Connecticut Ave., N.W.
Washington Printmakers, 1833 Jefferson Pl., N.W.

Music

A trip to Washington offers the music lover an embarrassment of riches, no matter what the season or type of music preferred. Opera, symphony, choral, string quartet, band, piano, organ, guitar, rock and roll, soul, blue grass and jazz freaks can find an offering to please the tenderest palate. Here are some suggestions on places to go for your musical evening. Look for others in the daily newspaper.

SUMMER BAND CONCERTS

During the summer months service bands (U.S. Army, Navy, Marine and Air Force) perform nightly except weekends on a rotating basis on the steps of the West Terrace of the Capitol, at the Sylvan Theater on the lawn south of the Washington Monument or on the Ellipse. Because the schedule is likely to change from season to season it is best to check your newspaper for where and when. All concerts are free of charge. The concerts held at the Sylvan Theater and on the Ellipse provide a wonderful opportunity to take along a picnic supper; arrive early for a good seat.

Plan ahead for two outstanding summer events. *The Spirit of America*, a pageant which traces important events and personalities of American history from Revolutionary times to the present, takes place at the Capital Centre in Landover, MD. The U.S. Army Band, "Pershing's Own", and the Third Infantry join forces in June to present this colorful program. Write for free tickets at least a month in advance to: Spirit of America, Fort McNair, Washington, DC 20319.

The U.S. Marine Band, "The President's Own," presents an outdoor retreat ceremony Friday evenings, mid-May–Sept. at the Marine Barracks on 8th and Eye Sts., S.E. Call 433-6060 to reserve seats. A few unreserved seats are passed out at the Barracks on a first-come, first-served basis. Arrive by 6:30 P.M. to ensure seating.

SUMMER SPECIALS

WOLF TRAP FARM PARK FOR THE PERFORMING ARTS AND THE BARNS OF WOLF TRAP, 1624 Trap Rd., Vienna, VA. Opened in 1971, this is the first national park for the performing arts. During the summer festival season (June through early September) performances of a varied nature are held at the 3,786-seat Filene Center; 3,100 additional seats are available on the lawn. The variety of entertainment is astonishing, from symphony orchestras, to musical comedies, to ballet companies. Picnic suppers are popular, but supper under a tent is an alternate possibility. Ticket prices for under-the-roof seating range from $8–$30; lawn seats are $6–$10. For tickets call 255-1860 or the Ticket Center, 466-2666.

The Barns of Wolf Trap is a smaller 350-seat theater located in a converted pre-Revolutionary structure on the Wolf Trap grounds. It operates *year-round* with American and international programs. For tickets, call 255-1939.

To drive to Wolf Trap take the Beltway (495) to Exit 10W (Route 7W/Leesburg Pike), then turn left on Towlston Road at the Wolf Trap sign. (Allow about 45 minutes from downtown.)

MERRIWEATHER POST PAVILION, Columbia, MD (982-1800) presents the Baltimore Symphony Orchestra, jazz ensembles and a variety of musical programs. Open May–Sept.

CARTER BARRON AMPHITHEATER, 16th St. and Colorado Ave., N.W. in Rock Creek Park, features a seven-week summer festival with popular singers and entertainers, jazz and soul music and rock concerts. Call 829-3200 or 426-6837 for program and ticket information. Concerts are presented from mid-June to the end of August on Sat. and Sun. nights at 8:30 P.M. Tickets are low-priced (about $5) and go on sale a week before the performance. Call Ticketron (789-6552) for the nearest outlet, and arrive early for the performance as seating at this 4,500-seat outdoor theater is on a first-come, first-served basis.

GLEN ECHO PARK, MacArthur Blvd. and Goldsboro Rd., (492-6282) is the suburban setting for music and dance performances.

THE SPANISH BALLROOM AT GLEN ECHO PARK, MacArthur Blvd. and Goldsboro Rd. This large, cavernous ballroom will bring back fond memories of bygone days to square and folk dance devotees (Fri. and Sun. nights at 8:00 or 8:30 P.M. and to ballroom dancers on Sat. nights at 9:00 P.M.). Admission is $3.50 to $5.50. Call 492-6282 to check on the schedule. It is apt to be erratic. The dances are usually held from mid-May through Sept.

WINTER SEASON

THE NATIONAL SYMPHONY ORCHESTRA, conducted by Mstislav Rostropovich, performs a regular series of concerts from October through April at the Kennedy Center Concert Hall (254-3776).

THE PHILLIPS COLLECTION, 1612 21st St., N.W. (387-2151) has free concerts and recitals Sundays at 5:00 P.M., mid-Sept. through May in the living room of this small and choice gallery. No reservations; only 120 seats (free), so come early.

THE NATIONAL GALLERY OF ART, 6th St. and Constitution Ave., N.W., offers free concerts Sundays at 7:00 P.M. in the East Garden Court of the West Building. No reservations and limited seating; free. Starting in late Sept. and continuing through most of June, you may combine an evening of art and music enjoyment; cafeteria open for supper. (737-4215).

WASHINGTON OPERA performs a full season of operatic performances during the fall and winter season. The productions are lavish (and the tickets are expensive). See the newspaper for program information or call the Kennedy Center Opera House (254-3770).

THE LIBRARY OF CONGRESS, 1st St. and Independence Ave., S.E. (393-4463) has chamber music concerts by the Juilliard String Quartet and other distinguished ensembles and soloists several nights a week in Coolidge Auditorium, which seats 550, Sept. through May. For concert and ticket information call 287-5502.

THE SMITHSONIAN MUSEUM OF NATURAL HIS-TORY (357-3030) and the **SMITHSONIAN MUSEUM OF AMERICAN HISTORY** (357-2700), Constitution Ave. between 10th and 14th Sts., N.W. offer many and varied musical programs during the year. Call for program and ticket information.

FOLGER CONSORT, 201 E. Capitol St., S.E., (at the Folger Library) provides thrice-weekly medieval and Renaissance music performed on authentic instruments of the period (544-7077).

LISNER AUDITORIUM, 21st and H Sts., N.W. (676-6800) provides a stage for many types of entertainment from ballet (you will always find Tchaikovsky's *The Nutcracker* here at Christmas time) to Julian Bream, classical guitarist.

CAPITAL CENTER in Landover, MD (350-3400) hosts popular singers, rock groups and occasional symphony orchestras and ballet.

THE NETHERLANDS CARILLON, "From the People of the Netherlands to the People of the United States," expresses the gratitude of the Dutch people for American aid received during and after World War II. It is located on the Virginia shore of the Potomac River, opposite the capital and bordering the northern end of Arlington National Cemetery, a short distance from the U.S. Marine Corps War Memorial (the Iwo Jima Statue). Carillon concerts are presented by outstanding carillonneurs every Saturday from 2:00–4:00 P.M. from Apr. through Sept. Free; no tickets required.

Presidents and Vice-Presidents

References throughout the text to Presidents of the United States suggest that the following list will be useful in identifying them and their periods of service:

No.	Name	Party	Term	Age at Inaug.	Vice-Pres.
1	George Washington	Fed.	1789–97	57	John Adams
2	John Adams	Fed.	1797–1801	61	T. Jefferson
3	Thomas Jefferson	Dem.-Rep.	1801–09	57	Aaron Burr George Clinton
4	James Madison	Dem.-Rep.	1809–17	57	George Clinton Elbridge Gerry
5	James Monroe	Dem.-Rep.	1817–25	58	D. Tompkins
6	John Quincy Adams	Dem.-Rep.	1825–29	57	John Calhoun
7	Andrew Jackson	Dem.	1829–37	61	John Calhoun M. Van Buren
8	Martin Van Buren	Dem.	1837–41	54	R.M. Johnson
9	William Henry Harrison*	Whig	1841–41	68	John Tyler
10	John Tyler	Whig	1841–45	51	
11	James Knox Polk	Dem.	1845–49	49	George Dallas
12	Zachary Taylor*	Whig	1849–50	64	M. Fillmore
13	Millard Fillmore	Whig	1850–53	50	
14	Franklin Pierce	Dem.	1853–57	48	William R. King
15	James Buchanan	Dem.	1857–61	65	J. Breckinridge
16	Abraham Lincoln*	Rep.	1861–65	52	H. Hamlin A. Johnson
17	Andrew Johnson	Union	1865–69	56	
18	Ulysses S. Grant	Rep.	1869–77	46	S. Colfax Henry Wilson
19	Rutherford B. Hayes	Rep.	1877–81	54	W.A. Wheeler
20	James A. Garfield*	Rep.	1881–81	49	Chester Arthur
21	Chester Arthur	Rep.	1881–85	50	
22	Grover Cleveland	Dem.	1885–89	47	T. Hendricks
23	Benjamin Harrison	Rep.	1889–93	55	Levi P. Morton
24	Grover Cleveland	Dem.	1893–97	55	A.E. Stevenson
25	William McKinley*	Rep.	1897–1901	54	Garret Hobart T. Roosevelt

No.	Name	Party	Term	Age at Inaug.	Vice-Pres.
26	Theodore Roosevelt	Rep.	1901–09	42	C. Fairbanks
27	William H. Taft	Rep.	1909–13	51	J.S. Sherman
28	Woodrow Wilson	Dem.	1913–21	56	T.R. Marshall
29	Warren G. Harding*	Rep.	1921–23	55	C. Coolidge
30	Calvin Coolidge	Rep.	1923–29	51	Charles Dawes
31	Herbert C. Hoover	Rep.	1929–33	54	Charles Curtis
32	Franklin Delano Roosevelt*	Dem.	1933–45	51	John N. Garner Henry Wallace Harry Truman
33	Harry S Truman	Dem.	1945–53	60	Alben Barkley
34	Dwight David Eisenhower	Rep.	1953–61	62	Richard Nixon
35	John F. Kennedy*	Dem.	1961–63	43	L.B. Johnson
36	Lyndon B. Johnson	Dem.	1963–69	55	H.H. Humphrey
37	Richard M. Nixon	Rep.	1969–74	56	Spiro T. Agnew Gerald Ford**
38	Gerald Ford**	Rep.	1974–77	61	Nelson Rockefeller**
39	James Earl Carter, Jr.	Dem.	1977–81	53	Walter F. Mondale
40	Ronald Reagan	Rep.	1981–	69	George H.W. Bush

* Died in office
** Not inaugurated—sworn in pursuant to 25th Amendment

Theaters

The cultural boom of the past ten years in Washington has been of staggering proportions. Especially noteworthy are the Kennedy Center for the Performing Arts, with its Eisenhower Theater, Opera House, Concert Hall, Terrace Theater and Film Theater; Wolf Trap Farm Park, in nearby Vienna, VA—(open summer months only); and a new phenomenon, the dinner-theater, which has become a popular way to combine dining-out with theatrical entertainment.

Space limitations prevent our listing many of the fine college and community groups offering commendable productions. Some of the theaters we mention are seasonal. We urge you to peruse the "Style" section of the morning *Washington Post* newspaper, particularly "Weekend" appearing in each Friday's edition. The monthly *Washingtonian* magazine has a section called "Where and When", where information on current happenings may be found. It is often possible to make reservations by telephone and charge your tickets to one of the major credit card companies.

Hint: Popular performances at the Kennedy Center and elsewhere are often sold out, but it is possible to pick up tickets before the performance from individuals unable to attend who stand by the box office an hour or so before curtain time. These are not scalpers, and you will usually pay them exactly what they paid for the tickets.

Tickets are sold at:

Ticketplace, F St. Plaza between 12th and 13th Sts., N.W. Open NOON–2:00 P.M., Mon.; 11:00 A.M.–6:00 P.M., Tues.–Sat. Call 842-5387 for recorded message. Half-price tickets (on the day of the performance only) are for sale to Washington-area productions; cash only. Full-price tickets in advance are also available.

Ticketron sells tickets for most performances. Call 659-2601 for locations around town or 626-1000 to charge tickets to major credit cards.

Ticket Centre, 904 17th St., N.W. Call 466-2666.

Instant Charge. Call 857-0900.

YEAR ROUND

Eisenhower Theater at the Kennedy Center, 2700 F St., N.W. (254-3670). Theater seats 1,150. Evening performances at 7:30 P.M.; matinees at 2:00 P.M.

Opera House at the Kennedy Center, 2700 F St., N.W. (254-3770), offers theatrical, ballet, opera and musical perform-ances in elegant, red three-tiered hall seating 2,300. Evening performances at 8:00 P.M.; matinees at 2:00 P.M.

Terrace Theater at the Kennedy Center, 2700 F St., N.W. (254-9895), offers theatrical presentations in a smaller, more intimate setting.

Concert Hall at the Kennedy Center, 2700 F St., N.W. (254-3776), presents symphony concerts, choral groups, dance and other types of musical entertainment and seats 2,700. The acoustics are near perfect. Performances are at varied hours.

The American Film Institute Theater at the Kennedy Center, 2700 F St., N.W. (785-4600) is located in the Hall of States and seats 240. Film "classics"—old and new—shown in rep-ertory nightly. Tickets are for sale at box office under the Tiffany shade.

National Theater, 1321 E St., N.W. (628-3393), has operated at the same location since 1835. Pre- and post-Broadway plays are presented in a richly decorated and handsomely renovated theater seating 1,150.

The *Arena Stage* (theater-in-the-round) and its step-brother, the *Kreeger Theater* at 6th and M Sts., S.W. (488-3300) in the southwest redevelopment area, house the 37-year-old professional resident company, widely acclaimed for its presentations of classic and original plays. Season is Sept. to July. Performances at 8:00 P.M. (7:30 on Sun.); Sat. matinees at 2:30 P.M.; Sun. at 2:00 P.M. on occasion.

Ford's Theatre at 511 10th St., N.W. (347-4833) has been restored to the way it was on the night of April 14, 1865, when President Lincoln was assassinated while sitting in the Presidential box. Shows suitable for families usually presented; they are often musicals.

Shakespeare Theater at the Folger at 201 East Captiol St., S.E. (546-4000) presents both new and classic plays as well as innovative productions of Shakespeare in this small (198 seats) Elizabethan theater. Poetry readings, evening lectures and other events are often held on Monday evenings.

New Playwright's Theater, 1742 Church St., N.W. (232-1123). This professional theater promotes new works by American playwrights between Oct. and June each year. Five to seven plays are produced; many of them continue on to New York or other parts of the United States.

The Source Theater Company has productions at different locations around town throughout the year. Its largest space is at *Warehouse Rep*, 1835 14th St., N.W., between S and T Sts.; the medium-sized *Source Main Stage* is at 1809 14th St. between S and T Sts., N.W. The city's best local artists star in productions under the direction of the talented actor/director/producer Bart Whiteman. See newspaper for program information, or call 462-1073.

SUMMER ONLY

Olney Theatre, Route 108, Olney, MD (924-3400) offers summer stock in a 722-seat house located in a small town in the Maryland countryside about 50 minutes north of Washington.

The Sylvan Theatre on the Washington Monument grounds offers free Monday-night big band concerts during the summer months (June–Aug.). (426-6700 or 426-6690). A dance floor is set up in front of the stage. Concerts start at 8:00 P.M., but arriving by 7:00 P.M. to ensure a good seat is advisable. Picnic suppers are in order.

DINNER THEATER

Dinner theaters abound in the Washington suburbs. Following a buffet supper, with the actors and actresses serving, a shortened version of a musical comedy is presented. Some of the old favorites produced are: *I Do, I Do*, *Camelot*, *Jesus Christ Superstar*, *Oliver*, *South Pacific* and *A Funny Thing Happened on the Way to the Forum*. Prices range from $22 to $25 per person. Most of the dinner theaters listed below are within a 45-minute trip from downtown, but it is best to call ahead for reservations and how to get there.

Burn Brae Dinner Theater, Route 29 at Blackburn Rd., Burtonsville, MD (384-5800).

Harlequin Dinner Theater, 1330 Gude Dr., Rockville, MD (340-8515).

Hayloft Dinner Theater, 10501 Balls Ford Rd., Manassas, VA (631-0230).

Lazy Susan Inn Dinner Theater, Woodbridge, VA (550-7384).

Petrucci's, 312 Main St., Laurel, MD (725-5226).

West End Dinner Theater, 4615 Duke St., Alexandria, VA (370-2500).

Don't
Overlook. . .

CONGRESSIONAL CEMETERY, at 18th and E Sts., S.E., served as the semi-official burying ground for Senators, Congressmen and public officials during much of the 19th century. Today it presents a curious sight, well off the beaten track.

The strange-looking pyramidal affairs lined up side by side over Congressional graves are cenotaphs designed by Benjamin Latrobe, an architect of renown in the early 19th century. Senator Hoar of Massachusetts remarked in 1877 that the prospect of being interred beneath one of these atrocities added a new terror to death—a sentiment that may have been directly responsible for the decline of the cemetery as a popular final resting place for government officials.

Among the distinguished citizens buried here are Thornton, Hadfield and Mills, all architects of importance in the founding years of the capital, and Elbridge Gerry, a signer of the Declaration of Independence. You can also see the grave of John Philip Sousa, the March King, who died in 1932. Try to find the late Victorian sculpture of Marion Kahlert, aged 10, who in 1904 became Washington's first victim of a motor vehicle. (It is located in the southwest section.)

Since 1973 the National Park Service has maintained this historic site as a national landmark. You may visit the grounds seven days a week; inquire at the gatekeeper's house for maps and information on the location of grave sites.

THE GOVERNMENT PRINTING OFFICE, at North Capitol St. between G and H Sts., N.W., offers the public an opportunity to buy an amazing assortment of books and pamphlets printed by the government on almost any and every topic. Do-it-yourselfers will enjoy the search for unlimited help in how to can, fix, plant, exterminate, grow, repair, learn, observe, preserve, tear down, build up and make just about anything.

THE GRANT MEMORIAL, at the east end of the Mall on 1st St. between Pennsylvania Ave. and Maryland Ave., constitutes one of Washington's most important sculptures. Gigantic in size and concept, the sculptural grouping was, at the time of its dedication on April 27, 1922, the largest ever cast in the United States. General Ulysses S. Grant (1822–86), the first full general in American history, and military leader for the Union during the Civil War, is depicted as a relaxed warrior, sitting astride his famous mount "Cincinnatus." To the north of Grant the *Cavalry Group* of seven horsemen making a charge onto the field of battle is considered to have "more dramatic interest and suspense than any other sculpture in the city, and indeed in the nation." To the south the *Artillery Group* shows a caisson carrying a cannon and three soldiers being pulled by three horses. Before starting work on his great opus, the sculptor Henry Merwin Shrady made a meticulous study of Civil War history and military trappings. Shrady died of strain and overwork two weeks before the memorial's dedication.

GRIEF, more properly called the *Adams Monument*, is located in Section E of Rock Creek Cemetery, Rock Creek Church Rd. and Webster St., N.W. Henry Adams, the historian, teacher, author and journalist commissioned the famous sculptor Augustus Saint-Gaudens to create a memorial to his wife, Marian, who died in 1885. The six-foot-high bronze figure, neither male nor female, is seated on a rock, shrouded in a full-length cloak, the face deeply shadowed by the hood, the eyes staring downward. There is a remarkable sense of harmony between the sculpture and the landscape. You will step from the sunlit open cemetery to the dappled shade of the small sanctuary; seated on a bench before the figure you will sense a feeling of calm, repose and closeness to nature. Saint-Gaudens called his work *The Mystery of the Hereafter* and *The Peace of God that Passeth Understanding*. The incorrectly used name of "Grief" came from Mark Twain's remark that the figure embodied all of human grief. Alexander Woollcott described the memorial as "the most beautiful thing ever fashioned by the hand of man on this continent."

Many other distinguished monuments may be found in this cemetery. Among the famous people buried here are Montgomery Blair, an early owner of the Blair House, Alexander Shepherd, last territorial governor of the District, Chief Justice Harlan Fiske Stone, William Vandevanter and John Marshall Harlan of the Supreme Court.

THE NATIONAL INSTITUTES OF HEALTH in Bethesda, MD, represent an exciting development in medicine—an assault organized under federal funds on the most critical of our national health problems. More than 14,000 employees fill more than 50 buildings on a 306-acre campus in Bethesda. This year the budget of NIH will be $6 billion.

The 13 institutes, nearly all of which conduct research in laboratories at NIH, are listed below:

National Cancer Institute

National Eye Institute

National Heart, Lung and Blood Institute

National Institute on Aging

National Institute of Diabetes and Digestive and Kidney Diseases

National Institute of Allergy and Infectious Diseases

National Institute of Arthritis and Musculoskeletal and Skin Diseases

National Institute of Child Health and Human Development

National Institute of Dental Research

National Institute of Environmental Health Sciences

National Institute of General Medical Sciences

National Institute of Neurological and Communicative Disorders and Stroke

National Center for Nursing Research

Chief points of interest are the exteriors of the modern, campus-like buildings, the three-wing general office building and the symbolic "Pools of Bethesda" outside the Clinical Center. The 500-bed Clinical Center is a combined laboratory-hospital in which intensive study of actual cases advances the research of the institutes. Professional visitors are welcome, and may visit the Clinical Center and perhaps see a showing of the color film explaining its functions. The Special Events Office will arrange tours for appropriate groups of members of the health professions. The unusual looking National Library of Medicine, the world's largest research library in a single scientific and professional field, is on the NIH grounds.

THE NAVAL OBSERVATORY, Massachusetts Avenue at 34th St., N.W. (653-1543) offers 1½–2 hour tours every Monday night on a first-come, first-served basis. Up to 140 passes are distributed at the gate at 7:30 P.M., Oct. 21–April 27, and 8:30 P.M., April 28–Oct. 20. Call before 5:30 P.M. Mondays to find out whether the tour will take place. On the tour you will look through the Observatory's largest telescope, a 26-inch refractor, and see the atomic clock used by the Observatory to determine standard time for the United States.

THE PENTAGON, located across the 14th Street Bridge in Arlington, VA, serves as the headquarters for the Department of Defense, and thus for the Army, Navy, Air Force and Joint Chiefs of Staff. (695-1776). Metro: Pentagon. The Pentagon is so named because it has five sides. It also has five stories and five separate concentric rings connected by ten spoke-like corridors.

Everything about the Pentagon is big, even the stories about it. You may have heard of the young Western Union messenger who entered the Pentagon to deliver a telegram. By the time he found his way out, he had been promoted to Lt. Colonel.

The Pentagon is the world's largest office building, with 3.7 million square feet of floor space, more than three times that of New York's Empire State Building. The daily work force of 27,000 approximates the population of Parkersburg, WV, or Pocatello, ID. Through the building run 17½ miles of corridors, yet you can reach the most distant point in it within six minutes—if you know your way.

A guided tour leaves from the concourse every half hour from 9:00 A.M. to 3:30 P.M. Mon.–Fri. A 13-minute film precedes the walk-a-thon. Great for older children.

THE TAFT MEMORIAL is located on the U.S. Capitol grounds, between Constitution, New Jersey and Louisiana Aves., N.W. The bell tower commemorating Senator Robert A. Taft is the only memorial building on Capitol Hill. The 100-foot Tennessee marble shaft, housing 27 well-matched bells, stands at the center of a five-acre plot halfway down Capitol Hill on the northwest side. Douglas W. Orr designed it and Wheeler Williams sculptured the 11-foot statue of the Senator at the west base of the tower.

Senator Taft began his public life in 1921 in the Ohio House of Representatives. He served in the U.S. Senate from 1938 until his death in 1953. A three-time unsuccessful candidate for his party's nomination for the Presidency, he was known as "Mr. Republican." The Senator's father, William Howard Taft, served as the 26th President of the United States and Chief Justice of the Supreme Court.

THE VOICE OF AMERICA, located at 330 Independence Ave., S.W., has guided tours Mon.–Fri. (except holidays) at 8:45, 9:45 and 10:45 A.M., 1:45 and 2:45 P.M. Tours last about 35 minutes. Tour reservations are preferred; call 485-6231 for information. Metro: Farragut West or Farragut North.

At the Voice of America (VOA) you will learn how the U.S. Information Agency tells America's story to the people of other countries. You will see radio programs being broadcast in many different languages, samples of the nearly 400,000 letters sent to VOA by foreign listeners each year, VOA's Master Control and the newsroom.

Almost every nation is engaged in international broadcasting. The Voice of America is the official international radio broadcaster of the U.S. government. Nearly all VOA programs originate from Washington. Facilities include 32 studios, recording equipment and the Master Control.

VOA has more than 100 transmitters in the United States and abroad with a total power of more than 22 million watts. It broadcasts over 1,300 hours per week in 42 languages via short and medium wave, targeting the peak listening times of its audiences. Additionally, VOA and field-produced USIA radio programs are broadcast by local radio stations in other countries. About 120 million people worldwide listen to VOA regularly.

Part IV

Where to Stay, Eat and Shop; Transportation

Hotels and Motels

HOTELS

With more than 18 million visitors to Washington each year, tourism is now one of the capital's principal industries. Occupancy rates are high at all seasons of the year, and visitors should not come without advance reservations. Most major hotels are located in the downtown area, within a short ride of the sightseeing areas, the government buildings and the business district. There are some motels in the city, but most of them are to be found along the major approaches to the city within a 25 to 30 minute drive from downtown. Many fine motels are located in Virginia (Rosslyn, Arlington, Crystal City and Fairfax), with access to the Metrorail system.

Some of the older downtown hotels with the proper pedigrees have recently undergone extensive renovations. Listed below are hotels in different price ranges. Weekend bargain rates are available at many of the top hotels, and it is worth making inquiry about them. The Washington Convention and Visitors Association, 1575 Eye Street, N.W., Washington, DC 20005 (789-7000) will send you a list of hotels and their current rates.

Top Rates: $115–$235, single; $135–$260, double.
Somewhat less expensive: $85–$135, single; $120–$190, double.
Moderately priced: $40–$70, single; $65–$90, double.

Space limitations allow only a representative number of hotels and motels in Washington to be listed. A listing in the *Guide* does not represent an endorsement. Most of the hostelries mentioned are located within the downtown area of the District and in nearby Virginia. The outlying suburbs of Bethesda and Silver Spring, MD, and Fairfax, Alexandria and Falls Church, VA contain innumerable motels of first-rate quality that are within a 25-minute drive of downtown. Your travel agent will be of help in choosing your accommodations and making reservations. Many of the newer hotels and motels in the suburbs are near Metro stops, or within short walking distance. When no Metro stop is indicated, the hotel is not near a stop.

Canterbury, 1733 N St., N.W., DC 20036, (202)393-3000 or (800)424-2950—a small gem of a hotel with charming decor; only 99 rooms; quiet street just off Connecticut Avenue. Excellent restaurant, *Chaucer's*. Metro: Dupont Circle.

Dolley Madison, 15th and M Sts., N.W., DC 20005, (202)862-1600 or (800)424-8577—an annex to the older Madison Hotel; top prices, and with it, top amenities (rooms with Ming vases, personalized service, English furniture). Metro: three blocks north of McPherson Square.

Embassy Row, 2015 Massachusetts Ave., N.W., DC 20036, (202)265-1600 or (800)424-2400—one of Washington's luxury hotels; fine location on tree-lined street not far from Embassy area; rooftop pool. Metro: Dupont Circle, Q St. exit.

Four Seasons, 2800 Pennsylvania Ave., N.W., DC 20007, (202)342-0444 or (800)268-6282—A top-flight Georgetown hotel with continental touches such as a concierge, stunning public rooms and fine restaurants.

Hay-Adams, 800 16th St., N.W., DC 20006, (202)638-6600 or (800)424-5054—finest location of all, overlooking Lafayette Square and White House; older hotel of quiet distinction, paneled lobby, well-appointed rooms. Metro: Farragut West.

Hyatt Regency on Capitol Hill, 400 New Jersey Ave., N.W., DC 20001, (202)737-1234 or (800)228-9000—large with dramatic architecture; a short walk to Capitol; good restaurants. Metro: Union Station.

Jefferson Hotel, 1200 16th St., N.W., DC 20036, (202)347-2200 or (800)368-5966—an older, small (100 rooms) hotel of great charm and distinction; well-located near National Geographic. Metro: three blocks east of Farragut North.

Madison Hotel, 15th and M Sts., N.W., DC 20005, (202)862-1600 or (800)424-8577—luxury level hotel; contender for Washington's finest; medium size, fine service, nicely furnished rooms in good taste, and nary a convention. Metro: three blocks north of McPherson Square.

Marriott, J.W., 1331 Pennsylvania Ave., N.W., DC 20004, (202)393-2000 or (800)228-9290—ideal location half way between the Capitol and the White House. Within walking distance of the Mall. This flagship hotel (774) rooms) is near the Pavilion at the Old Post Office, the National Theatre, and adjacent to The Shops at National Plaza. Health club with indoor pool, fine restaurants, including *Celadon* (French/Chinese cuisine), and free transportation to and from National Airport. Metro: Federal Triangle or Metro Center.

The Ritz-Carlton, 2100 Massachusetts Ave., N.W., DC 20008, (202)293-2100 or (800)424-8008—smallish "exclusive" European-type hotel in pleasant tree-lined area of Massachusetts Avene; concierge; fine restaurant, the *Jockey Club*. Metro: two blocks northwest of Dupont Circle (Q St. exit).

Sheraton Carlton, 923 16th St., N.W., DC 20006, (202)638-2626 or (800)325-3535—another old-timer with status, fine location near White House; beautifully refurbished; tasteful and elegant. Metro: McPherson Square.

Sheraton Washington, 2660 Woodley Rd., N.W., DC 20008, (202)328-2000 or (800)325-3535—a huge hotel in park-like setting. A favorite for conventions. Near Rock Creek Park; concierge service; two outdoor heated swimming pools (seasonal); 1,505 rooms. Metro: Woodley Park–Zoo.

Watergate, 2650 Virginia Ave., N.W., DC 20037, (202)965-2300 or (800)424-2736—the hotel part of THE Watergate is luxury level; on Potomac River, adjacent to Kennedy Center, with *Les Champs* shopping mall downstairs; some rooms with kitchens. Metro: three blocks west of Foggy Bottom, GWU.

Westin, 2401 M St., N.W., DC 20037, (202)429-2400 or (800)228-3000—a brand new and super luxurious hotel with every comfort; health club. Metro: three blocks north of Foggy Bottom, GWU.

Willard Inter-Continental, 1401 Pennsylvania Ave., N.W., DC 20024, (202)628-9100 or (800)327-0200. This beautiful renovation of a great landmark deserves a look-see even if your pocketbook does not allow you to stay here. Edwardian elegance; every amenity; near White House. Metro: Metro Center.

Anthony House Hotel, 1823 L St., N.W., DC 20036, (202)223-4320—in the heart of the downtown business, shopping and entertainment districts. Rooms include complete kitchen. Metro: Farragut North.

Capital Hilton, 1001 16th St., N.W., DC 20036, (202)393-1000—large, modern, well-located hotel with excellent convention facilities; a few blocks from the White House. *Trader Vic's* restaurant. Metro: Farragut North.

Dupont Plaza, 1500 New Hampshire Ave., N.W., DC 20036, (202)483-6000 or (800)421-6662—medium-size hotel at Dupont Circle, and within walking distance of lower Connecticut Avenue business and shopping districts, pleasant restaurant. Metro: Dupont Circle, Q St. exit.

Georgetown Dutch Inn, 1075 Thomas Jefferson St., N.W., DC 20007, (202)337-0900—on pleasant side street just down from busy M Street in old Georgetown; small, with pleasant rooms (some with kitchens).

Georgetown Inn, 1310 Wisconsin Ave., N.W., DC 20007, (202)333-8900 or (800)424-2979—smallish hotel on colorful Wisconsin Avenue in heart of shopping area of Georgetown; known for its unusually attractive rooms.

Highland Hotel, 1914 Connecticut Ave., N.W., DC 20009, (202)797-2000 or (800)424-2464—"fashionable" hotel with convenient location near embassies, shopping and fine restaurants. Metro: three blocks north of Dupont Circle.

Howard Johnson's Wellington Hotel, 2505 Wisconsin Ave., N.W., DC 20007, (202)337-7400 or (800)368-5696—smallish hotel just north of Georgetown and within walking distance of Cathedral; part residential; some rooms with kitchenettes.

Loews L'Enfant Plaza, 480 L'Enfant Plaza, S.W., DC 20024, (202)484-1000 or (800)223-0888—luxury hotel in rather unusual "grand" setting amidst some of the most imposing government office buildings; near Smithsonian Museums and Mall; within walking distance of waterfront. Metro: L'Enfant Plaza.

Mayflower, 1127 Connecticut Ave., N.W., DC 20036, (202)347-3000 or (800)468-3571—a Washington institution; large, traditional decor, in heart of lower Connecticut Avenue business area; always bustling with conventions and activity. Metro: Farragut North.

Omni Shoreham, 2500 Calvert St., N.W., DC 20008, (202)234-0700 or (800)THE-OMNI—a very large, sprawled out hotel on edge of Rock Creek Park; another favorite for conventions; a ten-minute ride downtown. Metro: Woodley Park.

Washington, 515 15th St., N.W., (at F St.) DC 20004, (202)638-5900, or (800)424-9540—large, with graciousness of by-gone times; refurbished rooms and lobbies; just a stone's throw from White House and across the street from the Treasury Department; best location for inaugural parade; marvelous view from rooftop restaurant. Metro: Metro Center.

Washington Hilton, 1919 Connecticut Ave., N.W., DC 20009, (202)483-3000—a hotel of gigantic proportions (1,154 rooms) both inside and out; tennis courts and pool in summer; caters to conventions; short ride to downtown. Metro: Woodley Park–Zoo or Dupont Circle.

MODERATELY PRICED:

Bellevue, 15 E St., N.W., DC 20001, (202)638-0900—small, recently remodeled hotel just three blocks from the U.S. Capitol building and one block from the Metro and Amtrak. Metro: Union Station.

Gralyn, 1745 N St., N.W., DC 20036, (202)785-1515—reconverted town houses with charm of a European pension; antiques; some rooms without private bath; garden; one of the area's prettiest residential streets. Metro: Dupont Circle.

Harrington, 11th and E Sts., N.W., DC 20004, (202)628-8140 or (800)424-8532—somewhat old-fashioned, but centrally located in heart of downtown shopping area; haven for high-school groups on spring outings, and family groups; excellent cafeteria. Metro: Metro Center.

Holiday Inn Capitol, 550 C St., S.W., DC 20024, (202)479-4000 or (800)HOLIDAY—large (529 rooms), convenient to the Hill and Amtrak; concierge, shopping mall and health club. Metro: Judiciary Square.

Holiday Inn Central, 1501 Rhode Island Ave., N.W., DC 20005, (202)483-2000 or (800)HOLIDAY—pleasant location, convenient to downtown but not in heart of business or sightseeing area. Metro: three blocks east of Dupont Circle.

Holiday Inn, Connecticut Ave., 1900 Connecticut Ave., N.W., DC 20009, (202)332-9300 or (800)HOLIDAY—just north of business district on Connecticut Avenue and near huge Washington Hilton; a few blocks from charming residential-Embassy area at Kalorama Circle. Metro: Woodley Park or Dupont Circle.

Holiday Inn at Thomas Circle, Massachussetts Ave. at Thomas Circle, N.W., DC 20005, (202)737-1200 or (800)HOLIDAY—unusual architecture, with covered swimming pool before hotel's main entrance; fairly large. Metro: three blocks north of McPherson Square.

Howard Johnson's Motor Lodge, 2601 Virginia Ave., N.W., DC 20037, (202)965-2700—near Watergate Hotel and short walk from Kennedy Center; only H.J. Motor Lodge in downtown Washington. Metro: Foggy Bottom, GWU.

Marriott Motels—motels of known qualities at Key Bridge, #29/211, Arlington, VA 22209; Twin Bridges, U.S. 1 & I-95, Arlington, VA 20001; also at Bethesda, Crystal City and Dulles Airport. (800)228-9290.

Normandy Inn, 2118 Wyoming Ave., N.W., DC 20008, (202)483-1350 or (800)424-3729—European type hotel near embassies; just off Connecticut Avenue, three blocks north of Washington Hilton; quiet. Metro: Woodley Park.

Park Terrace Hotel, 1515 Rhode Island Ave., N.W., DC 20005, (202)232-7000 or (800)424-2461—recently remodeled medium-size hotel (189 rooms) in convenient downtown location near Scott Circle; excellent restaurant. Metro: four blocks northeast of Farragut North.

Quality Inn-Capitol Hill, 415 New Jersey Ave., N.W., DC 20001, (202)638-1616 or (800)228-5151—a good value near Capitol Hill. Metro: Union Station.

Quality Inn-Downtown, 1315 16th St. at Scott Circle, N.W., DC 20036, (202)232-8000 or (800)368-5689; medium size (135 rooms), well located. (Other locations in Washington area.) Metro: four blocks northeast of Farragut North.

Skyline Inn, 10 Eye St., S.W., DC 20024, (202)488-7500—medium-size motel in southwest redevelopment area not far from Arena Stage, and within ten-minute drive of Mall and downtown sightseeing attractions. Metro: some distance from Federal Center S.W.

Tabard Inn, 1739 N St., N.W., DC 20036, (202)785-1277—a small inn (50 rooms) with lots of atmosphere for the appreciative guest; some rooms share bath. Metro: Dupont Circle.

Restaurants

When the first edition of this book was published in 1963, we kept to ourselves our personal opinion that Washington was not a distinguished restaurant city and that there were only a few restaurants of merit on an international scale. This pessimism is no longer merited, if it ever was.

We suggest below a list of restaurants which, on general excellence, or a specific point of merit, appeal to us. It is not a compendium of all the Washington restaurants. The authors have neither the appetite nor the waistline to undertake a comparative evaluation of all restaurants. Furthermore, even within cuisines there is no attempt to make direct comparisons. We list very elegant and expensive restaurants which can please the most discriminating and challenge the most lavish expense account. In the same category we may include a modest family restaurant, or even a carry-out, because we think it has merit.

We acknowledge a pleasant debt of gratitude to a number of friends skilled and interested in wine and food matters who have suggested restaurants for inclusion.

The authors use only two symbols, which are by way of explanation rather than rating. A heart means that we like the restaurant, as a personal matter, and you may or may not agree. A star means that the restaurant has been chosen to host a dinner of the International Wine and Food Society within a recent period.

We have made a special effort to include in our list moderately priced and "adequate but inexpensive" restaurants. Visitors from most parts of the United States (not including New York) will find Washington restaurant prices in the better restaurants quite expensive. It is quite easy to spend more than $85 for a dinner for two at a very expensive restaurant, even with a careful selection of wine. A moderate dinner will cost between $35 and $60, and an inexpensive dinner can cost $35 for two, unless you make a particular effort to be frugal. Generally, restaurants have a luncheon menu that is less expensive than the dinner menu. Your bill will vary with whether you have drinks or wine, the number of courses and the like. Some of the finest Washington restaurants offer a prix-fixe, pre-theater dinner at relatively modest prices, but you must eat at an early hour.

For at least the expensive and very expensive restaurants, reservations are necessary for both lunch and dinner. Take the time to call and avoid disappointment. Arrive on time.

A big caveat: tastes differ and restaurants and temperaments also vary from day to day. We confess a prejudice for small family-run restaurants and restaurants which, as compared to those in their native country, come off authentically well. We defend our comments and welcome yours.

- ♥ *means a favorite of the authors. This is not a rating, but strictly a personal preference.*
- ★ *means chosen for a dinner by the Washington Chapter of the International Wine and Food Society. Note, however, that the Society's dinners do not follow the printed menu, but are specially prepared and served by the host chef(s).*

Note well: the Washington restaurant scene is like the movable feast. Be forewarned that the chef, owner or restaurant we love today may be gone tomorrow, but new and worthy ones emerge for your consideration.

We have added a new feature, "Restaurant Rows" for those of our readers who want to window shop a bit and make their own on-the-spot choice of cuisine and restaurant. The emphasis here, of course, is on a wide choice of restaurants within walking distance of each other. We can recommend the area, and do list some of the restaurants, but it will be your inclination and mood that will determine your selection.

These concentrations of restaurants occur: along and just north of the 1800 block of M Street, N.W.; Latin Row, primarily in and adjacent to the 1700–1800 blocks of Columbia Road, N.W.; wall-to-wall restaurants on M Street in Georgetown and along Wisconsin Avenue, just to the north. We have included a few Capitol Hill restaurants for visitors to this area.

♥ *Bootsie, Winky & Miss Maud*
2026 P St., N.W.
887-0900

A "find" for gallery-goers in the Dupont Circle area; small, charming, fine American cuisine. Moderate.

Café Burgundy
5031 Connecticut Ave., N.W.
686-5300

Pleasant family restaurant in upper Connecticut Avenue area; inexpensive.

♥ *Café Splendide*
1521 Connecticut Ave., N.W.
328-1503

Small, unsophisticated, "down-home" atmosphere; delicious soups and entrees; home-made desserts; no microwave, no credit cards. Inexpensive.

Florida Avenue Grill
11th St. and Florida Ave., N.W.
265-1586

For soul-food lovers you'll find scrapple, ham hocks, collard greens, corn muffins and other favorites; inexpensive; no credit cards.

Martin's Tavern
1264 Wisconsin Ave., N.W.
333-7370

Booths, college-style, budget restaurant in heart of Georgetown. Good seafood; American menu; inexpensive.

Mel Krupin's
1120 Connecticut Ave., N.W.
331-7000

An all-American menu: steaks, lamb chops, calves liver, broiled seafood. Closed Sundays; very expensive.

Morton's of Chicago
3251 Prospect St., N.W.
342-6258

A blue-ribbon winner (*Washingtonian* magazine) for being a "national class meat and potatoes restaurant;" masculine atmosphere; no reservations after 7:00 P.M.; very expensive.

♥ *Mrs. Simpson's*
2915 Connecticut Ave.,
N.W.
332-8300

Black and white décor à la Edward the Eighth and Mrs. Simpson; delicious "new American" menu; friendly atmosphere and fine service; expensive.

Nora
2132 Florida Ave., N.W.
462-5143

Fresh vegetables; meats without additives; soups from scratch; fresh bright appearance; moderate to expensive.

Potomac
K and Thomas Jefferson Sts., N.W. (Georgetown)
944-4200

The glitziest place in town; huge (seats 1,000); wonderful view of Potomac River and downtown Washington; from hamburgers to haute cuisine; moderate.

Sholl's Colonial Cafeteria
1990 K St., N.W.
296-3065

Consistently great value; inexpensive.

Sir Walter Raleigh Inn
8011 Woodmont Ave.
Bethesda, MD
652-4244
and 2001 Wisconsin
Ave., N.W.
338-1000
(other locations in telephone book)

Williamsburg-style decor; fire in cocktail lounge; always popular, with simple menu choice of steaks, baked potato, open salad bar and delicious home-baked breads. Inexpensive to moderate.

Tabard Inn
1739 N St., N.W.
785-1277

Small, limited menu; fresh produce; outdoor café in warm weather; inexpensive.

★*Watergate Terrace*
2650 Virginia Ave.,
N.W.
298-4455

International; fine terrace; good for conversation; expensive.

West End Café
1 Washington Circle,
N.W.
293-5390

Quiet, airy, good-for-
conversation restaurant with
live entertainment; salade
gourmande a specialty;
moderate.

CHINESE

Golden Palace
720 7th St., N.W.
783-1225

A consensus favorite in
Washington's Chinatown;
Cantonese dishes; inexpensive.

House of Hunan
1900 K St., N.W.
293-9111

An attractive Chinese
restaurant with unusual dishes
in the heart of restaurant
competition; moderate.

Ruby
609 H St., N.W.
842-0060

Another consensus favorite in
Washington's Chinatown;
Cantonese duck and lemon
chicken specialties;
inexpensive.

Szechuan
615 Eye St., N.W.
393-0130

Chef Lam Thoung Khong is
credited with serving the best
Szechuan-Hunan food in the
city according to
Washingtonian magazine;
inexpensive.

SUBURBS:

China Coral
6900 Wisconsin Ave.
Bethesda, MD
656-1203

Hong Kong dim sum, seafood
dumpling soup, Chinese
seafood plus unusual seasonal
specialties; moderate.

Golden Hunan
4550 Montgomery Ave.
Bethesda, MD (in North
Air Rights Bldg.)
657-1897

Quiet; elegant decor; classic
menu, helpful service;
moderate.

♥*House of Kao*
7500 Old Georgetown
Rd.
Bethesda, MD (at
Bethesda Metro exit)
657-8868

Crispy sesame beef a specialty.
Unhurried; gracious service;
orchid for the ladies; sherbet
between courses. Moderate.

North China Restaurant
7814 Old Georgetown
Rd.
Bethesda, MD
656-7922

Crowded and popular; carryout
service of merit. Moderate.

Shanghai
5157 Lee Highway
Arlington, VA
563-7446

Although the Yah-Ming Soh's
Cantonese restaurant can be
described as inexpensive, we
suggest you be expansive and
try Shanghai soup, Champagne
fish, beef with snow peas,
Szechuan style shrimp and Lee
chi.

FRENCH

There are several very expensive French restaurants of the
highest standards, each of which has a devoted following.
Jean-Louis in the Watergate Hotel, 2650 Virginia Ave., N.W.
deserves special mention with its fine chef and his nouvelle
cuisine.

♥★*Dominique's*
1900 Pennsylvania Ave.,
N.W.
452-1126

Contributes a well-run
restaurant, unusual foods
(including live trout and exotic
dishes such as rattlesnake and
buffalo); owner Dominique
d'Ermo and manager Diana
Damewood provide a warm
welcome; expensive.

Jean-Pierre
1835 K St., N.W.
466-2022

An "in" restaurant now built
around its staff; top flight; very
expensive.

Jockey Club
2100 Massachusetts
Ave., N.W.
659-8000

On all lists for a number of
years; elegant; in Ritz Carlton
Hotel; very expensive.

★*Le Lion D'Or*
1150 Connecticut Ave.,
N.W. (entrance on 18th
St. near M)
296-7972

Jean-Pierre Goyenvalle's very
successful top-drawer
restaurant; considered to be
"one of the best French
restaurants in America." Very
expensive.

★*Le Pavillon*
1050 Connecticut Ave.,
N.W.
833-3846

Yannick Cam is considered to
be Number One practitioner of
nouvelle cuisine in the country,
with an enthusiastic following;
very expensive.

Maison Blanche
1725 F St., N.W.
842-0070

Consistently superb classic
French cooking; seafood, beef
and lamb dishes; very
expensive.

Montpelier Room
Madison Hotel
15th and M Sts., N.W.
862-1712

Well-proven, elegant and
formal; hotel restaurant; very
expensive.

Expensive restaurants, but less so than the group above include:

★*Jacqueline's*
1990 M St., N.W.
785-8877

Mme. Jacqueline Rodier's
restaurant has a rustic
modernity and continues to
have a following of Gallic food
devotees; expensive.

La Brasserie
239 Massachusetts Ave.,
N.E.
546-9154

Converted town house on
Capitol Hill; intimate; a real
French bistro; moderate.

♥ *La Chaumière*
2813 M St., N.W.
338-1784

Full of atmosphere evoked by
French country inn; tasty
specialties; expensive.

♥ *La Colline*
400 N. Capitol St., N.W.
737-0400

The best restaurant on Capitol
Hill; outstanding daily specials
at this attractive bistro;
expensive.

La Fourchette
2429 18th St., N.W.
332-3077

M/Mme. Chauvet have a tiny
restaurant of great ambiance in
an interesting transitional
neighborhood; moderate.

★*La Marée*
1919 Eye St., N.W.
659-4447

A restaurant of ambiance and
emphasis on foods of the sea;
more moderate in price.

★*La Nicoise*
1721 Wisconsin Ave.,
N.W.
965-9300

Informal and fun; in upper
Georgetown; songs; waiters on
roller skates; excellent fare;
expensive.

Le Caprice
2348 Wisconsin Ave.,
N.W.
337-3394

A new "insider's" restaurant; a
small storefront that seats only
40; prix-fixe lunches and
dinners, good values; closed
Tuesdays; expensive.

♥ *Le Gaulois*
2133 Pennsylvania Ave.,
N.W.
466-3232

Excellent French fare in close
quarters and simple decor—but
much appreciated and popular;
reservations required;
expensive.

1789 Restaurant
1226 36th St., N.W.
965-1789

Pleasant and comfortable early
American decor; near
Georgetown University;
expensive.

♥ *Tout Va Bien*
1063 31st St., N.W.
(Georgetown)
965-1212

Pleasant small French bistro
with first-rate specialties;
inexpensive.

And there is excellence in the suburbs:

Chalet de la Paix
4506 Lee Highway
Arlington, VA
522-6777

A pleasing, sophisticated yet rustic restaurant; food from the south of France, with terrines a specialty; moderate.

Henry Africa
607 King Street
Alexandria, VA
549-4010

Edwardian decor; a charming dining out spot in Old Town Alexandria; closed Monday; expensive.

♥ *L'Auberge Chez François*
332 Springvale Road
Great Falls, VA
759-3800

Natives who make reservations well in advance can have the good fortune of dining in François Haeringer's charming Alsatian country inn near Great Falls; a half-hour ride from downtown. Especially delightful in warm weather when outdoor dining is a special feature; expensive.

♥ *La Ferme*
7101 Brookville Rd.
Bethesda, MD
986-5255

A charming French inn in suburban setting; outstanding menu and service; closed Tuesdays; expensive.

Le Chardon d'Or
116 S. Alfred St.
Alexandria, VA (in the Morrison House Hotel)
838-8008

Recently rated as "the best French restaurant in northern Virginia; elegant setting; the best of nouvelle cuisine from the talented chef, Jim Papovich; very expensive.

GERMAN

♥ *Café Mozart*
1331 H St., N.W.
347-5732

A combination German carry-out Deli in the front, and a small Viennese restaurant in the back; live music; perfect for pre-Ford's Theatre; inexpensive.

★*Old Europe*
2434 Wisconsin Ave.,
N.W.
333-7600

Schnitzels, red cabbage, apple
strudel and other specialties.
Rathskeller and entertainment.
Try the Rhinehesse wines;
inexpensive to moderate.

GREEK

★*Astor*
1813 M St., N.W.
331-7994

Delicious lamb dishes, great
values in downtown location;
popular. Bouzouki music
upstairs; inexpensive.

♥*Taverna the Greek
Islands*
307 Pennsylvania Ave.,
S.E.
547-8360

For an introduction to Greek
specialties, try the appetizer
plate; inexpensive.

SUBURBS:

♥*Taverna Cretekou*
818 King St.
Alexandria, VA

White washed with garden;
delightful; brunch; moderate to
expensive.

HUNGARIAN

★*Csiko's*
3601 Connecticut Ave.,
N.W.
362-5624

The best known Hungarian
restaurant; full line of
Hungarian dishes and wines;
upper Connecticut Ave. in
Broadmoor Apartments;
moderate.

INDIAN

Apana
3066 M St., N.W.
965-3040

Great ambiance; some dishes
adapted for American taste;
expensive.

Bombay Palace
1835 K St., N.W.
331-0111

On K Street's restaurant row;
attractive decor; vegetable
curries, tandoori prawns and
chicken; a *Washingtonian* two-
star restaurant; expensive.

244

Madurai
3318 M St., N.W.
333-0997

Their Sunday buffet is a fine
introduction to the delicious
vegetarian cuisine of South
India; made-to-order bread;
inexpensive.

Tandoor
3316 M St., N.W.
333-3376

Specializing in dishes cooked in
the tandoor oven; moderate.

ITALIAN

Anna Maria's
1737 Connecticut Ave.,
N.W.
667-7461

Cheerful; open late;
entertainment; inexpensive.

♥ *Cantina D'Italia*
1214-A 18th St., N.W.
659-1830

As long as Joseph Moran de
Assereto runs the Cantina, it
will not have an equal.
Northern Italian cuisine and
wines of quality; expensive.

♥ *Floriana*
4936 Wisconsin Ave.,
N.W.
362-9009

This always-popular
neighborhood Italian
restaurant offers a large
selection of appetizers amongst
other good dishes; inexpensive.

Galileo
2014 P St., N.W.
293-7191

Small, top-rated northern-
Italian dishes with unusual
pastas and main courses; very
expensive.

Gusti's
1837 M St., N.W.
331-9444

A long established traditional
Italian restaurant with
catacombs of rooms and a
good sidewalk café; moderate.

Marrocco's
1120 20th St., N.W.
331-9664

Wonderful homemade pastas
and seafood platters are
favorites at this newly located,
attractive restaurant;
moderate.

♥ *Petitto's*
2653 Connecticut Ave.,
N.W.
667-5350

Pastas with more than 30
vegetable, fish and meat
sauces; charming townhouse;
moderate.

Roma
3419 Connecticut Ave.,
N.W.
363-6611

A relaxed neighborhood
restaurant with enjoyable
outdoor facilities; good family
restaurant; inexpensive to
moderate.

Tiberio
1915 K St., N.W.
452-1915

Amongst the leading northern
Italian restaurants; one can
talk and enjoy; very expensive.

Vincenzo
1606 20th St., N.W.
667-0047

Purist Italian seafood
restaurant of high aspirations
in a well remodeled house;
very expensive.

SUBURBS:

Geranio
722 King St. Alexandria,
VA
548-0088

Chef-owner Lucio Bergamin's
relaxed and cheerful restaurant
offers fine Italian dishes; the
veal scallopini is especially
good; moderate.

Pines of Rome
4709 Hampden Lane
Bethesda, MD
657-8775

Very informal; southern
Italian; crowded; moderate.

JAPANESE

Japan Inn
1715 Wisconsin Ave.,
N.W.
337-3400

Amongst the oldest and best
authentic Japanese restaurants
in the city; tatami rooms
upstairs; moderate.

♥ *Mikado*
4707 Wisconsin Ave.,
N.W.
244-1740

Plain decor—oustanding food;
owner-chef; remarkable range
of authentic foods, including
raw fish; moderate to—on a
gourmet level—expensive.

Sushi-Ko
2309 Wisconsin Ave.,
N.W.
333-4187

For the serious sushi lovers;
teriyaki, tempura and main
course soups also available;
moderate.

SUBURBS:

♥ *Matuba-Bethesda*
4918 Cordell Ave.
Bethesda, MD
652-7449

Always reliable; sushi bar,
teriyaki, tempura; reasonable
prices.

Nara
7756 Wisconsin Ave.
Bethesda, MD
986-9696

One of the best authentic
Japanese restaurants in the
suburbs; small, simple;
inexpensive.

MEXICAN

Enriqueta's
2811 M St., N.W.
338-7772
1832 Columbia Rd.,
N.W.
328-0937

Flair and variety; authentically
busy in decor and activity; try
new dishes; inexpensive.

MIDDLE EASTERN

Bacchus
1827 Jefferson Pl., N.W.
785-0734

One of *Washingtonian*
magazine's "50 best;" try the
lamb-kabobs and molded pilafs
of rice; moderate.

Calvert Café
1967 Calvert St., N.W.
232-5431

Mama Ayesha's place is
painfully plain but mighty good
and fun; closed Mondays;
moderate.

♥★*Iron Gate Inn*
1734 N St., N.W.
737-1370

This remodeled carriage house
is pleasing and good value; fine
outdoor facilities; inexpensive.

POLYNESIAN

Trader Vic's
Capital Hilton Hotel
16th and K Sts., N.W.
393-1000

This was Richard Nixon's
favorite restaurant; very
expensive.

247

We have difficulty with recommendations, apart from the excellent *Crisfield* (which may be the most popular seafood restaurant in town), *Aux Fruits de Mer*, 1329 Wisconsin Ave., N.W. (965-2377) and *Vincenzo's*, 1606 20th St., N.W. (667-0047). Most of the French restaurants we have listed are noted for their fine seafood dishes. Several seafood restaurants along the waterfront are:

Gangplank
600 Water St., S.W.
554-5000

Le Rivage
1000 Water St., S.W.
488-8111

Hogate's
9th St. & Maine Ave.,
S.W.
484-6300

Phillips Flagship
Restaurant
900 Water St., S.W.
488-8515

SUBURBS:

Bethesda Crab House
4958 Bethesda Ave.
Bethesda, MD
652-3382

Crisfield
8012 Georgia Ave.
Silver Spring, MD
589-1306

SPANISH (Latin)

El Bodegon
1637 R St., N.W.
667-1710

Fun and a bargain; not in the high rent district; paella is the chef's specialty; moderate.

El Tio Pepe
2809 M St., N.W.
337-0730

Consistently applauded and enjoyed as one of the best Spanish restaurants in Washington; expensive.

Torremolinos
1624 U St., N.W.
667-2377

Authentic Andalusian food; even baby eels; moderate.

The "Latin Row" along Columbia Road is something special and includes authentic cuisines and bargains. See "Latin Row" below.

Independence Day fireworks display on the grounds of the Washington Monument, seen from the Tidal Basin.

Within the Lincoln Memorial (seen below at night) sits the brooding, gigantic figure of our sixteenth President.

One wall of the Vietnam Veterans Memorial
points toward the Washington Monument, the
other toward the Lincoln Memorial.
Nearby stands the group of three servicemen.

The Jefferson Memorial, viewed across the Tidal Basin at night . . .

. . . Within the building, Jefferson's colossal statue and his words, taken from the Declaration of Independence.

(Above) The U.S. Supreme Court, directly opposite the Capitol . . . (Right) The statue of Simon Bolivar, liberator of Venezuela, Colombia, Ecuador, Peru, Bolivia, and Panama.

(Above) Clark Mills' statue of President
Jackson in Lafayette Park and (below)
Theodore Roosevelt Memorial Park on Theodore
Roosevelt Island in the Potomac River.

From Cumberland, Md., 184 miles away, the Chesapeake and Ohio Canal reaches the Potomac, passing in its last mile through historic Georgetown, where cyclists can be seen riding its towpath.

A few miles west of the city, the Great Falls of the Potomac

The Great Hall of the National Building Museum, housed in the historic Pension Building. At its highest point it measures 159 feet, the height of a 16-story building.

The interior of the recently restored Old Post Office Building, which now contains shops and restaurants.
(Credit: Maxwell MacKenzie)

The majestic and elegant Willard Hotel, exterior and interior, recently re-opened for use. It was in the original Willard that Julia Ward Howe wrote the "Battle Hymn of the Republic"

The Vietnamese restaurants provide a great addition to Washington in terms of excellence and in terms of value. Of interest and value are:

★*Germaine's*
Upstairs at 2400
Wisconsin Ave., N.W.
(upper Georgetown)
965-1185

Asian cooking, including
Vietnamese; also dishes from
Indonesia, Hawaii, Japan and
China. Elegant setting, zestful
fare; expensive.

Viet Château
2637 Connecticut Ave.,
N.W.
232-6464

Vietnamese fare of several
regions in pleasant
surroundings near Sheraton
Washington; moderate.

Viet Huong Café
2928 M St., N.W.
(Georgetown)
337-5588

Simple, good Vietnamese
restaurant just across Rock
Creek Park; inexpensive.

♥*Vietnam Georgetown*
2934 M St., N.W.
(Georgetown)
337-4536

Very simple restaurant with
tasty specialties such as grilled
meat on skewers and crêpes
stuffed with meat, egg and
bean sprouts; no credit cards;
inexpensive.

DON'T OVERLOOK:

Bamiyan
3320 M St., N.W.
338-1896

Splendid chicken, beef and
lamb kabobs; other Afghan
delicacies, including Aushak;
inexpensive.

Clyde's Omelette Room
3236 M St., N.W.
333-9180

Perfect after-the-theater spot,
with any kind of omelette
created before your very eyes;
the tasty hamburgers may be
the best in town; moderate.

The Foundry
1050 30th St., N.W.
(Georgetown)
337-1500

Pleasant restaurant on C&O
Canal serving well-prepared
American food; moderate.

♥ *Gadsby's Tavern*
138 N. Royal St.
Alexandria, VA
548-1288

This was once George Washington's hang-out for parties and dancing; today's restaurant serves delicious 18th-century food; entertainment nightly; moderate.

♥ *Kabul West*
4871 Cordell Ave.
Bethesda, MD
986-8566

The suburb's contribution to first-rate Afghan food; good vegeterian dishes; inexpensive.

Kramer Books & Afterwards Café
1517 Connecticut Ave., N.W.
387-1462

Come by for breakfast, lunch or a late snack; small, pleasant area for reading and snacking; day-long Sunday brunch; an institution; inexpensive.

Leo and Linda's
1075 Thomas Jefferson St., N.W. (in basement of Georgetown Dutch Inn)
333-0993

Intimate, candlelit surroundings; imaginatively prepared American food; moderate.

Nizam's
523 Maple Ave. Vienna, VA
938-8948

The chef spent 27 years with Abdullah's in Istanbul; worth the drive for Turkish food lovers; moderate.

Suzanne's
1735 Connecticut Ave., N.W. (also in the Phillips Collection, downstairs)
483-4633

Innovative continental menu; salmon and sole terrine; noteworthy desserts; closed Sunday; moderate.

DOWNTOWN RESTAURANTS

The major sightseeing areas around the Mall do not coincide with the restaurant areas. You will find the usual eateries in this area on your own. We have selected the following, most of which are not otherwise included in the book, because of location and some special feature. Most are moderately priced.

Fitch, Fox & Brown
Old Post Office Pavilion
1100 Pennsylvania Ave.,
N.W.
289-1100

Get away from the sightseeing crowds for lunch or dinner (American menu) at this attractive restaurant in the Old Post Office; moderate.

♥ *Garfinckel's Greenbrier Gardens Restaurant*
14th & F Sts., N.W.
628-7730

Excellent fare in delightful dining room; moderate.

Old Ebbitt Grill
675 15th St., N.W.
347-4800

Victorian saloon; an old landmark in a new location; elegant entrees; expensive.

Reeves Bakery
1209 F St., N.W.
347-3781

This is the place for an all-you-can-eat breakfast bar until 11:45 A.M.; great sandwiches; inexpensive.

Vita
1010 F St., N.W.
737-1212

A vegetarian, health food and vitamin store with a small counter space; garden fresh salads and homemade honey ice cream.

Woodward & Lothrop Tea Room
10th & 11th, F & G Sts.,
N.W.
347-5300

Buffet and regular meals in Woodie's downtown store; inexpensive.

CAFETERIAS:

Air and Space Museum Cafeteria
Independence Ave. &
7th Sts., S.W.

All States Cafeteria
1750 Pennsylvania Ave.,
N.W.

Gigantic and popular.

Chamberlin Cafeteria
819 15th St., N.W.

In financial district; lunch only; small.

*Commerce Department
Cafeteria* (Aquarium)
14th St. between E St. &
Constitution Ave., N.W.

*The James Madison
Memorial Building of the
Library of Congress*
(6th floor)
101 Independence Ave.,
S.E.

One of the most attractive
government cafeterias;
breakfast and lunch only.
Buffet Dining Room next door
with excellent prix-fixe lunches
and great views; weekdays
only.

Kennedy Center Cafeteria
Rock Creek Parkway at
New Hampshire Ave.
and F St., N.W.

Open for lunch and dinner;
good view of city even if not
attending a performance.

Kitcheteria
11th and E Sts., N.W.

In the Harrington Hotel; great
for families.

*National Gallery
Cafeteria*
Constitution Ave. & 6th
St., N.W.

Stunning cafeteria in
underground passageway
between old National Gallery
and the East Building;
waterfall.

*National Museum of
American History
Cafeteria*
Constitution Ave.
between 12th & 14th
Sts., N.W.

*Patent Pending in the
National Museum of
American Art*
8th & G Sts., N.W.

Limited menu; charming, small
restaurant.

Sholl's Colonial Cafeteria
1990 K St., N.W.

For years Sholl's Cafeteria has
been one of the best buys in
town; enjoy fresh vegetables
and homemade desserts;
inexpensive.

Supreme Court Cafeteria
E. Capitol & 1st Sts.,
N.E.

SEE ALSO:

Washington Hotel Roof 15th St. and Pennsylvania Ave., N.W. 638-5900	For cocktails with view; also dining.

RESTAURANT ROWS

In our "Restaurant Rows" section, our idea is not to recommend every restaurant, but to show areas in which there may be within a short distance a wide range of worthy restaurants with a variety of cuisines and prices, so you can make your choice on the spot.

THE 1800 M STREET BLOCK

There are over two dozen restaurants in the vicinity of the 1800 block of M Street, Jefferson Place and adjoining blocks of 19th Street and Connecticut Avenue, N.W. Starting from Connecticut and M and proceeding counter-clockwise around the block there are:

★*Astor* 1813 M St., N.W. 331-7994	Greek; inexpensive.
El Palacio 1827 M St., N.W. 785-8228	Mexican style; moderate.
Gusti's 1837 M St., N.W. 331-9444	Large, popular, Italian; outdoors in summer; inexpensive to moderate.
Flaps Rickenbacher's 1207 19th St., N.W. 223-3617	Pub.

Pierce Street Annex 1210 19th St., N.W. 466-4040	American; inexpensive to moderate.
♥ *Bread Oven* 1220 19th St., N.W. 466-4264	French; limited, good menu, wine and bakery goods; moderate.
The Palm 1225 19th St., N.W. 293-9091	D.C. version of the New York steak house; very expensive.
Bacchus 1827 Jefferson Place, N.W. 293-3122	Simple; Italian; inexpensive.
Trattu 1823 Jefferson Pl., N.W. 466-4570	Italian; limited but good menu; popular; moderate.
Le Souperb 1221 Conn. Ave., N.W. 347-7600	Good soups and sandwiches; inexpensive.
♥ *Cantina d'Italia* 1214-A Conn. Ave., N.W. 659-1830	The first-rate expensive but worth-it Italian restaurant.
Joe & Moe's 1211 Conn. Ave., N.W. 659-1211	Known for its beef dishes. Enhanced by the personality of hosts and staff; very expensive.
Le Lion d'Or 1150 Conn. Ave., N.W. (entrance on 18th St.) 296-7972	Top flight French; very expensive.

LATIN ROW

In the "Latin Row," primarily along Columbia Road, in the 1700–1800 block, and adjacent Champlain Street, 18th Street and Adams Mill Road, there are a dozen interesting and quite inexpensive restaurants, primarily Cuban (and Latin) and a dozen more carry-outs which offer limited restaurant service.

Recent newcomers to this area are many fine Ethiopian restaurants, a few of which we have listed. In order of street address approaching from Columbia Road and Connecticut Avenue, there are:

Omega
1856 Columbia Rd.
745-9158

Well established.

El Caribe
1828 Columbia Rd.
234-6969

South American foods, somewhat more expensive than neighbors.

El Rincon Espanol
1826 Columbia Rd.
265-4943

Tiny, hospitable.

Carlos Gardel
1759 Columbia Rd.,
N.W.
797-8704

Ecuadoran-Argentinian.

Asmara
1725 Columbia Rd.,
N.W.
332-2211

Ethiopian food including *wats* (stews prepared with chicken or lamb); inexpensive.

Meskerem
2434 18th St., N.W.
462-4100

More Ethiopian treats; inexpensive.

Red Sea
2463 18th St., N.W.
483-5000

An award winning Ethiopian restaurant; friendly staff; inexpensive.

Other restaurant/carry-outs have a variety of Latin, Chinese and Italian cuisines. Try especially *Scott's Bar-B-Que Pit*, a carry-out at 3066 Mt. Pleasant St., N.W., for barbecued meats and poultry, collard greens and corn bread. There are also groceries and delis of note.

GEORGETOWN RESTAURANTS

M Street in Georgetown, from the 2800 block through the 3300 block is wall-to-wall hairstylists, art shops and interesting restaurants. Starting with the first block in Georgetown, 28th and M Street, N.W.:

★*El Tio Pepe*
2809 M St., N.W.
337-0730

Fine Spanish restaurant; Flamenco dancing; expensive.

Enriqueta's
2811 M St., N.W.
338-7772

Mexican; interesting; moderate.

♥ *La Chaumière*
2813 M St., N.W.
338-1784

With wine bar; moderate.

The Guards
2915 M St., N.W.
965-2350

American Grill; charcoal meat and fish; ambiance and excellence; expensive.

Geppetto
2917 M St., N.W.
332-2602

Italian café; carry-out for pizza; moderate.

Viet Huong Café
2928 M St., N.W.
337-5588

Vietnamese; inexpensive.

Vietnam Georgetown
2934 30th St., N.W.
337-4536

Vietnamese; inexpensive.

Charing Cross
3027 M St., N.W.
338-2141

Now Italian; try the shrimp in lemon and garlic, and veal dishes; moderate.

Georgetown Seafood House
3056 M St., N.W.
342-1925

Soft-shell crabs; lobsters; inexpensive.

♥ *Chez Grand-Mère*
3057 M St., N.W.
337-2436

Unpretentious and rather sedate; simple menu of well cooked and attractively served dishes; expensive.

Le Steak
3060 M St., N.W.
965-1627

Serves its name; fabulous French fries; moderate to expensive.

Apana
3066 M St., N.W.
965-3040

Indian; good ambiance; some dishes adapted for American taste; expensive.

Mr. Smith's
3104 M St., N.W.
333-3104

A traditional Georgetown pub.

Bistro Français
3128 M St., N.W.
338-3308

Delicious chicken cooked on a spit; moderate.

Nathan's
3150 M St., N.W.
338-2000

Another of the well-known pubs.

Clyde's
3236 M St., N.W.
333-9180

Yet another of the well-known pubs.

Le Duck
3280 M St., N.W.
338-0900

Timbered room with stuccoed walls; poultry cooked in imaginative ways; fish dishes; moderate.

Crazy Horse
3259 M St., N.W.
333-0400

Pub.

Paul Mall
3235 M St., N.W.
965-5353

Pub.

El Caribe Georgetown
3288 M St., N.W.
338-3121

The Georgetown version of the Latin Row restaurant; expensive.

Tandoor
3316 M St., N.W.
333-3376

Indian; dishes cooked in the tandoor oven; moderate.

Bamiyan 3320 M St., N.W. 338-1896	Fine Afghan food; inexpensive to moderate.

On Wisconsin Avenue just north of M Street in Georgetown there are several restaurants worth noting:

The American Café 1211 Wisc. Ave., N.W. 337-3600	Simple menu of good soups, salads, sandwiches and desserts; pleasant; moderate.
Martin's Tavern 1264 Wisc. Ave., N.W. 333-6778	For decades a Georgetown institution; informal; moderate.
Aux Fruits de Mer 1329 Wisc. Ave., N.W. 965-2377	A real French café exactly as should be in the heart of Georgetown; seafood; moderate.
Au Pied de Cochon 1335 Wisc. Ave., N.W. 333-5440	The companion French café; deservedly popular; moderate.

THE HILL

In the past the Hill has not been a restaurant area. There are now a few good restaurants and the trend may be starting. We list the ones we know because so many visitors may be in the area at lunch time:

On Pennsylvania Avenue, S.E.:

209½ 209½ Pa. Ave., S.E. 544-6352	Good for conversation; attractive; moderate.
Jenkins Hill 223 Pa. Ave., S.E. 544-6600	Pub; Hill staffers; inexpensive.
Taverna the Greek Islands 307 Pa. Ave., S.E. 547-8360	First-rate Greek cuisine; moderate.

On Massachusetts Ave., N.E.:

American Café
227 Mass. Ave., N.E.
547-8500

Soups and sandwiches;
moderate.

♥*La Brasserie*
239 Mass. Ave., N.E.
546-9154

Fine Hill addition; French;
moderate.

Also:

The Broker
713 8th St., S.E.
546-8300

Swiss, interesting dishes; well
managed; imaginative
architecture; moderate.

Market Inn
200 E St., S.W.
554-2100

Seafood; an old timer in
popularity; moderate.

Shopping

Not too many years ago Washingtonians traveled to New York when they had "serious" shopping to do. All that has changed. Besides Washington's own fine department stores, New York's Bloomingdale's, Lord and Taylor and Saks Fifth Avenue have opened branches here. Dallas has contributed a Neiman Marcus store, and a branch of California's I. Magnin is located in the beautiful White Flint Shopping Mall on Rockville Pike, Bethesda, MD. Clusters of antique shops may be visited in Kensington, MD, (on Connecticut Avenue) and a concentration of quality Oriental rug stores is to be found on Wisconsin Avenue extended in Bethesda, MD.

PRINCIPAL SHOPPING AREAS

Central Downtown—centers at 14th and F Sts., N.W., and extends northwest to about 15th and Eye Sts., and east to Pennsylvania Ave. The Old Post Office Pavilion, 1100 Pennsylvania Ave., N.W., houses numerous gift shops, boutiques and restaurants. The shops and restaurants (over 85) at National Place on Pennsylvania Ave. between 13th and 14th Sts., N.W. are worth visiting.

Lower Connecticut Ave.—centers around Connecticut Ave. and K St.

Georgetown—between 28th and 34th Sts. on M St., and Wisconsin Ave. from M St. to Q St. (and streets to right and left of Wisconsin Ave. within this area).

Friendship Heights—Western and Wisconsin Aves. (Chevy Chase Center).

Around the Beltway—the Beltway, Routes 495 and 95, encircles the greater Washington area for a distance of 60 miles. More than a half-dozen gigantic shopping malls, most of them with branches of the large department stores, may be found within a few minute's drive of a Beltway exit. Four of the finest suburban shopping centers are Montgomery Mall (Democracy Blvd., Bethesda, MD), White Flint Mall (Rockville Pike, Bethesda, MD), Tysons Corner (Route 123, McLean, VA) and Fair Oaks Mall (Route 50 and I-66, Fairfax, VA).

WHAT YOU WILL FIND WHERE

CENTRAL DOWNTOWN DEPARTMENT STORES

Garfinckel's, 14th and F Sts., N.W.—large department store, nationally known for its high quality apparel and decorative accessories.

Woodward and Lothrop, 11th and F Sts., N.W.—known as "Woodies" by the natives; shop here with confidence for everything from clothes to kitchen gadgets. The 1986 renovation makes a stunning contribution to downtown's "uplift."

The Hecht Co., 12th and G Sts., N.W.—a new Hecht's opened at Metro Center in 1985; an "old reliable" for just about everything.

LOWER CONNECTICUT AVENUE—*Mostly for Men*

Arthur Adler, 1101 Connecticut Ave., N.W.—fine quality men's clothing with traditional styling.

Brooks Brothers, 1840 L St., N.W.—where those who have never forsaken the Ivy Look replace their buttondowns and three-inch ties; a branch of their Madison Avenue emporium. Some ladies' clothing with traditional Brooks Brothers tailoring.

Joseph A. Bank Clothiers, 1118 19th St., N.W.—provides clothes conscious men with slimmer wallets but champagne taste an excellent selection of coats and suits; a branch of renowned Baltimore store.

Camalier and Buckley, 1141 Connecticut Ave., N.W.—offers fine quality leather goods, games and household accessories.

GEORGETOWN

Along M Street

American Needlework Center, Inc., 2803 M St., N.W., is Mecca to the needlepoint and crewel freaks who disdain kits and appreciate excellent, original designs and imported canvasses and hand-dyed yarns; knitting, too. Closed in August.

The *Junior League Shop of Washington*, 3307 M St., N.W., donates the proceeds of their quality second-hand clothing donated by League members to Washington charities. Here's a good opportunity to pick up a fur, designer clothes, children's wear, jewelry and accessories for a bargain basement price.

Georgetown Park Mall, at the junction of Wisconsin Ave., N.W. and M St., offers a great variety of fine shops in an intimate Victorian setting. Scattered amongst the three shopping levels is a mini-Garfinckel's, Abercrombie and Fitch, Conran's, Crabtree and Evelyn, Liberty of London and F.A.O. Schwarz; also, several restaurants including the Samurai, Clyde's, Houlihan's and Vittorio's. Open 10:00 A.M.–9:00 P.M. Mon.–Sat.; NOON to 6:00 P.M. Sunday.

Laura Ashley, 3213 M St., N.W., offers charming, distinctive floral-design fabrics, wallpapers, accessories and feminine-looking clothes reminiscent of Edwardian England.

GOING UP WISCONSIN AVENUE

Georgetown Coffee, Tea and Spice, 1328 Wisconsin Ave., N.W., will entice you inside with the aroma of freshly ground coffee, imported from Africa, Central and South America; candies in bins and a host of spices, chocolates and gadgets.

Appalachian Spring, 1415 Wisconsin Ave., N.W., sells all manner of pottery, wooden items, toys, patchwork pillows and other crafts made (much of it by hand) in the Appalachians.

Little Caledonia, 1419 Wisconsin Ave., N.W., has been a Georgetown favorite for many years, with its six or seven small rooms, each devoted to a different specialty—material by-the-yard for curtains and upholstery, cards and wrappings, china and glassware, lamps and small pieces of furniture, kitchen items and a roomful of children's toys.

The *Christ Child Opportunity Shop*, 1427 Wisconsin Ave., N.W., is a paradise for the browser in search of antiques and quality china, pictures, silver, jewelry and bric-a-brac, all on consignment (second floor). Open weekdays from 10:00 A.M. to 3:45 P.M.; closed August.

The Phoenix, 1514 Wisconsin Ave., N.W., tempts the aficionado with "the best from Mexico," from hand-embroidered dresses, skirts and blouses to exquisite jewelry and unusual household items.

The French Market, 1632 Wisconsin Ave., N.W., will provide the gourmet cook with every kind of kitchen utensil, all from France, and a little grocery store next door.

Audubon Naturalist Book Shop, 1621 Wisconsin Ave., N.W., has, you guessed it, everything to do with and about birds—books, records, notepaper, paintings, callers and calendars.

FRIENDSHIP HEIGHTS

Lord & Taylor, 5255 Western Ave., N.W., brings one of New York's choicest stores to Washington; everything for men, women and children as well as furniture and gifts.

Neiman Marcus, in the Mazza Gallerie, 5300 Wisconsin Ave., N.W. at the District line. Many other distinctive specialty stores are located here.

Saks Fifth Avenue, 5555 Wisconsin Ave., N.W. is another Fifth Avenue gift to the capital, with an expensive selection of ladies' designer fashions plus fine quality wear for men.

Transportation Guide

TAXIS

Taxis are plentiful (except in rains) and reasonable. A zone plan controls rates in the District. It is relatively easy to hail a cruising cab in Zone 1, which includes almost all the downtown sights; there are more than 10,000 in service! For travel in all eight zones fares range from $2.10 to $8.05. A zone map displayed in each cab will help you to determine your fare. An additional $1 is charged during the evening rush hour from 4:00 to 6:30 P.M. For each additional passenger after the first, $1.25 is charged. A charge is made for large suitcases, trunks and more than one grocery bag.

In Maryland and Virginia the fare is based on mileage rather than zones. Some of the larger cab companies are: Diamond (DC) 387-6200; Diamond (Arlington, VA) 578-1111; Diamond (Alexandria, VA) 549-6200; Barwood (MD) 984-1900.

Cabs may be hired by the hour for sightseeing, but be sure to settle on the cost in advance. Drivers with guide's licenses charge considerably more per hour.

AUTOMOBILES

As the volume of traffic in the city increases year by year, driving becomes ever more frustrating for the natives; for the unsuspecting visitor it is hazardous. Most downtown parking lots, if you're lucky enough to find one that takes transient cars, charge dearly for an hour's or a day's parking.

Fringe parking is often available at lots near bus stops and the Metro, though lots are often filled to capacity early in the morning. If you have arrived in the Washington area in your car, we would strongly urge you to consider riding the Metro downtown, and taking advantage of the Tourmobile once you are in the heart of the sightseeing area. (See write-up immediately below.) Many streets are one-way in the morning and reverse directions in the evening rush hour. A right turn on red is allowed except where indicated to the contrary. Only a veteran who has studied artful dodging knows the terrors of negotiating one of the city's attractive but dangerous circles. In any case, should you persist in taking your car downtown, arm yourself with the best map you can find, and avoid rush hours, 7:00–9:30 A.M. and 4:00–6:30 P.M. (3:00 P.M. in Mall area). Almost no downtown street parking is allowed at those times; parking fines are $10 and up, and should your car be towed away, a likely possibility if you're parked on one of the main arteries, it may cost you $50 plus towing charges (and a call to the local police precinct to locate its where-abouts) to retrieve it. Washington police collect more than $28 million a year in revenue from parking violations.

Driving to sights in the suburbs and environs of the city should present no particular problems. Note that right turns on red are allowed in D.C., Maryland and Virginia.

Call the following numbers for help: fines for booting/tow-away, 727-5000; repossession of motor vehicles, 576-6585.

TOURMOBILE

You will find the Tourmobiles, smooth-riding shuttle trams carrying 88 passengers, the most efficient way to sightsee in the principal Mall-Monument area, and Arlington Cemetery. A narrator gives you historical facts. Your ticket is your board-ing pass, good all day, and may be bought on board the Tourmobile. You may get on and off as many times as you wish during the day of your ticket purchase. Call 554-7950 for tour information, as some tours are seasonal and hours vary. (Price of tickets is subject to change.) Here is your choice of the four tours available:

Tour No. 1: The Combination Tour. (The U.S. Capitol, Wash-ington Mall and Arlington Cemetery.) Adult: $9; children (3–11): $4.50.

Tour No. 2: The Arlington Cemetery Tour. (Purchase ticket at the Arlington Visitors' Center.) Adult: $2.25; children: $1.

Tour No. 3: Mount Vernon-Washington-Arlington Tour. Daily, Apr.–Oct. Ticket good for two days' use. Leaves at 10:00 A.M., NOON and 2:00 P.M. Purchase ticket by 2:00 P.M. and depart from Arlington Cemetery, Lincoln Memorial or Washington Monument. Ticket includes admission to Mount Vernon estate. Adult: $20; children: $10. Mount Vernon Tour may be purchased separately. Adult: $12.50; children: $6.25.

Tour No. 4: Frederick Douglass Home-Washington-Arlington Combination Tour. Daily, June 15 through Labor Day. Ticket

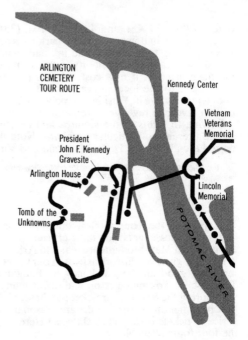

ARLINGTON CEMETERY TOUR ROUTE

Kennedy Center

Vietnam Veterans Memorial

President John F. Kennedy Gravesite

Arlington House

Lincoln Memorial

Tomb of the Unknowns

POTOMAC RIVER

good for two consecutive days' use. Visit the home of Frederick Douglass, an ex-slave, statesman, orator and advisor to Presidents. Cedar Hill has a spectacular view of the city and represents upper-class living about 1880. Adults: $14; children: $7. Departures at 10:00 A.M. and 1:00 P.M. Douglass Home Tour may be purchased separately. Adults: $5.; children: $2.50. Note: Be sure to buy combination tickets before 2:00 P.M. from Tourmobile ticket booths or drivers. *Make reservations* in person for Mount Vernon or Douglass Home Tours at Arlington Cemetery, Lincoln Memorial or Washington Monument Tourmobile ticket booths.

The Tourmobiles stop at the following sites:

U.S. Capitol Building
Washington Monument
National Air and Space Museum
Union Station
National Arts and Industries Building

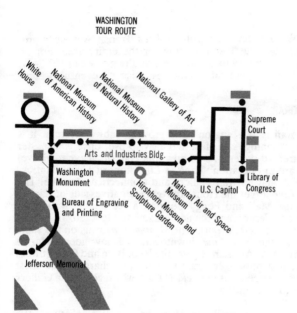

WASHINGTON
TOUR ROUTE

West Potomac Park (free visitor parking)
National Gallery of Art
Museum of Natural History
Museum of American History
Bureau of Engraving and Printing
Jefferson Memorial
Lincoln Memorial
Arlington Cemetery
White House
Kennedy Center

In Arlington Cemetery the Tourmobile stops at these sites:

President John F. Kennedy Gravesite
Senator Robert F. Kennedy Gravesite
Tomb of the Unknowns (Guard changing)
Arlington House (formerly Custis-Lee Mansion)
Visitors' Center

BUS

The Washington Metropolitan Area Transit Authority provides public bus transportation for the entire area. For information on how to get to where you're going call 637-2437. It will be busy, but hang in there, a voice will eventually come to your rescue.

METRORAIL

Metrorail is Washington's still-growing subway system. It is clean, stunning, safe, fast and easy to use, once you master the farecard system. As of now four (out of an eventual five) lines are in operation: The *Red Line* stops at Union Station, the National Portrait Gallery and Connecticut Avenue. The *Blue Line* serves the House of Representatives side of Capitol Hill, the Mall and Foggy Bottom, a reasonable walk from Kennedy Center, and the nearest stop to Georgetown. Its last stop is National Airport. The *Orange Line* runs on the same track as the *Blue Line* downtown, and now goes as far as Vienna, VA. At *Metro Center* the Red, Blue and Orange lines cross, and passengers may transfer (no charge). The most recent line opened is the *Yellow Line*, which goes from Gallery Place to Alexandria, VA.

Hours for Metrorail are Mon.–Fri., 6:00 A.M.–MIDNIGHT; Sat., 8:00 A.M.–MIDNIGHT; Sun., 10:00 A.M.–MIDNIGHT. Metrorail stations have vending machines that sell farecards between 80¢ and $20. Hold on to your card, as you will need it when you exit. Unused portions of farecards are not refundable. A free copy of *All About Metro* is available at kiosks in the stations. Consult the charts near the farecard machines before buying your card; fares differ according to the time you are traveling. Note: All Metrorail stations have elevators to accommodate wheelchairs. No smoking, eating or drinking is allowed on the Metro; playing radios or tape records is also forbidden. Rules are strictly enforced. Work continues on Metro and new lines open up as they are completed. Check for further openings and changes in hours.

BOATS

The Washington Boat Lines provide a pleasant way to travel to Mount Vernon. Their spring, summer and fall schedules vary, and it is best to call their offices for reservations and

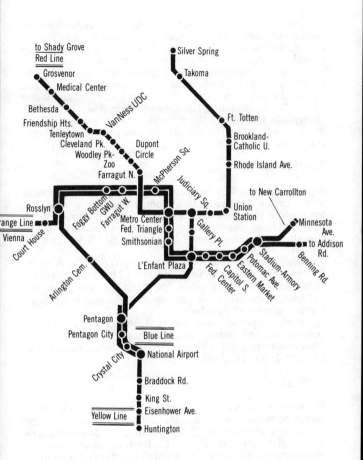

to Shady Grove
Red Line
Grosvenor
Medical Center
Bethesda
Friendship Hts.
Tenleytown
Cleveland Pk.
Woodley Pk-
Zoo
Farragut N.
VanNess UDC
Dupont
Circle
McPherson Sq.
Judiciary Sq.
Silver Spring
Takoma
Ft. Totten
Brookland-
Catholic U.
Rhode Island Ave.
to New Carrollton
Rosslyn
Orange Line
Vienna
Court House
Foggy Bottom
GWU
Farragut W.
Metro Center
Fed. Triangle
Smithsonian
Gallery Pl.
Union
Station
Minnesota
Ave.
to Addison
Rd.
Benning Rd.
Stadium-Armory
Potomac Ave.
Eastern Market
Capitol S.
Fed. Center
L'Enfant Plaza
Arlington Cem.
Pentagon
Pentagon City
Crystal City
Blue Line
National Airport
Braddock Rd.
King St.
Eisenhower Ave.
Yellow Line
Huntington

METRO SYSTEM

information: 554-8000. Besides the trips to Mount Vernon, visitors may enjoy an hour round-trip cruise from either the Lincoln Memorial or Georgetown Dock. Licensed tour guides provide commentary on the points of interest.

Besides the waterfront shuttle cruise there is a moonlight dance cruise, a city lights cruise, a luncheon buffet cruise and a student dance cruise. Boats leave from Pier 4, 6th and Water Sts., S.W., Washington, DC (just off Main Ave., next to the *Gangplank* restaurant). Reservations for all groups of 25 or more are necessary. Individual tickets are sold on a first-come, first-served basis.

SIGHTSEEING TOURS

Sightseeing tours of course relieve you of parking problems and planning the route. Most companies offer a variety of tours—four to eight hours in length. Free pick-up service at your hotel can usually be arranged. For a list of companies consult "Sightseeing Tours" in the Classified Telephone Directory.

Highly recommended are the tours given by NFAA, the *National Fine Arts Associates, Inc.*, 4801 Massachusetts Ave., N.W., Suite 400, Washington, DC 20016; tel. 966-3800. Special tours to special places with expert guides may be arranged for any number of people.

Another top-flight company is *Washington à la Carte*, "a custom-designed touring service for the sophisticated tourist." They may be reached at 1706 Surrey Lane, N.W., Washington, DC 20007; tel. 337-7300.

AIRPORTS

Washington is served by three major air terminals. The Washington National Airport has the distinciton of being (except in rush hours) only some 15 minutes from the downtown area. Metrorail serves this airport. Dulles International Airport, Washington's striking jet terminal in Chantilly, VA, is about 45 minutes and 28 miles west of downtown. Baltimore-Washington International Airport (BWI), some 31 miles and 45–50 minutes to the northeast, serves Baltimore and Washington. Airport buses and limousines take passengers from the airports to downtown hotels and suburban motels. Private taxis to or from Dulles or BWI Airports are exorbitantly expensive.

Part V
History and Government

A Capsule History

1608   Captain John Smith, probably the first white man in the area, explores the Potomac River as far as Great Falls.

1790   Compromise between North and South leads to location of the Federal District on the Potomac, almost exactly halfway between New England and Georgia. George Washington chooses the precise site at the head of the tidewater, far enough inland to protect against surprise attack but accessible for ocean vessels. In 1791 Pierre Charles L'Enfant chosen to establish a plan for the city. Maryland gives 69.25 square miles of land, and Virginia, 30.75 square miles to form the District of Columbia.

1800   Congress and the rest of the federal government move to new capital from Philadelphia. The Capitol is under construction. On June 3, 1800, President John Adams moves to the unfinished President's house. Total federal employees: 137.

1814   British troops invade the city and burn the Capitol, President's house and other buildings. A torrential rainstorm saves the rest of the city.

1815–16   Treaty of Ghent, ending the War of 1812 signed at Octagon House, President Madison's temporary residence. Congress moves to "Brick Capitol" on grounds of present Supreme Court building (funds raised by private subscription) while original Capitol is rebuilt.

1824   General Lafayette visits America as guest of the nation, and is accorded tremendous welcome; receives $200,000. gift from Congress.

1846   Residents in the portion of the Federal District south of the Potomac River, seeking a better chance to develop, succeed in having that area returned to Virginia. (Since then the District of Columbia has comprised about 69 square miles on the Maryland side of the river, instead of its original 100 square miles.) Washington is a sleepy town, with excitement only during Congressional sessions. Smithsonian Institution chartered by Congress.

1848–50 Chesapeake and Ohio Canal (started in 1828) is completed between Georgetown and Cumberland, MD—184.5 miles. Steam trains come to the city, foreshadowing the end of the canal's usefulness.

1850s The city is subject to increasing national division on tariff and slave issues and struggle between state's rights and central government. Washington Monument construction is halted when less than one-third completed. Treasury Building is under construction.

1861 The city overnight becomes the center of the Civil War effort; barracks and hospitals are found in all open spaces. Horace Greeley describes the capital as "a place of high rents, bad foods, disgusting dust, deep mud and deplorable morals."

1864 Confederate troops threaten the capital from the north. Lincoln is under fire while visiting front lines at Ft. Stevens.

1865 Greatest parade in Washington's history celebrates the end of the Civil War; Federal troops parade for two days and nights down Pennsylvania Avenue.

1871–74 Territorial form of government under Governor Alexander R. ("Boss") Shepherd is established. The L'Enfant plan is resurrected. Streets are paved; water, gas and sewer mains are laid; parks are developed and trees are planted—all resulting in a huge ($20,000,000) debt.

1878 The commission form of government is reestablished (three commissioners appointed by the President, and responsible to Congress).

1901	The McMillan Park Commission reaffirms and extends L'Enfant's plan; the main axis of the city is extended three-quarters of a mile westward to the Potomac banks; plans are made for the Lincoln Memorial and Arlington Bridge, to develop the Mall and remove its railroad tracks, and to create 640 acres of Potomac parklands from a swamp. The city burgeons; population now 300,000.
1910	The National Commission of Fine Arts is established to oversee the orderly and esthetic development of the capital.
1926	The largest public building program ever adopted and carried out by any nation (including an expenditure of over $400,000,000) leads to many of the present downtown federal buildings.
1932	Washington's population (and the number of civil servants in Washington) spurts sharply upwards with the coming of the New Deal and the growth of federal agencies.
1941–45	Washington bursts at its seams with the war effort. The Pentagon is built.
1960s	The population of the greater metropolitan area is over 2 million—and Washington faces the same gamut of problems as other cities of its size. The southwest redevelopment program, including a major series of contemporary office buildings and some exciting residential architecture, rehabilitates the blighted southwest section of the capital. Some decentralization of government buildings takes place in area, the Dulles International Airport is in service and the John F. Kennedy Center for the Performing Arts is all but completed.
1970s	The federal budget soars; the government has one of its most agonizing Constitutional crises; new federal activities further increase the impact of the government; additions to the Mall museums make that area the most exciting in the world to visit.

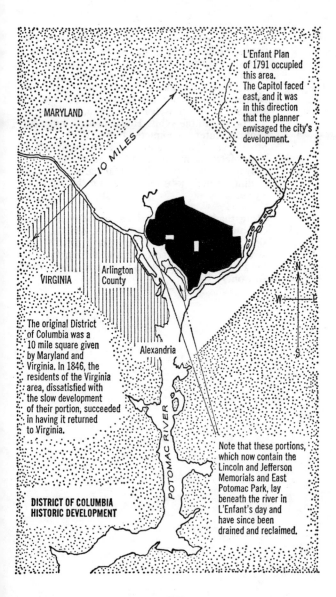

L'Enfant Plan of 1791 occupied this area. The Capitol faced east, and it was in this direction that the planner envisaged the city's development.

MARYLAND

10 MILES

Arlington County

VIRGINIA

N
W — E
S

The original District of Columbia was a 10 mile square given by Maryland and Virginia. In 1846, the residents of the Virginia area, dissatisfied with the slow development of their portion, succeeded in having it returned to Virginia.

Alexandria

POTOMAC RIVER

Note that these portions, which now contain the Lincoln and Jefferson Memorials and East Potomac Park, lay beneath the river in L'Enfant's day and have since been drained and reclaimed.

DISTRICT OF COLUMBIA HISTORIC DEVELOPMENT

1980s   The rapid growth of downtown Washington continues. Space in the prime professional district is almost exhausted. Almost 100 trade associations a year move their headquarters to Washington. The Pennsylvania Avenue Development Corporation contributes two new parks between 13th Street and 15th Street on Pennsylvania Avenue, adding grace and beauty to the White House area. A huge convention center is completed between 9th and 11th Streets, and H Street and New York Avenue, N.W. The Metro is having a profound effect on the growth of the city with 40,000 passengers commuting to their jobs in the city on the Red Line alone.

More than 3,000 professional and business associations are based in Washington. On the down side, however, a *Forbes* magazine article ranks Washington as "the second most unfriendly city in the United States in which to do business." (First: Boston.)

Government

"All legislative Powers. . .shall be vested in a Congress of the United States. . ."

CONSTITUTION OF THE U.S. ART. I SEC. I

The executive Power shall be vested in a President. . ."

CONSTITUTION OF THE U.S. ART. II SEC. I

The judicial Power of the United States shall be vested in one supreme Court, and in such inferior Courts as the Congress may from time to time ordain. . .

CONSTITUTION OF THE U.S. ART. III SEC. I

Your tour of the Capitol, the White House, the Supreme Court and your glimpses of the dozens of government office buildings can give you only a small idea of how the government works—or of its extraordinary size and complexity. The federal office buildings you pass enroute from the Capitol to the State Department provide headquarters for most of the 3.5 million federal employees—who hold one out of every 25 jobs in the United States. From these sprawling buildings and the Pentagon is spent the federal budget in the $740 billion range, almost one-fourth of the gross national product.

You may well wonder how an enterprise of this size functions at all. It works, in fact, amazingly well. The constitutional separation of powers into three "separate" but "equal" branches, the Executive, the Legislative and the Judicial, has stood the test of two centuries and has recently been re-affirmed. The checks and balances between the three branches have evolved with the passage of time, but continue to function effectively. And the federal giant continues to respond to the changes in political leadership dictated by the voters in the federal elections.

Each of the branches, however, reacts quite differently to a change in political control. This difference in "reaction time" comes partly from the different ways in which governmental personnel are selected and partly from size. The Legislative branch, for example, jumps quickly when the voter speaks: the elections fix directly and promptly how many Republicans and Democrats sit in Congress. The federal judiciary, on the other hand, responds slowly: the President can make appointments to the bench only as vacancies occur through death or retirement or as new judgeships are created.

Paradoxically enough, and principally because of its size, the Executive Branch responds both quickly and slowly. Think of the Executive Branch in layers, with an upper thin slice of "politically sensitive" jobs placed over a huge lower layer which varies little from administration to administration. The thin layer includes 2,000 or so jobs, such as cabinet and sub-cabinet and some 1,600 "policy" jobs filled with men the President hires and fires at his pleasure. Below this razor-thin stratum, however, the President's direct influence decreases. He can, for example, appoint federal commissioners and name the chairman of commissions, but he cannot usually remove such men during the term of their appointment. A new administration frequently tries to push out the employees in the top pay grades. However, the top three Civil Service grades number only some 5,400 jobs in all, and even so, pressure is usually not successful. Below these grades, the vast bulk of the federal bureaucracy changes little. Almost all federal employees in the United States are under Civil Service and normally keep their jobs regardless of the party in power.

The President is by far the highest paid official—he receives $200,000 a year taxable, plus an allowance of $50,000 for expenses resulting from his official duties. Top cabinet officials receive salaries comparable to those of private industry vice presidents of small companies. Congress has finally attempted a long range solution to the inadequacies at the executive pay levels by creating a commission on Executive, Legislative and Judicial salaries. The commission meets every four years and makes recommendations which, if implemented by the President, will be law unless vetoed by Congress.

The comments concerning inadequate salaries apply only to the executive levels. Lower level jobs have been relatively better treated and in fact recent studies have raised the possibility that some grade levels are overpaid in relation to private industry.

You may feel that the federal establishment is infinitely complicated. If you do, the authors have succeeded in achieving their purpose. You *must* recognize the government for what it is. Such size and complexity make it even more necessary for you to try to understand and visualize the workings of the government as you tour the capital.

THE EXECUTIVE BRANCH

The President and the Vice-President, elected every four years, head the Executive branch. Of the 3,058,711 civil employees in the Executive branch and the postal service, they are the only two officials elected by the voters. Ex-President Ford and former Vice-President Rockefeller were special exceptions, under the 25th Amendment to the Constitution.

The President's personal staff is called the Executive Office of the President. The size and power of the President's Executive Office has grown dramatically. One of the most important—and least understood—of the several permanent organizations within the Executive Office is the Office of Management and Budget. This important agency not only serves as the President's budget planner, but also as the President's man Friday for a variety of other jobs, such as clearing legislative proposals for Congress and keeping the activities and programs of the federal agencies and departments in step. The Executive Office also includes "inner ear" advisory councils on important and sensitive matters. The cabinet departments are the 13 traditional agencies of the Executive branch. All but two deal with internal and domestic affairs of government. The first established was the Department of State in 1789; the most recent development has been the reorganization of the Department of Health, Education and Welfare into the Department of Health and Human Services and the Department of Education.

The demands of a cold war have called into being a series of agencies dealing with our national security. In addition to Departments of State and Defense, these national security agencies include the Central Intelligence Agency, the Department of Energy, the Federal Emergency Management Agency and the National Aeronautics and Space Administration.

A final category of government is the independent commissions. These are expert groups that work independently within the area of their expertise and reach their own decisions, which usually can be challenged only in court. Because the President appoints the commissioners, their policies are apt to be affected by a change in administration. The major regulatory agencies have well-established procedures for making rules and arriving at rate and regulatory decisions. The commissioner and board members usually serve for a fixed number of years after appointment, which gives them additional independence. The major regulatory agencies are the Civil Aeronautics Board, the Federal Communications Commission, the Federal Energy Regulatory Commission, the Federal Trade Commission, the Interstate Commerce Commission and the Securities and Exchange Commission.

THE LEGISLATIVE BRANCH

How do 100 strong-minded Senators manage to work together? How do 435 Representatives each looking after their own set of constituents coordinate their legislative work? How does Congressional leadership change with the elections?

Party organization provides the answers, in a setting of years of tradition.

At the start of each Congressional session, the political party in power in the Senate elects the Majority Leader and his deputy, the Majority Whip. The other party elects the Minority Leader and its Minority Whip. These are powerful men; they influence their party's position on legislation and the work the Senate will consider. They speak for their party and supervise the floor debates.

The majority party also controls the Senate committees. It appoints the majority of the members of each committee and elects the chairman. By tradition, the latter is the party member with the longest continuous service on that committee. You can see why Senators rarely change committees. Once they have assignments of their choice, they seek seniority and increasing influence within the committee. There are 15 standing (permanent) committees in the Senate. Each Senator has assignments to two committees, and sometimes to a select and special committee.

The House organizes itself similarly. Each session the majority party elects a Majority Leader and a Majority Whip; on the other side of the aisle the Minority Leader and Minority Whip are elected. The House Committee system resembles that of the Senate. Because there are 435 Representatives, many can be assigned only to one of the 21 standing or permanent committees. House committees tend to be larger and to have more formal procedures and organization than their Senate counterparts.

The Vice-President of the United States presides over the Senate. During his absence, the President *pro tempore* presides, or appoints another Senator to preside. The House elects its presiding officer—the Speaker—each session. The Speaker often is the most effective leader in the majority party of the House; traditionally he has influenced House actions more than the Vice-President has in the Senate.

The same party does not always control the Senate, the House and the Presidency. Under President Nixon as in the latter years of the Eisenhower Administration, the President was a Republican, but the Senate and House were Democratic. Because House members are elected every two years, and thus stand for election during a presidential election, the House and the Presidency frequently are controlled by the same party. Senators, on the other hand, serve for six years. At each election only one-third of the Senators need stand for reelection. Thus the Senate responds more slowly to changes of the political climate.

Each chamber requires a number of such supporting offices as the legislative counsel, which helps draft bills and does research, the official reporters of debates, and the sergeant at arms. Some surprising activities, the administration of the Botanic Garden, for instance, come under legislative direction. In addition, the Congress supervises these important activities:

Congressional Budget Office—determines each year for Congress the appropriate level of federal revenues, spending and debt.

General Accounting Office—the accounting arm of the Congress.

Government Printing Office—the world's largest printer. The products and services provided by GPO amount to over $775 million a year.

Library of Congress—perhaps the world's largest library. Its foremost function is to serve the needs of members of Congress.

Office of Technology Assessment—analyzes complex issues involving science and technology for the Senate and House committees.

THE HOUSE OF REPRESENTATIVES

The Speaker

Majority Leader   Minority Leader

Special Offices:

Majority Whip

Minority Whip

Parliamentarian
Chaplain
Clerk
Sergeant at Arms
Doorkeeper
Postmaster
Official Reporters
Legislative Counsel
Architect of the Capitol

House Standing Committees:

Agriculture	Interior & Insular Affairs
Appropriations	Judiciary
Armed Services	Merchant Marine & Fisheries
Banking, Finance & Urban Affairs	Post Office & Civil Service
Budget	Public Works & Transportation
District of Columbia	Rules
Education & Labor	Science & Technology
Energy and Commerce	Small Business
Foreign Affairs	Standards of Official Conduct
Government Operations	Veterans' Affairs
House Administration	Ways & Means

There are also almost three dozen commissions, conferences, etc. (some with Senate members). They include such different activities as the Consumer Products Safety Commission and the Interparliamentary Union.

THE SENATE

President of the Senate
(Vice President of the United States)

President Pro Tempore

Majority Leader   Minority Leader

Special Offices:

Majority Whip
Majority Secretary

Minority Whip
Minority Secretary

Chaplain
Secretary
Sergeant at Arms
Legislative Counsel

Senate Standing Committees

Agriculture, Nutrition & Forestry	Finance
Appropriations	Foreign Relations
Armed Services	Governmental Affairs
Banking, Housing & Urban Affairs	Judiciary
Budget	Labor & Human Resources
Commerce, Science & Transportation	Rules & Administration
Energy & Natural Resources	Small Business
Environment & Public Works	Veterans' Affairs

There are also ten select and special committees of the Senate. These include the Democratic and Republican Policy Committees; and the select committees on Ethics; Intelligence; and Indian Affairs. With the House there are also powerful joint committees, such as the Joint Committee on Taxation and the Joint Economic Committee.

The judiciary is the smallest and the most independent of the three branches of government. Fewer than 1,000 judges (including bankruptcy judges) staff the entire federal court system. Once he has been appointed by the President and confirmed by the Senate, each judge (except for three judges serving in the territories outside the United States) serves for life. The courts are organized into trial courts, appellate courts and the Supreme Court.

The trial courts are the ones with which you are familiar; a single judge presides to determine and apply the legal principles. In appropriate cases, a jury determines facts in dispute. In the absence of a jury the judge determines the facts. At least one such federal district court sits in each state. Large states have several such courts—hence a total of 94.

The loser in the trial court has a right to take his case to the Court of Appeals for his area, but only on questions of law. Questions of fact found in the trial are final. A party aggrieved by an administrative order of one of the federal commissions or agencies can also appeal to the Circuit Court of Appeals.

The loser in the appellate court usually finds himself at the end of the road. Normally he has no "right" to a further appeal to the Supreme Court. He may, however, petition the Supreme Court to hear him. If he can show that his case is especially significant, the Supreme Court may grant his petition.

The three-level hierarchy permits the courts to apply the laws uniformly. A decision of the Circuit Court of Appeals becomes binding for the trial courts under it. If the trial court does not follow it, it can be "reversed" on appeal. Similarly, the Supreme Court can review decisions of the Circuit Courts of Appeals, and thus resolve any differences in rulings between one circuit and another. Decisions of the Supreme Court are binding on all federal courts.

In practice, the Supreme Court has freedom to concentrate on only the most important cases. The Supreme Court is required to hear only certain cases involving constitutional and federal issues; otherwise, it selects from the many issues offered it, those on which its decisions will have the most far-reaching effect.

	SUPREME COURT OF THE U.S.
SUPREME COURT	Original Jurisdiction
	States, Ambassadors, Public Ministers and Consuls as Parties
	Appellate Jurisdiction
	Review otherwise by permission of Court (most cases)
	Appeals on constitutional questions
	Special review for certain constitutional cases in District Courts (rare)
APPEAL COURTS	U.S. COURTS OF APPEALS
	Appeals from District Courts (and federal agencies) on questions of law
TRIAL COURTS	U.S. FEDERAL DISTRICT COURTS
	Appeal on questions of law
	Final decision on questions of fact

1986 SALARIES OF FEDERAL OFFICIALS

The Congress	The Courts	The Executive Branch
		$200,000—President of the U.S.—plus taxable $50,000 for expenses and support from budgets of agencies*
$97,900 —Speaker of the House; plus taxable $10,000 for expenses	$108,400 —Chief Justice of the Supreme Court; Associate Justices $104,000	$91,000—Vice President of the U.S.—plus taxable $10,000 for expenses (Vice-Pres. presides over Senate)
		Executive Schedule Level I, $80,100—all Cabinet members
$97,900 —Senate and House majority and minority leaders		
$75,100 —All other Senators and Representatives	$83,200 —Judges of the U.S. Courts of Appeals	
	$78,700 —Judges of U.S. Federal District Courts	

*Congress has provided lifetime pensions of $69,630 a year for former Presidents. He (or she) is also entitled to free mailing privileges, free office space and up to $96,000 a year for office help.

SALARIES OF THE CIVIL SERVICE
(CAREER RATINGS)

Average Level in 1986	
GS- 1	$ 9,533
GS- 2	10,855
GS- 3	12,241
GS- 4	14,230
GS- 5	16,268
GS- 6	18,452
GS- 7	20,235
GS- 8	22,895
GS- 9	24,519
GS- 10	27,898
GS- 11	29,879
GS- 12	36,163
GS- 13	43,518
GS- 14	51,747
GS- 15	61,635
GS- 16	67,933
GS- 17 and	
GS- 18	68,700

In 1986 there were 286,914 civilian federal workers in Washington. Their average salary was $32,210.

Let us oversimplify a complicated subject and suppose you are a Congressman who wants to pass a particular bill—let us say to compel the Commissioner of Internal Revenue to acknowledge receipt of each income tax return by a personal thank-you note.

You would first need a properly drafted bill. Drafting might be done by your personal staff, by the professional staff of the committee that will have jurisdiction over the bill, by the Legislative Reference Service of the Library of Congress or even by a constituent who backs your idea.

You "introduce" your bill by dropping it in the box provided for new bills on the House floor, called the "Hopper." The Speaker of the House then assigns the bill to the committee having jurisdiction, let us say the Ways and Means Committee. Now assume you are successful in persuading the Ways and Means Committee to vote favorably on your bill. It then "reports it out" to the whole House of Representatives, accompanied by a carefully prepared report on the bill. The report is printed promptly and distributed to all members of the House. The Rules Committee of the House then schedules the bill for floor debate and vote. By this time the House Republican and Democratic party organizations will have decided whether to support or oppose your bill.

In your case, let us assume you persuaded one of your Senate colleagues to introduce the bill in the Senate at the time you introduced it in the House. In the language of the Hill, the Senate bill would be a "companion" bill, and the Senate Finance Committee could proceed to consider it (and the Senate to vote on it) without necessarily waiting for House approval first. Of course, if no such companion bill is introduced, the House bill would be automatically referred upon passage to the Senate, where it would have to survive much the same series of steps as in the House; but you would obtain no Senate consideration of your bill before the House had completed its action.

Should the Senate pass a version of the bill different from that passed by the House, the presiding officers of the two Chambers appoint conference committees. They then meet together to compromise the differences and have the bills repassed by their respective Chambers in the agreed-upon form.

At this point, in Hill language, the "authorizing legislation" for your proposal has passed both houses, and will be a law

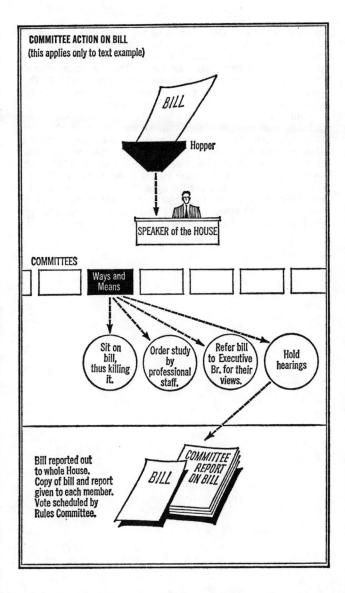

COMMITTEE ACTION ON BILL
(this applies only to text example)

BILL

Hopper

SPEAKER of the HOUSE

COMMITTEES

Ways and Means

Sit on bill, thus killing it.

Order study by professional staff.

Refer bill to Executive Br. for their views.

Hold hearings

Bill reported out to whole House. Copy of bill and report given to each member. Vote scheduled by Rules Committee.

BILL

COMMITTEE REPORT ON BILL

as soon as the President signs it. If you need money to make your bill work, however, your job is only half done. You must arrange for a second piece of legislation to be introduced and passed which appropriates the funds. This "appropriations" bill must go through each of the steps of the original bill. This time the committees that will approve or disapprove your funds will be the powerful House and Senate Appropriations Committees.

Each bill requiring funds must survive this eight-step Congressional review. The bill must be reported out by the House committee having jurisdiction and the Senate committee having jurisdiction (steps 1 and 2) and voted favorably by the full House and Senate (steps 3 and 4) before the bill can go to the President for his signature; then funds must be provided by approval of the House Appropriations Committee and the full House (steps 5 and 6) and the Senate Appropriations Committee and the full Senate (steps 7 and 8).

Master Index

304

313

MORE WAYS TO ENJOY YOUR TRAVEL IN THE MID-ATLANTIC REGION:

ADVENTURE VACATIONS IN FIVE MID-ATLANTIC STATES.
Hiking, riding, canoeing, fishing, painting, weaving, lending a hand and digging for artifacts are some choices in this comprehensive guide to adventure in PA, MD, VA, WV and NC. $9.95

GENERAL LEE'S CITY.   An illustrated guide to the historic sites of Confederate Richmond. Seventeen maps and 150 photographs help you relive the city's turbulent life from 1861–1865. $16.95

INNS OF THE SOUTHERN MOUNTAINS.   The first comprehensive guide to the 100 best hostelries of the Appalachians from Virginia to Georgia. $8.95

WALKING TOURS OF OLD WASHINGTON AND ALEXANDRIA.
A treasury of Paul Hogarth watercolors depicting 200 years of our Capital's finest old buildings. Engaging text; exquisite gift. $24.95

PHILADELPHIA ONE-DAY TRIP BOOK.   Norman Rockwell Museum, Daniel Boone Homestead, Covered Bridges and Amish Farms are among 101 fun things to see after the Liberty Bell. $8.95

VIRGINIA ONE-DAY TRIP BOOK.   Jane Ockerhausen Smith, one of the most experienced Mid-Atlantic travel writers, guides you to the variety, beauty and history of the Old Dominion. $8.95

WASHINGTON ONE-DAY TRIP BOOK.   101 fascinating excursions within a day's drive of the Capital Beltway—out and back before bedtime. $7.95

ONE-DAY TRIPS THROUGH HISTORY.   200 historic sites within 150 miles of the nation's capital. Where our forebears lived, dramatic events occurred and America's roots took hold. $9.95

FLORIDA ONE-DAY TRIPS (from Orlando).   What to do after you've done Disney. $5.95.

(see next page for convenient order blank)

CALL IT DELMARVALOUS. How to talk, cook and "feel to hum" on "thisseer" Delaware, Maryland and Virginia peninsula. $7.95

GOING PLACES WITH CHILDREN. More than 400 things for kids to see and do in Washington, D.C. A bestseller for three decades. $5.95

FOOTNOTE WASHINGTON. Tracking the surprising, humorous bypaths of capital history. $7.95

MR. LINCOLN'S CITY. In text and photos, a guide to the sites of Civil War Washington. $14.95

ORDER BLANK. Mail with check to:

EPM Publications, Box 490, McLean, VA 22101

Title	Qty	Price	Amount
	Subtotal		
Virginia residents add 4½% tax			
Add $2 shpg. first book, $1 ea. add'l.			
	Total		

Name _____

Street _____

City _____ State _____ Zip _____

Remember to enclose names, addresses and enclosure cards for gift purchases. Prices are subject to change. Write or call for free catalog: 703-442-7810.